West German Film
in the course of time

West German Film
in the course of time

Reflections on the Twenty Years since Oberhausen

ERIC RENTSCHLER

Redgrave Publishing Company
Bedford Hills, New York

Library of Congress Cataloging in Publication Data

Rentschler, Eric.
  West German film in the course of time.

  Bibliography: p.
  Includes index.
  1. Moving-pictures--Germany (West)--History
2. Moving-picture plays--History and criticism. I. Title.
PN1993.5.G3R44   1984   791.43'0943   84-9833
ISBN 0-913178-00-4

©1984 Redgrave Publishing Company, Bedford Hills, New York 10507

All rights reserved.

Printed in the United States of America
91 90 89 88 87 86 85 84 6 5 4 3 2 1

ISBN 0-913178-00-4

To Jeanie

CONTENTS

Preface i

PART ONE
History Lessons: An Introduction 1

Chapter One
Continuity and Subversion:
Toward a Reception History of West German Film

    The Construction Site 4
    Different Kinds of Film History 5
    Integrating Past and Present: History and Effect 7
    Suppressed Demands of the Sixties 9
    Film in the Spectator's Head 12
    From the Distance I See This Cinema 16

PART TWO
Two Views: Inland and Abroad 29

Chapter Two
West German Film's Precarious Course in Time:
Misère-en-scène in the Federal Republic

    The Redemption of (West) German Reality 32
    1962: Taking Leave of Yesterday 35
    1966: First Signs of Life 39
    1971: The Second Awakening of Young German Film 43
    1975: West German Film in the Cities 49
    1979: Coming of Age 54

Chapter Three
American Friends and the New German Cinema:
Patterns of Reception

    From Young German Film to New German Cinema 64
    West German Film at Home and on the Road 65
    Once Every Year at Lincoln Center 75

Products, Texts, and Stars:
The Packaging of New German Cinema 78
New German Cinema: Auteurism's Last Stand? 89

PART THREE
Texts and Contexts, *Auteurs* and Others:
Three Challenges 101

Chapter Four
Calamity Prevails over the Country:
Young German Filmmakers Revisit the Homeland

The Illusory Idyll 103
Origins and Development of the *Heimatfilm* 105
The Rise of the Critical *Heimatfilm* 109
The Subversion of a System 113
Radical Picture Stories from the Homeland 119
The Subsequent Path of the *Heimatfilm*: Coming Home .. 123

Chapter Five
Germany before Autumn:
The Literature Adaptation Crisis

The Big Mess 129
The State of Things: An Inventory 131
Word and Image: Literature in German Film History 135
Adaptations and Transformations 138
Pictures from an Exhibition:
Phasing Discourse out of Story 142
Last Words: After the Fall 150

Chapter Six
The New Sensitivity and the New Filmmakers:
Subjective Factors

Autorenkino: Dead or Alive? 158
The Melancholic Left in the
Wake of the *Tendenzwende* 162
The Collapse of Collectivity 163

The Presentiment of Terrorism	164
Peter Handke's *The Left-Handed Woman*: Specularity and Hunger for Experience	166
Wim Wenders's Rerouting of Handke's *Wrong Move*	174
Why Herbert Achternbusch Runs Amok	179

Epilogue
Life with Fassbinder:
The Politics of Fear and Pain

Private Psychodrama or Public Passion Play?	191
Melancholy Becomes Mourning	193
Autorenkino and Cooperative Cinema: Same Difference	195
Body Politics and the Discourse of Terrorism	198
The Subjective Factor in the Course of Time	200

PART FOUR
Appendices	203

Appendix A
West German Film since Oberhausen:
A Year-by-Year Checklist (1962-1981) 205

Appendix B
Readings in English on West German Film:
A Selected Bibliography 235

Index of Films 255

PREFACE

This book is the product of a dialogue initiated in the late sixties during my studies in West Germany. In those days the names Fassbinder and Herzog, whose early films I remember first encountering in student club showings and out-of-the-way houses, were on few people's lips. I became a spontaneous defender of the ambitious works when talking with sceptical student friends in the Federal Republic of Germany. Back in the United States, I assumed the role of an enthusiast, telling chums that there *really* were some fantastic things taking shape in the Young German cinema, no matter what they thought about German films. The days have long since passed when West German films needed advocates or PR-managers; there are more than plenty of them now, both here and abroad. Over the years as I repeatedly visited the Federal Republic of Germany (FRG) to keep current (and continue my studies), I began to have mixed feelings about the media ebullience and cultish fervor increasingly devoted to several *Jungfilmer* whom one had in the meanwhile discovered. Filmmakers I had long revered suddenly enjoyed considerable attention. The pages of various New York weeklies and numerous film journals sported coverage of the recent breakthroughs of New German Cinema and feature articles on the key directors. As early as the mid-seventies, I was struck by how watered-down this foreign version of West German film culture was, how these renderings left out so much and concentrated on a very small circle of films and directors.

Over the years I grew even more dissatisfied with the mythologies about these filmmakers, with the denial, for instance, that they had anything to do with German history or had any links with their own cultural tradition. If one more person quoted an *auteur* saying, "We started out of a vacuum," or "We had to begin from zero," I thought I would run amok. I have even less patience for the widespread tendency to scream about a small number of superstars and ignore the rest. In time my initially wholehearted veneration of Young German Film — born of the belief that it continued the "other" Germany which first had led me to study German literature and philosophy — was somewhat tempered. I still rarely agreed with most West German film critics and scorned their tendency to either rave about or ravage certain directors. (Fortunately I did gain a respect for the more balanced FRG commentators.) Conversing with cineastes at home more recently, I cannot share the excitement for Herzog's latest trek to the jungle and the obligatory tales of high adventure. At a conference several years ago, I reproached a well-meaning colleague for her defense of Syberberg, raging at the wider American acceptance of the primadonna's stories of suffering and his self-serving fustian. Syberberg: "the pariah of New German Cinema?" I seethed when I considered so many other noteworthy filmmakers who had had it so much harder, about whom one knew nothing in this country.

Clearly, this is not the "official history" referred to by Alexander Kluge,[1] the rags-to-riches narrative recounted in a host of commentaries. Background studies abound, in a number of languages. We already have John Sandford's introductory survey in English,[2] a comprehensive handbook by Hans Günther Pflaum and Hans Helmut Prinzler, a copiously illustrated volume by Robert Fischer and Joe Hembus, much less the latter's eclectic collage-compendium, all in German.[3] Comparable studies exist in French and Italian.[4] And, without a doubt, more critical literature remains to follow: James Franklin's survey in the Twayne series as well as rigorous readings of New German Cinema by Thomas Elsaesser and Timothy Corrigan. Besides these volumes are more specialized ones devoted to individual directors (Hellmuth Costard, Rainer Werner Fassbinder, Werner Herzog, Jean-Marie Straub/Danièle Huillet, and Wim Wenders), a forthcoming anthology of essays on various *auteurs,* and numerous special issues devoted to New German Cinema.[5] Circulating at academic gatherings and film festivals in the United States, one hears constant mention of other works in the offing, dissertations on Straub/Huillet and Herzog, English translations of articles written by West German filmmakers, a monograph on Volker Schlöndorff, a study of Bertolt Brecht's impact on film culture in the FRG, among a host of projects. (At least ten colleagues have told me in the last three years they were working on a book devoted to New German Cinema.) If one includes the substantial body of literature written in French, Italian, and German as well as the veritable glut of scholarship in English, one must truly wonder: why then this book?

If the present study is neither an introduction nor a critical work centering on significant directors, just what is it? First of all, it is *a work in progress,* a modest part of a larger and more encompassing task, the endeavor Kluge speaks of as a "subterranean history" of West German film, an exploration into the less surveyed reaches of film culture in the

FRG. Second, the following essays are short on objectivity and impartiality. A decided bias has shaped these pages, a pronounced regard for the rougher edges of West German filmmaking since 1962. Clearly, many New German films have recently broken out of their arthouse ghettos and gained wide commercial exposure in the FRG and abroad. By all indications, a film industry of considerable proportions has just about reshaped itself in West Germany. As a result, German films are being made with a distinct international appeal. Wolfgang Petersen's *Das Boot* (1981) and Ulrich Edel's *Christiane F. —Wir Kinder vom Bahnhof Zoo/Christiane F.* (1980) are the first harbingers of things to come. But this book is not interested in repeating the success stories or predicting even larger breakthroughs.[6] It shies away from the highflown phrases that have become stock usages in American to-do about the New German Cinema.

This study is as open-ended as the subject with which it is concerned. I consider the work as a balancing act that tries to mediate certain tensions. Among these are texts and contexts, my American background and my years in West Germany, my deep regard for films from the FRG and a desire not to be seen as just another American friend of the New German Cinema. The project began in the autumn of 1977. Since then I have received help from a number of sources. The Ohio State University Graduate School and College of Humanities awarded me generous and frequent study and research stipends. The OSU Department of German released me from teaching duties during the spring of 1981 so that I might complete a first draft. Both the American Council of Learned Societies and the German Academic Exchange Service provided the means for summer sojourns abroad. For all of these I am most grateful.

A host of institutions aided my investigations, allowing me access to films and documents: the *Deutsches Institut für Filmkunde* (Wiesbaden), the Film Library of the Embassy of the Federal Republic of Germany (Washington, D.C.), the *Filmverlag der Autoren* (Munich), the Goethe House New York, various other branches of the Goethe Institute (Chicago, Munich, and San Francisco), *Hessischer Rundfunk* (Frankfurt), the *Hochschule für Fernsehen und Film* (Munich), Inter-Nationes (Bonn), the International Forum of the Young Film (West Berlin), New Line Cinema (New York), and New Yorker Films. The following individuals in particular were extremely helpful in my search for background materials: Ramona Curry, Klaus Denicke, Konrad and

Herbert Jopp, Hilmar Hoffmann, Friedrich Kahlenberg, Ulrich Kurowski, Klaus Lakschéwitz, David Löwenherz, Ingrid Scheib-Rothbart, and Ulrike Storch.

Beyond hours spent in the dark and at editing tables viewing films as well as days huddled over back issues of periodicals and DIN-A-4 notebooks full of newspaper clippings, I recall a number of conversations in many different places over the last five years which equally fueled my thinking. I gained considerably from insights offered in a myriad of dialogues, especially those with Thom Andersen, Reinhard Baumgart, Russell Berman, Walter Bockmayer, Timothy Corrigan, R.C. Dale, Wolf Donner, Jörg Drews, Alfred Edel, Christian Friedel, Frieda Grafe, Wilhelm and Birgit Hein, Ronald and Dorothea Holloway, Andreas Huyssen, Anton Kaes, Gertrud Koch, Norbert Kückelmann, Wolfgang Längsfeld, Claudia Lenssen, Lindsay Michimoto, Ulrike Ottinger, B. Ruby Rich, Herbert Rimbach, Wilhelm Roth, Paul Sauerländer, Karl Saurer, Karl Schedereit, Henry Schmidt, Walter Schobert, Wolfram Schütte, Karsten Witte, and Klaus Wyborny. Above all, I am indebted to my friends and colleagues Miriam Hansen and Judith Mayne for sharing their sharp minds, sympathy, and time with me while I pursued this project.

Although the book presents a sustained argument over its six chapters, it stems in part from studies that have already appeared. I thank the editors of *Ciné-Tracts, Discourse, Kino: German Film, New German Critique,* and *The Quarterly Review of Film Studies* for allowing me to use portions of the volume whose earlier versions were published in those journals. My thanks as well to Gray City Films for the cover photograph.

Irvine, California
December 1982

NOTES

[1] Klaus Eder and Alexander Kluge, *Ulmer Dramaturgien. Reibungsverluste* (Munich: Hanser, 1980), p. 5.

[2] John Sandford, *The New German Cinema* (Totowa, N.J.: Barnes & Noble, 1980).

[3] Respectively: Pflaum/Prinzler, *Film in der Bundesrepublik Deutschland* (Munich: Hanser, 1979); Fischer/Hembus, *Der neue deutsche Film 1960-1980* (Munich: Goldmann, 1980); and Hembus, *Der deutsche Film kann gar nicht besser sein: Ein Pamphlet von gestern. Eine Abrechnung von heute* (Munich: Rogner & Bernhard, 1981).

[4] See Francis Courtade, *Jeune Cinéma allemand* (Lyon: Serdoc, 1969) and Bernard Eisenschitz, "Le Cinéma allemand, aujourd'hui," in *Documents: Revues des questions allemands,* September 1976, pp. 81-168; also, Manuela Fontana, *Film und Drang: Nuovo cinema tedesco* (Florence: Vallecchi, 1978). For a Swiss account, see "Deutscher Film im Lauf der Zeit," *Cinema* (Zürich), No. 3 (1976), pp. 3-69.

[5] See "Special Issue: New German Cinema," *Literature/Film Quarterly,* Vol. 7, No. 3 (1979); "New German Cinema," *Wide Angle,* Vol. 3, No. 4 (1980); "West German Film in the 1970s," *Quarterly Review of Film Studies (QRFS),* Spring 1980; and "Special Double Issue on New German Cinema," *New German Critique,* No. 24-25 (Fall/Winter 1981-2). For further references, see Appendix B.

[6] For examples of such high-spiritedness, see Ronald Holloway's various editorials in the West Berlin journal *Kino: German Film.* Holloway's regular notices in *Variety* likewise have been marked by similar enthusiasm.

PART ONE
History Lessons: An Introduction

> "The problem of film history, then, is not primarily one of missing data, but of a lack of adequate conceptual models to apply to the data we have. And the kind of film history we are now looking towards is the kind which will not simply produce more information but which will also offer accounts of the relationships between the 'facts' of film history and other kinds of phenomena. The object would be to show not just that certain things occurred, but why they occurred, and why these and not others."
> —Edward Buscombe

> "For it is not a question of presenting . . . works in the context of their time, but rather of describing the time which recognizes them, i.e. our own time, by evolving the time that gave rise to them."
> —Walter Benjamin

Chapter One

Continuity and Subversion: Toward a Reception History of West German Film

> *"There is an official history of the so-called New German Film and a subterranean one. The so-called New German Film is measured by the public in terms of its more conspicuous successes. The roots of these successes lie however in its side-paths."*
> —Alexander Kluge[1]

> *"We have film historians, but something less than film history."*
> —Edward Buscombe[2]

> *"The critic-historian, no less than the filmmaker, is a storyteller, reworking material from the near and further past (choosing, indeed, which past shall be of service), projecting the home society's unacknowledged conflicts, exposing, rejecting, denouncing for, and on behalf of, readership and audience."*
> —Sylvia Lawson[3]

The Construction Site

The present examination centers on West German film as a function of two key phenomena: continuity and subversion. Unlike previous commentators who subscribe to the zero-point thesis (the contention that West German directors, lacking a viable national tradition after World War II, had to start all over), I believe one of the major accomplishments of the *Jungfilmer* was their rediscovery of German film tradition, a process that took some rather circuitous routes, but one that amounted to a regaining of a left-for-lost legacy. One rebelled against the feeble likes of *Papas Kino* for starters, but soon recognized the legitimate points of cultural continuity inherent in the less immediate past, especially in the films of the Weimar Republic and in the work of emigrants who had taken flight to Hollywood. Subversion, though, came as a function of distrust of dominant forms of expression, a disdain toward a bankrupt cultural heritage and its official histories, a continuing anger about the falsifications of the establishment media, and, further, a love-hatred toward the conventions of commercial cinema. The only common denominator that stands for the majority of films by young directors in the FRG since 1962—be they the products of filmmakers as different as Werner Herzog or Werner Nekes, Klaus Wyborny or Klaus Wildenhahn, Helma Sanders-Brahms or Helke Sander—is the quest for alternative images and counter-representations.

Kluge has already announced a future *Bestandsaufnahme* (taking of stock) of the New German Film and its various paths since Oberhausen.[4] The present investigation can, at best, attempt something analogous from the distance, but only as a modest start to what demands a larger and many-faceted project. More specialized studies will be needed to draw attention to the unique circumstances surrounding *"das andere Kino"* in the FRG, the experimental and avant-garde sector, a sphere all but unknown in the U.S. outside of occasional screenings in New York City and Berkeley. Right now several people have begun an examination of feminist filmmaking in West Germany, a subject rarely broached in the scrutiny of New German films. (This forthcoming work will deal with an important other history of West German film only marginally accounted for in these pages.) Further, one still looks for in-depth discussions of the particulars connected with the relationship of film and television, a matter every bit as unexplored as the evolution of documentary filmmaking in that country. Both of these factors have had significant bearing on the overall direction of narrative productions in the FRG; both areas have given rise to considerable debate in the last decade, a dialogue that very much has circumscribed the development of New German Cinema—and one that has received little note from American observers.

If the topic is somewhat clearer, the approach still is not. Given the large amount of controversy over the question of film history during the recent decade, some comments regarding methodology are in order. As Geoffrey Nowell-Smith has argued, we doubt the conventions guiding previous film histories, yet we still lack any real sense of an alternative approach:

> No one now accepts accounts of film history (or of film in history) which pass blandly from one 'fact' to another, alternately making technology the cause of style, directorial intention the cause of a film's reception or public taste the arbiter of economic demand, without ever posing the problem of the articulation of different orders of structures and events. And yet no one knows how to do much better, except at the cost of a sceptical unwillingness to do anything.[5]

A similar crisis atmosphere governs Hans Robert Jauss's essay on the fallen status of literary history in our time, "Literary History as a Provocation to Literary Studies" (1967),[6] an important article analyzing a discipline's decline and its deplorable present state. A piece issuing from the same dissatisfaction with official histories which spirited the Young German filmmakers and the student movement as a whole, the polemic contains valuable insights, ones that I will attempt to use for this project.

Different Kinds of Film History

The malaise articulated by Jauss readily applies for film history. The Constance professor maintains that modern would-be literary histories neither come to terms with literature or history, preferring as they do mere chronologies of individual works within generic or epochal contexts or, further, unilinear accounts of central figures in a "life and work" setting. Both approaches, ones duplicated by the majority of popular film histories, refuse to make qualitative or critical judgments; one isolates the object at hand (texts and creators) outside of mundane temporality and projects oneself into the historical past while ignoring the interpreter's present. The hindsight of history, previous judgments, an exegete's operating assumptions—all of these factors remain peripheral and superfluous concerns for historical studies defined in these traditional terms.

The impasse outlined by Jauss haunts film historians more than ever. Numerous expressions of discontent with previous scholarship in this field have resounded in recent years. Invariably, those involved in the discussion describe the problem in terms of different kinds of film history, which although not mutually exclusive have somehow rarely been integrated. The work at hand represents a piecemeal rather than a synthetic approach. Commentators repeatedly speak of contrasting pairs, squaring off histories of style with socio-economic studies of the film industry[7] or juxtaposing theoretical and more practical discourse, "emic" and "etic" perspectives.[8] No doubt these antinomies restate in various ways and on different axes Christian Metz's distinction between "filmic" and "cinematic" study, i.e. the scrutiny of the activities and institutions surrounding films and filmmaking as opposed to investigations of cinematic texts themselves, their signs and codes. Some film historians come under attack for their exclusive concern with artistic matters and their neglect of socio-political conditioning factors.[9] It is conversely argued how sociological accounts have overstressed film's "relevance quotient" and, in so doing, have dealt with concrete films in less than medium-specific terms.[10] (The first criticism might apply to Lotte H. Eisner's *The Haunted Screen;* the second objection has been raised in reference to Siegfried Kracauer's *From Caligari to Hitler: A Psychological History of the German Film.* [11]) Thus far, no one has found a bridge between these clearly related, yet somehow discrete activities. We lack "a workable means of correlating politics and art, reality and realism,"[12] a way of mediating the formal integrity and complexity of individual films and the concrete historical station from which they issue and on which they act.

No one has demanded film historians start from ground zero. Many, though, have recognized the need for more viable paradigms. "It is not," submits Edward Buscombe, "that film history lacks theory or methodology, though much of it does. Rather, it lacks any agreement either about the usefulness of these theories, or about how they might fit together."[13] Seeking a more well founded and sophisticated film historiography, David Bordwell acknowledges the need to consider "film style, the film industry, and the social matrix in one complex whole." Such sweeping and encompassing analysis promises much more satisfactory results than the impressionistic grab-bags of data, directors, and short descriptions so endemic to many so-called "standard works" of film history. (Roger Manvell and Heinrich Fraenkel's *The German Cinema,* the only work in English or German which accounts in a single volume for the entire course of German film history, provides an unfortunate example of this kind of writing.) But how to realize Bordwell's ambitious resolve? "Nothing less than a theory of art in culture is required."[14]

Integrating Past and Present: History and Effect

Jauss's attempt to maneuver between the Scylla and Charybdis of aestheticism and historicism does not totally resolve the methodological stalemate outlined above. His stress, though, on the communicative aspect of the aesthetic experience within its historical dimension *does* offer a crucial point of departure thus far only in part acknowledged and otherwise undeveloped by film scholars. Rather than reconstructing the past, Jauss seeks an *integration* of past and present, of interpreter and text, thus bringing forth a hermeneutically-reflected approach to the historicity of literature as well as of its audiences. Reception theory concerns itself "with the historical conditions of the aesthetic effect of works of art."[15] Anything but a monolithic discipline, one solely applicable to literary study, reception theory is a dialogical science. As Jauss stated in an interview, it

> does not exclude the standpoint and activity of the subject, but rather includes him as the condition of knowledge, and this concept is to that extent specific to all sciences which would understand meaning, which proceed from the assumption that meaning is a yielded truth—and not a given one.[16]

For Jauss the subject is every bit as time-bound as any given text; an encounter between the two elements gives rise to a dialogue, an exchange Jauss describes as a relation between history and (literary) effect. He elevates the historicality of understanding to the status of a hermeneutical principle, and, in so doing, presents compelling arguments against the limits of both aestheticism's and historicism's tendency to seal their objects off from the present or from the course of intervening time. Each approach would separate the work of art and the perceiving subject as closed monads isolated from one another. Central to Jauss's notion of effective history stands the desire "to make the focus of interest the communicative and thereby socially formative function of literature, over and above its representational dimension."[17]

Up to this point film historians have done little work with reception aesthetics, for the most limiting their few inquiries in this direction to empirical studies of audience sociology on the one hand and theoretical discussions of spectator-text relations on the other.[18] Conventional film history, while stressing the artistic merits of selected films, isolates its object, the "films themselves," in a vacuum; it attends only vaguely to the production background, social context, audience appeal, and critical reception of a film, instead preferring to believe "that however the work got to be what it is, it is what it is." Such practitioners assume "that a film can exist for us concretely on a screen today exactly as it might have existed ten or twenty or sixty years ago."[19] More recent discussants have recognized the naiveté of this methodology and have called for "a truly reflexive film studies" that would lead to "a systematic appreciation of the subjective nature of any historical writing."[20] While designing the film history of the future, one does well to consider past attempts. As Robert C. Allen indicates, one must realize

> that film historians' concepts of the nature and function of film determine, in some measure at least, the kinds of materials they choose for analysis, the kinds of events they see as significant, and, perhaps, most importantly, what patterns of cause and effect they infer from their data.[21]

If one can agree at least nominally that the major task of film history is to depict how and under what conditions films produce meaning, then one does well to heed Hans-Georg Gadamer's caveat that history does not belong to us, but we to it.[22] We do not stand beyond tradition, but rather exist within it. And history should not amount to a chronicle of completed events, a narrative that tells us all, instilling in the reader the feeling that nothing has been left out. The impetus at hand in a good number of Young German films and the insight central to reception theory is a common one: history is a process engaging the subject in a dynamic relationship. It is, as Walter Benjamin once said, "a structure whose site is not homogeneous, empty time, but time filled by the presence of the now [*Jetztzeit*]."[23] With these notions in mind, I would like to outline Jauss's programmatic call for a reception history, to point out its advantages and problems, before elaborating on its worth for a history of West German film.

Suppressed Demands of the Sixties

Young German Film enjoyed its first successes at roughly the same time Jauss formulated his seven controversial theses. Both phenomena issued from an atmosphere of ferment, from a period of intense dissatisfaction with dominant modes of discourse. "The problem of application," Jauss submitted in an interview a decade later,

> put another way, the insufficiency of a mere reconstruction of the past 'as it really was,' of an interpretation or description of a text 'for its own sake,' and the effort to mediate past literature in the experiential horizon of our own present—was a suppressed demand, and it is the real content of that turn toward the aesthetics of reception which occurred in the mid-sixties and which, evidently, was successful.[24]

Reception theory in its numerous guises had enjoyed only a marginal existence in German scholarship prior to Jauss. True, previous generations had produced volumes like Fritz Strich's *Goethe und die Weltliteratur* (1946) or Wolfgang Leppmann's *The German Image of Goethe* (1961), as well as sundry studies of author reputation, mainly marked by a positivistic or hagiographical impulse.

Various factors, nonetheless, had historically limited any rigorous pursuit of reception studies in Germany. First of all, up to the mid-sixties, the classical notion of the autonomy of the artist held sway, obtaining—albeit for different reasons—in the case of *textimmanent* adherents, New Critics, and Theodor W. Adorno.[25] The primacy of the text made reception at best a secondary, indeed undignified activity, one that drew attention away from the sanctity of the aesthetic representation.[26] Second, a concomitant belief in the integrity of discrete historical epochs (which the literary historian was to scrutinize on their own terms as phenomena valid unto themselves) likewise fostered a scholarly curatorship of the past, a conservative attitude toward tradition.[27] Finally, the legacy of Wilhelm Dilthey and *Geistesgeschichte* continued to urge the exegete to commune with his/her object of study via an act of empathy toward its creator; the interpreter's task involved nullifying the temporal gap separating him/her from the artist by reexperiencing *(nacherleben)* a work's origin as it had evolved in its shaper's mind. The preoccupation with the temporal gap, a central emphasis of reception aesthetics, was perceived until recently as an "affective fallacy," offering nothing new, or at best a subjective interpretation that in no way affects the ineluctable presence of the text and the authority of the artist.[28]

These assumptions underwent extreme criticism during the late sixties in West German universities. Students began to disdain a detached mode of discourse which uncritically duplicated tradition, a legacy they perceived to be more often than not that of history's victors—and today's rulers. Anyone merely concerned with describing the world could not change it. Jauss's program issued from a period of opposition to previous socio-cultural models, a discontent articulated mainly by the student left that called the conservative intellectual heritage into question (just as the Young German Film rebelled against *Papas Kino*), laying bare its failure to mediate past experience and contemporary praxis.[29] Syncretic in its design, Jauss's program posed a liberal alternative to the rarified ivory tower ways of past legitimators of cultural tradition and the more radical impetus of contemporary leftist critiques.[30] He sought an Hegelian sublation of numerous impulses (Gadamer, Karl Kosík, Russian Formalists of the teens and twenties, Karl Mannheim, Karl Popper, Lucien Goldmann, among others), a unique blend that endeavored to renew current discourse by recognizing the seminal role of tradition, insisting the whole while that we confront this past *only in the present*. The goal is to make this encounter a productive—and not a reproductive—one, a merging of horizons.

Jauss most explicitly appropriates the insights of Gadamer's *Wahrheit und Methode/Truth and Method* (1960), in particular three main points[31]: the productive role of prejudice, the shaping function of horizon, and question-and-answer as a central factor in all interpretation. Drawing on Martin Heidegger's notion of *Vorverständnis* (pre-understanding), Gadamer argued that all understanding involves a certain set of predispositions we bring with us into the text, a collection of assumptions which the act of reading causes us to examine.[32] That we exist within a certain horizon—"the range of vision that includes everything that can be seen from a particular vantage point"[33]—need not be considered a liability, but rather offers an advantage, one that enables us to fuse past and present experience. Instead of obscuring the dialectic, Gadamer made it the basis for any historical understanding:

> In fact the horizon of the present is being continually formed, in that we have continually to test all our prejudices. An important part of this testing is the encounter with the past and the understanding of the tradition from which we come. Hence the horizon of the present cannot be formed without the past. There is no more an isolated horizon of the present than there are historical horizons. Understand-

ing, rather, is always the fusion of these horizons which we imagine to exist by themselves."[34]

The exegete carries on a dialogue with tradition, a question-and-answer activity that tests his/her assumptions. Temporal distance is helpful because it serves as a filtering process. "It not only lets those prejudices that are of a particular and limited nature die away, but causes those that bring about genuine understanding to emerge clearly as such."[35] Jauss intends to go beyond previous literary-historical ventures of materialist critics (in his account equatable to a vulgar Marxist theory of realism) and the formalist school by focussing on the historicity of both text and reader. In a series of theses, he outlines "how literary history might be methodologically justified and rewritten" (p. 171).

The central concept informing Jauss's project is *Erwartungshorizont*, i.e. expectation horizon, a notion borrowed from Karl Mannheim.[36] All texts, as all interpretations, issue from a distinct temporal vantage point. Literature, fundamentally dialogic in nature (for no text exists without a reader), stands within, questions, and often seeks to revise the shared assumptions and accepted traditions of a given historical moment. The novel exemplifies perhaps most dramatically how a specific mode of discourse forms an institution, one reflecting and influencing human praxis. The literary historian's—and Jauss speaks with this audience in mind and not a wider readership[37]—task involves not only recreating the expectation horizon of author and contemporary audience, but also opening these up to a conversation with present and past interpreters. This endeavor also includes the possibility of a reader's growing relationship in time to a text, the *process* of grappling with a work of art over a number of years. In a similar context, Jonathan Rosenbaum has suggested how this last insight applies to the work of a film critic:

> How can my subject be solid when half of it is me, the other half an external object, and memory has intervened to confuse any firm notion of barriers between us? How can the movie and I be regarded as discrete entities—the implied presumption of most criticism—when each of us is undergoing constant fluctuations, perpetual shifts of mood and tone and focus, both individually and collectively, with each unreeling?[38]

Reconstructing the expectation horizon allows one to discern the questions for which a text provided an answer; it enables one to establish how previous readers understood the work as well as to apply the object to the reader's present situation. The procedure makes it clear that there exists—contrary to the Platonizing dogma of philological metaphysicians—no single definitive reading of any given work (p. 183). *Reception history above all means placing a text within the context of its multiple possible meanings and interpretations.*[39]

Sensitivity to the historicality of literature involves for Jauss three things. First, a work dare not only be seen in terms of its effective history; reception theory must account for its significance and position within the historical constellations—Jauss limits these to the literary context (p. 189)—framing it. Second, one must place literature at the cutting stone between the diachronic and synchronic, "to analyze the literary horizon of a certain historical moment as that synchronic system in which simultaneously appearing works" can be received in diachronical terms, i.e. as timely or anachronistic, epigonal or innovative, ephemeral or of lasting value (pp. 196-97). Finally, the task of reception history involves going beyond literature and clarifying a work's function in relation to the whole of human history, "as *special history* in its own unique relationship to *general history*" (p. 199). This step means a concrete application to the reader's present situation, and thus constitutes a move past the hermeticism of previous literary histories. At this juncture, Jauss speaks of literature's crucial power in becoming a part of a reader's experience horizon, shaping daily praxis and influencing social action. Here literature takes on "that truly formative function which belongs to literature as it competes with other arts and social forces in the emancipation of man from his natural, religious, and social ties" (p. 207).

Film in the Spectator's Head

Some unordered preliminaries on the consonance of Jauss's insights and the resolve of West German filmmakers: "The search for a new language in German cinema," Miriam Hansen reminds us, "seems to be moving, not so much towards an evolution of individual styles, but rather towards forms of mediation between personal experience and the structures of the public sphere."[40] The weight of the past on the present has informed a large number of films from the FRG since the mid-sixties—or even earlier if one takes such precursors of Young German Film as Ottomar Domnick's *Jonas* (1957) into account. *Brutalität in Stein (Die Ewigkeit von gestern)/Brutality in Stone (The Eternity of Yesterday)* is the title of the first short film Kluge directed with Peter Schamoni in 1960. A host of feminist filmmakers have most noticeably continued this historical project while they search for appropriate forms of female narration. Recha Jungmann, for instance, revisits her abandoned family home in *Etwas tut weh/Something Hurts* (1979), sifting through pieces of her own past, reliving her parents' experience under National Socialism, and attempting to reconstruct her childhood "and what it had represented."[41] The relation of individual history to a more encompassing—and mostly unwritten and repressed—general history: this point of focus remains a consistent perspective at hand in West German films, a body of work very concerned with the question of historical memory, with the trauma of an as yet unassimilated past. The burden of that past, Moishe Postone has argued in a related context,

> has been too heavy to be ignored; the attempt to push aside the past in order to confront the present has not worked. The repressed past has remained, has continued to operate subterraneously, and has helped determine the mode of dealing with the present.[42]

Another conspicuous earmark of West German films addressed by reception aesthetics is their emphasis on the relationship between film and spectator. No other national cinema has so provocatively insisted on producing works that leave room for audience participation, on making films whose meaning presupposes spectator investment. "The film in the spectator's head" forms the basis of Kluge's film aesthetics.[43] The film journal *Filmfaust,* official organ for the newcomers to West German cinema culture, has repeatedly voiced its desire to promote spectator criticism *(Zuschauerkritiken).* Fassbinder's comments likewise underline the way in which West German film narratives open themselves to the viewer:

> This is my special attitude toward film. The reason is that I don't want to create realism the way it's usually done in films, but rather that a realism should come about in the audience, in the head of the viewer. It's a collision between film and the subconscious that creates a new realism. If my films are right, then a new realism comes about in the head, which changes the real reality, so to speak.[44]

As a collective body, West German filmmakers have fostered an expanding sense of experiential horizons, be it in documentations and chronicles of the everyday found in the worker films or the works of Klaus Wildenhahn and Günther Hörmann, be it subversions and reworkings of generic conventions such as the *Anti-Heimatfilm,* or, more radically, avant-garde undertakings. Take, for example, Klaus Wyborny's resolve to decimate conventional narrative discourse,[45] Vlado Kristl's attempt to chase spectators out of cinemas while making films people should ideally hate, or the quest of Werner Nekes, a filmmaker seeking the creation of new relationships between things seen and things heard,

> the invention of new languages through re-arrangement, addition, omission and the amassing of familiar verbal material and ways of seeing, in order to achieve an extension of our expression of the environment; in brief, making possible thoughts that were hitherto unthinkable.[46]

Beyond this, no other national cinema has so passionately forefronted the problems encountered by the individual film director working to keep open a critical dialogue with one's own history, to produce images that challenge accepted assumptions. "Is it possible to make films in German today?" runs the query at the center of Hellmuth Costard's reflections on the organizational structures shaping and limiting alternative image-making in the FRG today (*Der kleine Godard an das Kuratorium junger deutscher Film/The Little Godard* [1978]). As a group, West German filmmakers stand ardently aware of the dynamics behind reception mechanisms. Take two representative examples:

> ...Probably the most important factor in my survival has been the reception of my films outside Germany— particularly in the United States—which has grown more and more through the years (Werner Herzog).[47]

> ...The New German Cinema is much more a foreign affair than a national German one....In fact, the New German Cinema, the appreciation of New German Cinema, has come through the English, or French or American response. People in Germany are still very suspicious; or even indifferent (Wim Wenders).[48]

So much for the preview of coming attractions. Before I move on to a more ordered delineation of the tasks ahead, let me return to Jauss. However helpful his program is for the matter at hand, it does have problems that one must confront. Challenges to the theses came from both conservative and leftist quarters. The main objections of the former can more readily be cast aside than the serious misgivings voiced especially by materialist commentators. Advocates of text-oriented approaches basically uttered an often-heard reproach: reception aesthetics, in its stress on individual response, fosters subjectivism and psychologism. It furthers no authentic interpretation, but rather a sort of relativism in which every interpreter provides a different—and equally valid—interpretation. Jauss successfully countered this charge by pointing to the more apparent subjectivism of *textimmanent* advocates who attempt to put their object and their activity beyond history while pursuing a meaning *an sich*. Reception history takes into account previous readings of a text; it wants to unify "different interpretations in which the meanings of works of art—yielded to us and always only partially concretizable—especially manifests itself."[49] To critics who maintained that reception theory was nothing new, at best a "swing of the pendulum" (Manfred Naumann) rather than a shift in paradigms, Jauss replied that the basic constellations of reception theory (author, work, public) have always obtained and in part been recognized. But nineteenth-century objectivism in its various guises militated against any thorough-going attention to "the historical conditions of the aesthetic effect of works of art."[50] Only recently has a more inclusive concept of reception been used in literary studies, one that grants application—and not isolation—a seminal role.

Jauss, while steering clear of objectivistic dead-ends, still maneuvers himself into a precarious position when he tries to navigate territory traditionally claimed by Marxist criticism. In fact, he can be faulted for his decidedly monolithic reproduction of Marxist aesthetics, one that reduces a complex, far-ranging, and historically diverse array of possibilities down to a stick-figure representation, a unilinear reflection theory *(Widerspiegelungstheorie)* which at best reflects Georg Lukács of the 1930s.[51] Jauss asserts that one must do more than just account for the interaction between literary and social praxis; literary history needs to transcend what he perceives as Marxism's failure to deal with the relation of literary works to each other in their own diachronic and synchronic dimensions as determined by production and reception (p. 163). More than one critic has taken issue with Jauss's loose and vague use of the words "history" and "society."[52] Although Jauss maintains that reception studies ultimately view literature as part of human history and as a potentially powerful social phenomenon, he does not consider the role of literature in everyday existence, its material (extra-artistic) production and consumption mechanisms and the historical factors that determine these (cf. pp. 199-207). Such aestheticized accounts of film history, we shall see, have been the rule in most discussions thus far of West German film by American commentators. Jauss's rarified notion of expectation horizon *(Erwartungshorizont)* does not allude to anything apart from literature-oriented activity. Henry Schmidt has aptly described the idealistic limitations of Jauss:

> The mechanisms of cultural transmission that he describes... remain essentially intrinsic phenomena, whose emancipatory function is centered in aesthetic experience... His preoccupation with aesthetic expectation horizons obscures the social basis of literary communication processes and the material conditions of distribution.[53]

With these exceptions in mind, I now want to describe just which issues—out of the many possible subjects worthy of investigation—will receive closer examination in the subsequent chapters.

From the Distance I See This Cinema

Some ways in which one can use reception theory to combine both social and aesthetic structures within their specific historical dimensions in a discussion of West German film since 1962:

(1) *Outlining the expectation horizon behind the Oberhausen Manifesto and the subsequent development of Young German Film.* Hardly deferent to the past abuse of the cinematic medium in Germany, the Oberhausen signatories framed their statement (Hans Rolf Strobel drafted the text) as a critique of existing film practice in the FRG and promised to create alternative forms. This dramatic prologue to the Young German Film was an act of reception; it pronounced the death of a moribund tradition and the birth of a "new German feature film." Historical distance provides numerous insights into the constellations surrounding the moment and the resulting consequences. One dare not—as is common practice—mythologize the event as a "pioneer act in the past."[54] *Papas Kino,* as Jan Dawson has convincingly shown, did not fall down and play dead just because a band of 26 upstarts thought it *passé.* And the young filmmakers hardly constituted an organized front, a coherent movement:

> Far from being a sign of organised group activity, the Manifesto in fact constituted virtually the *total* of that activity; united only in their frustrations and ambitions, its signatories lacked any common plan of campaign.[55]

Re-reading the press accounts devoted to the fledgling directors, one notes how factionalism, infighting, and competitiveness seemed more dominant than any shared program. Still, certain commonalities provided points of focus, continuities bound up in the German past. First, one had to take into account the shattered nature of the country's film tradition, a tradition broken by twelve years of Nazi control, a heritage undermined by the Allied postwar hegemony over the film economy, and one made even more problematic by virtue of the existence of the German Democratic Republic and its film culture that had evolved along independent lines. Further, one had to consider Germany's abiding and "deep-rooted distrust of sights and sounds which tell its own history" (Wim Wenders).[56] The country's most able image-makers had almost without exception left Germany, either in search of more favorable working conditions or out of dire necessity; no other nation has known such a powerful emigrant cinema.[57] Young German filmmakers harbored a broken relationship to their own film history, the memory of the definitive contributions made by German directors to the evolution of the cinematic medium on the one hand, a haunting awareness, though, of just how insidiously the powers of the medium had been debased and misused during the Third Reich and after 1945. A further matter markedly underestimated (at least initially) by the *Jungfilmer* remained the international stranglehold exercised by the American film industry over distribution and exhibition mechanisms. Even after they celebrated their first triumphs in enlisting state support of their projects (the founding of the *Kuratorium junger deutscher Film* and the subsequent Film Subsidies Bill of 1967), they found themselves in a situation where they had the funds to make their films, but no real means of distribution and no viable home market. In a country without a developed alternative film culture (unlike Great Britain, France, or the United States), the young directors searched for an audience in a land ill-disposed to alternative image-makers.

(2) *Viewing West German films within effective historical continuities beyond simply film-based considerations.* At various junctures in German cultural history, youth movements have risen out of stultified contexts, reacting to a stagnant climate of opinion with radical challenges. The battle cry "Papas Kino ist tot!" (Papa's cinema is dead!) heralded a generational rebellion that must be seen in connection with related grand refusals in the German past, as a successor to the Storm and Stress effusions of the Werther era, the progressive endeavors of Young Germany in the pre-1848 epoch, and the Expressionist and Activist pamphleteering of the 1910s and 1920s. The links between Young German Film and the organized student left are more than just fortuitous. Contrary to the often-repeated claim that West German film did not ever

really deal with the student movement, one can in fact point to a large number of productions concerned with it: a myriad of documentations by filmmakers in West Berlin, Hannes Fuchs's *Film '68* (1968), Günther Hörmann's *Aktiver Streik an der Frankfurter Universität/Active Strike at the Frankfurt University* (1969), Wim Wenders's *Polizeifilm/Police Film* (1970), as well as later works reflecting on the effect of the experience such as Helma Sanders-Brahms's *Unterm Pflaster ist der Strand/The Beach under the Sidewalk* (1974) and Helke Sander's *Der subjektive Faktor/The Subjective Factor* (1980). The massive discontent with the false representations of the Axel Springer press (such as the *Bild-Zeitung,* the FRG's largest daily newspaper) in 1967 formed a rallying point that led to major street altercations.[58] A similar critique of manipulative depictions moved the young directors, whose first films abound with documentary footage and counter-information.

The desire to provide alternative views of the FRG and German tradition beyond the representations of the media and cultural legitimators stands as one of the primary characteristics of West German film, which over the years has continued to fight against a dominant discourse that sands off reality's rough edges. Both documentary and feature-film directors have resolutely ferreted out the oppressed present and the suppressed past. As Alexander Kluge—the most articulate spokesperson for Young German Film since its inception—has pointed out,

> it's always the suppressed element in society that has to be described: the dominant element describes itself; there's no need to add to it in the cinema. It's much better to describe the sub-dominant element, the suppressed element.[59]

From the early stages, West German filmmakers have taken part in a search for history, an endeavor particularly prominent on an international level during the seventies:

> There is indeed an alternative search for tradition and history going on today which manifests itself in the concern with cultural formations not dominated by logocentric and technocratic thought, in the decentering of traditional notions of identity, in the search for women's history, in the rejection of centralisms, mainstreams and melting pots of all kinds, and in the great value put on difference and otherness.[60]

This book will concern itself with the specific terms of this quest within recent films in the FRG.

Continuity and Subversion 19

(3) *Discussing West German directors' relation to tradition in their attempt to fashion a viable alternative national cinema.* Previous accounts have tended to obscure the continuities between recent films from the FRG and German film tradition as a whole. One stresses the reaction against *Papas Kino,* expanding it to a thorough-going denial of German film history. Commentators as a rule undialectically affirm contentions from Herzog and Wenders which claim the young filmmakers operated out of a historical void, starting from zero without any dependence on German models.[61] In general critics point to West German filmmakers' love-hatred of Hollywood, at the same time forgetting a very crucial consideration: a great deal of what we think of as American film tradition came about due to the contributions of emigrant German directors. And the Hollywood films bear no small trace of a film language originally articulated in German.[62] Young German Film's initial ventures into the *film noir* (pre-1971 Fassbinder, the early Rudolf Thome, Roland Klick's *Deadlock* [1970], Hans W. Geissendörfer's *Eine Rose für Jane/A Rose for Jane* [1970], among others) amount to revisitations of a genre whose roots stretch back to Fritz Lang's Mabuse-films. The Alfred Hitchcock so revered by Wenders and Geissendörfer had likewise learned to make films while working in the UFA studio during the twenties.[63] Fassbinder's discovery of Douglas Sirk and his reshaping of the melodrama meant more than a celebration of an American director of "weepies"; in a circuitous way, it constituted a rediscovery of a filmmaker who had left Germany during the Third Reich as well as a new approach to one of the seminal Weimar genres, the *Kammerspielfilm* (chamber room film) besides a continuation of the domestic tragedy.[64]

It surprises one just how little attention has been paid to the lines of continuity between recent and older German films. The following examples suggest how ubiquitous the connections are:

- The *Strassenfilm* (street film): Uwe Brandner set out to update the genre in *halbe-halbe/Fifty-Fifty* (1977);[65]
- Alexander Kluge and Edgar Reitz's reworking of the big city symphony in their Frankfurt-film of 1974;[66]
- The refurbishing of the *Heimatfilm* by a host of young directors at the start of the seventies;
- Recent attempts to shape contemporary worker films *(Arbeiterfilme),* mainly by the Berlin School;[67]
- Various linkages with the Expressionist cinema, most definitively in the work of Werner Herzog.[68]

Numerous filmmakers have deferred to Fritz Lang. Volker Schlöndorff's first film, the short *Wen kümmerts/Who Cares* (1960), starts with a dedication to "the greatest living German film artist, Fritz Lang." Kluge gained his initial lessons about the workings of the German film industry while watching Lang labor in a Berlin studio.[69] Wenders once wrote an eulogy to the director; at key moments in *Im Lauf der Zeit/Kings of the Road* (1976), a photograph of the one-eyed countenance stares at the viewer. During Niklaus Schilling's *Die Vertreibung aus dem Paradies/The Expulsion from Paradise* (1976), a couple sits in a Munich cinema watching *Der Tiger von Eschnapur/The Tiger of Eschnapur* (1959). Earlier in Schilling's meta-film, we watch the protagonist stand on a roadside, framed between a sign pointing to Murnau and another in the director of Munich: the glorious past and the difficult present. Perhaps the most well-known homage to the classic period of German cinema is Herzog's *Nosferatu* (1978), an effort "to build a thin bridge back to that time, to legitimize our own cinema and culture" (Herzog.)[70] Volker Schlöndorff stood before a Hollywood audience in the spring of 1980, accepting the first Oscar ever won by a West German director in the name of "all those who worked here and whose tradition we want to pick up: Fritz Lang, Billy Wilder, Pabst, Murnau, Lubitsch."

There are yet other points of contact: think of Herbert Achternbusch's deference to the Bavarian film and stage comic, Karl Valentin,[71] Schlöndorff's fascination with the dancer and actress Valeska Gert, a survivor from the Weimar era,[72] or Fassbinder's and Wenders's recycling of German film stars from earlier epochs.[73] Ulrike Ottinger pays respect to Siegfried Kracauer in *Freak Orlando* (1981) and numerous directors (among them, Herzog and Sohrab Shahid Saless) have tipped their hats to the patron saint of German film history, Lotte H. Eisner.[74] In recent years, one notes an increasing amount of intertextuality between German films, summations of a nation's film legacy such as we find in Syberberg's *Hitler, ein Film aus Deutschland/Our Hitler—A Film from Germany* (1977). One finds quotations from colleagues' work, e.g. the references to Straub/Huillet and Peter Lilienthal in Wenders's *Falsche Bewegung/Wrong Move* (1974), much less the "preview" of Wenders's next film in Wilhelm's dream (he murmurs "Im Laufe der Zeit," pointing to *Kings of the Road)*. These considerations suggest a number of possible explorations; I will in particular pursue the question of continuities within German film history in light of the renaissance of the *Heimatfilm*.

(4) *Describing the precarious situation faced by West German filmmakers within a complex of public institutions and showing how socio-economics have conditioned the making of images in the FRG.* Attending to the reception of post-Oberhausen productions means studying the adversary relations between young filmmakers and a host of instances: the older film establishment (cinema owners, commercial distributors, exporting organizations, producers), film critics (for the most autodidacts writing for the bourgeois press, a great number of whom have no real commitment to the cinematic medium), government funding agencies (federal, state, and local) and public broadcasting networks (in both of the latter cases, West German directors, to make the films they want must also make arrangements with these institutions, bodies highly subject to political pressures), and rating boards. These tensions obviously have had economic as well as aesthetic consequences. The relative lack of box-office success enjoyed by West German films until very recently comes in great part as a result of these conflicts, not—contrary to many domestic observers in the FRG—as a simple consequence of filmmakers' esoteric indulgences, their arrogance toward popular audiences. Given Germany's historical disdain for its most critical talents, its "other tradition" of intellectuals persecuted by contemporaries, a brash and economically powerless independent cinema bent on remodeling accepted images and casting new ones was bound to suffer its fair share of challenges. A discussion of the literature adaptation crisis of 1976-1977 will attempt to demonstrate how tenuous the democratic framework is within which West German directors work and just what sort of creative constraints can evolve during a period of political exigency.

(5) *Explaining the key role of international critical reception in fashioning public images of West German films —and the consequences thereof.* The image "New German Cinema" enjoys internationally developed in time as directors like the triumvirate Fassbinder/Herzog/Wenders and several others travelled with their films to festivals outside of Germany. The counter public sphere lacking at home was found in Great Britain, North America, and France. Appreciations, homages, retrospectives, and eventually commercial distribution of works by these directors indicated the extent of foreign admiration, very much in contrast to the luke-warm, indeed often hostile, reception accorded the *Jungfilmer* inland. This approval, bounded in foreign experience of a cultural output viewed from the distance, has furthered a codified notion of West German film which appears as "New German Cinema." The next

two chapters will deal with the divergent critical climates within and outside of West Germany which have led to such different estimations of the body of films, attending to the specifics of the mass media perceptions in the FRG and the USA, showing how each context has fostered certain aspects of the national cinema while obscuring others.

This book as a whole concerns itself with the larger contours of West German film history since 1962. Unlike the more detailed textual analyses to be expected in Elsaesser's and Corrigan's forthcoming studies, the present investigation focusses on more general questions. It attempts "to relate the production of cinema to a social structure,"[75] more specifically to pursue the production of West German films in the light of recent West German experience. The hope is to provide insights and contextual information previously lacking in American discussions of the New German Cinema as well as to supply perspectives regarding the workings of these filmic texts thus far neglected for the most by West German commentators. This book appears as a counter-history, one presenting alternative images from the history of West German film meant to call into question the success-story rhetoric common to many American accounts, images of

- —West German film on dangerous ground, criticized by some critics for its lacking sense of history, by others in the FRG for its inability to attract popular audiences (chapter two);
- —the mixed blessings present in the enthusiasms of American friends of the New German Cinema, a reflection on just where these hurrahs have led (chapter three);
- —a distinctly German genre, a home-grown product rarely considered in American depictions (the *Heimatfilm* in chapter four);
- —the darker workings of a subsidy system generally hailed by foreign observers as a utopian arrangement for independent filmmakers (the literature adaptation crisis in chapter five); and
- —the radical tendency in West German films to shape personal experience, not just as—in American accounts—a function of artistic flamboyance, but rather as a way to reflect subjective history in its relation to a larger present and past (chapter six).

To supplement this reception history of West German film, I have appended a list of the important films made in the FRG since 1962 as well as an extensive bibliography of English-language literature on the subject.

NOTES

Portions of this chapter appeared as "Expanding Film Historical Discourse: Reception Theory's Use Value for Cinema Studies," in *Ciné-Tracts*, No. 13 (Spring 1981), pp. 57-68.

[1] Klaus Eder and Alexander Kluge, *Ulmer Dramaturgien. Reibungsverluste* (Munich: Hanser, 1980), p. 5.

[2] "A New Approach to Film History," in *The 1977 Film Studies Annual: Part Two* (Pleasantville, N.Y.: Redgrave, 1977), p. 1.

[3] "Towards Decolonization: Some Problems and Issues for Film History in Australia," *Film Reader 4* (1979), p. 64.

[4] See "Stichwort: Bestandsaufnahme," in *Ulmer Dramaturgien,* esp. Kluge's comments on pp. 86-87.

[5] "On the Writing of the History of the Cinema: Some Problems," *Edinburgh '77 Magazine,* p. 10.

[6] The original published version of the essay appeared in 1967 under the title "Literaturgeschichte als Provokation der Literaturwissenschaft," a piece that underwent some revision prior to its 1970 publication in the collection *Literaturgeschichte als Provokation* (Frankfurt: Suhrkamp, 1970), pp. 144-207. Parts V-XII were translated by Elisabeth Benzinger and appeared as "Literary History as a Challenge to Literary Theory," in *New Literary History,* Vol. 2, No. 1 (1970), pp. 7-37. Subsequent references to the text will be quoted according to page number following the Frankfurt version.

[7] See Edward Buscombe, "A New Approach to Film History," p. 2.

[8] Myron Loundsbury, " 'The Gathered Light': History, Criticism and *The Rise of the American Film,*" *QRFS,* Winter 1980, p. 53.

[9] Cf. Gerald Mast's discussion, "Film History and Film Histories," *QRFS,* August 1976, pp. 305ff.

[10] Bill Nichols, "Critical Approaches to Film Then and Now," *Cineaste,* Spring 1972, p. 8.

[11] See Barry Salt's diatribe, "From Caligari to Who?," *Sight & Sound,* Spring 1979, pp. 119-23.

[12] Nichols, p. 10.

[13] Buscombe, p. 2.

[14] David Bordwell, "Our Dream Cinema: Western Historiography and the Japanese Film," *Film Reader 4* (1979), p. 58.

[15] Rien T. Segers, "An Interview with Hans Robert Jauss," *New Literary History,* Vol. 11, No. 1 (1979), p. 83.

[16] Ibid., p. 86.

[17] Ibid., p. 89.

[18] Clearly, the investigations of Christian Metz and Jacques Lacan have played the central role in these discussions. Recent feminist theory, likewise, has addressed questions of spectatorship and the dynamics behind viewer-text relations.

[19] All three quotes in Mast, p. 299.

[20] Loundsbury, p. 54.

[21] "Film History: The Narrow Discourse," *1977 Film Studies Annual: Part Two*, p. 11.

[22] Buscombe, in his introduction to *Film Reader 4*, quotes E.H. Carr's similar insight from *What Is History?*: "...the facts of history never come to us 'pure,' since they do not and cannot exist in a pure form: they are always refracted through the mind of the recorder" (p. 12).

[23] "Theses on the Philosophy of History," in *Illuminations,* ed. Hannah Arendt (New York: Schocken, 1969), p. 261.

[24] "An Interview with Hans Robert Jauss," p. 84.

[25] "The study of impact neither touches art as a social phenomenon nor should it be allowed to dictate norms to art, a position it has usurped in the spirit of positivism," claimed Adorno in his *Aesthetische Theorie* in the *Gesammelte Schriften,* Vol. 7 (Frankfurt: Suhrkamp, 1970), p. 339. See Peter Uwe Hohendahl's discussion of Adorno's attitude toward reception studies in "Introduction to Reception Aesthetics," *New German Critique,* No. 10 (Winter 1977), pp. 31-33.

[26] See Karl Robert Mandelkow, "Probleme der Wirkungsgeschichte," in *Sozialgeschichte und Wirkungsästhetik,* ed. Peter Uwe Hohendahl (Frankfurt: Athenäum Fischer, 1974), pp. 83-85.

[27] Jauss discusses this in Section II of the essay, esp. pp. 153-54.

[28] Hohendahl, "Introduction to Reception Aesthetics," pp. 33-35.

[29] For expressions of the methodological state of siege, see *Ansichten einer künftigen Germanistik,* ed. Jürgen Kolbe (Munich: Hanser, 1969) and a sequel, *Neue Ansichten einer künftigen Germanistik* (1973). For an overview of the impact made by the student movement on West German intellectual life, consult *Nach dem Protest: Literatur im Umbruch,* ed. W. Martin Lüdke (Frankfurt: Suhrkamp, 1979).

[30] Henry J. Schmidt, " 'Text-Adequate Concretizations' and Real Readers: Reception Theory and its Applications," *New German Critique,* No. 17 (Spring 1979), p. 158.

[31] Gadamer will be quoted according to the translation of the second edition of *Wahrheit und Methode* by Garrett Barden and John Cumming (New York: Seabury, 1975).

[32] Gadamer, pp. 235ff.

[33] Ibid., p. 269.

[34] Ibid., p. 273.

[35] Ibid., p. 266.

[36] See Mannheim's study, *Man and Society in an Age of Reconstruction* (New York: Harcourt and Brace, 1940).

[37] The failure of numerous reception theoreticians to take real readers into account is a central point of Schmidt's essay quoted above.

[38] *Moving Places: A Life at the Movies* (New York: Harper, 1980), p. 59.

[39] See Mandelkow, p. 88.

[40] "Cooperative Auteur Cinema and Oppositional Public Sphere: Alexander Kluge's Contribution to *Germany in Autumn,*" *New German Critique,* No. 24-25 (Fall/Winter 1981-2), p. 42.

[41] Jungmann as quoted in Claudia Lenssen, *Women's Cinema in Germany* (Munich: Goethe Institute, 1980), p. 17.

[42] "Anti-Semitism and National Socialism: Notes on the German Reaction to *Holocaust*," *New German Critique*, No. 19 (Winter 1980), p. 104.

[43] Klaus Eder and Alexander Kluge, *Ulmer Dramaturgien. Reibungsverluste* (Munich: Hanser, 1980), p. 15. See also *Alexander Kluge & The Occasional Work of a Female Slave*, ed. Jan Dawson (Perth: Perth Film Festival, 1975), p. 31: "You could understand film history as merely the collected ideas of different *auteurs* or entrepeneurs. But it's not the basis, it's an abstraction, it's the median. Whereas the real mass medium is the people themselves, not the derivatives like cinema or television. And if you have a conception of film which means that it's the spectators who produce their films, and not the authors who produce their screenplay for the spectators, then you have a materialistic theory" (Kluge).

[44] John Hughes and Brooks Riley, "A New Realism: Fassbinder Interviewed," *Film Comment*, Nov.-Dec. 1975, p. 14.

[45] See Wyborny's essay, "Random Notes on the Conventional Narrative Film," trans. Philip Drummond, *Afterimage*, No. 8/9 (Spring 1981), pp. 112-32.

[46] Nekes speaking about his film *Lagado* (1977) in Ulrich Gregor, *The German Experimental Film of the Seventies* (Munich: Goethe Institute, 1980), n.p.

[47] "*Images at the Horizon*," ed. Gene Walsh (Chicago: Facets Multimedia, 1979), p. 10.

[48] Jan Dawson, *Wim Wenders* (Toronto: Festival of Festivals, 1976), p. 8.

[49] "An Interview with Hans Robert Jauss," p. 85.

[50] Ibid., p. 83.

[51] Jauss presents Marxist literary theory in a much less slanted way in the 1979 interview, being sure to distinguish between the rigid orthodoxy of the Stalinist period and more progressive recent theoretical work from the GDR (pp. 88-89).

[52] See Berndt Jürgen Warneken, "Zu Hans Robert Jauss' Programm einer Rezeptionsästhetik," in *Sozialgeschichte und Wirkungsästhetik*, p. 290.

[53] Schmidt, p. 158.

[54] Miriam Hansen cautions against such a reading in "Cooperative Auteur Cinema and Oppositional Public Sphere," p. 36. Sheila Johnston voices a similar caveat in "A Star is Born: Fassbinder and the New German Cinema," *New German Critique*, No. 24-25 (Fall/Winter 1981-2), pp. 57-58.

[55] Jan Dawson, "A Labyrinth of Subsidies: The Origins of the New German Cinema," *Sight & Sound*, Winter 1980/81, p. 14.

[56] "That's Entertainment: Hitler: Eine Polemik gegen Joachim C. Fests Film *Hitler-eine Karriere*," *Die Zeit*, 5 Aug. 1977. An example of Wenders's point is the consideration, for instance, that the anti-Nazi Hollywood films of Fritz Lang still do not have a commercial distributor in West Germany.

[57] See *German Film Directors in Hollywood: Film-Emigration from Germany and Austria*, ed. Ernst Schürmann (San Francisco: Goethe Institute, 1978).

[58] See Michael Ruetz, *"Ihr müsst diesen Typen nur ins Gesicht sehen." (Klaus Schütz, SPD): APO Berlin 1966-1969* (Frankfurt: Zweitausendeins, 1980), pp.

32-35. Interestingly enough, we see the protagonist of Sander's *The Subjective Factor* looking through the pages of this volume during the film's first sequence.

[59] *Alexander Kluge & the Female Slave,* p. 29.

[60] Andreas Huyssen, "The Search for Tradition: Avant-Garde and Postmodernism in the 1970s," *New German Critique,* No. 22 (Winter 1981), pp. 35-36.

[61] A typical example among many instances can be found in Peter Gambaccini's article, "The New German Film Makers," *Horizon,* June 1980, p. 22: "They [the young filmmakers] began virtually without mentors or models. There was no tradition, nothing to follow, and subsequently, no fear of duplication or triteness. People like Fassbinder, Herzog, and Wenders enjoyed an enormous and rare freedom; they did not have to compete with, or be intimidated by, any older masters, and they could be sure that whatever they attempted would be highly original." There are, fortunately, exceptions to the undialectical rule. See Jan-Christopher Horak, "Werner Herzog's *Écran Absurde,*" *Literature/Film Quarterly,* Vol. 7, No. 3 (1979), pp. 223-34; and Thomas Elsaesser, "Primary Identification and the Historical Subject: Fassbinder and Germany," *Ciné-Tracts,* No. 11 (Fall 1980), esp. 47-48.

[62] See *Elements of German Expressionism in American Films,* ed. Ernst Schürmann (San Francisco: Goethe Institute, 1981).

[63] See François Truffaut, *Hitchcock* (New York: Simon and Schuster, 1967), pp. 18-19. Asked by Truffaut to "single out a picture that made a special impression" during his apprenticeship, Hitchcock mentioned Lang's *Der müde Tod/Destiny* (1921). "*The Lodger* is the first picture possibly influenced by my period in Germany," Hitchcock claims later in the interview. That influence? "...I took a pure narrative and, for the first time, presented ideas in purely visual terms" (p. 31).

[64] For a discussion of the *Kammerspielfilm,* see Lotte H. Eisner, *The Haunted Screen,* trans. Roger Greaves (Berkeley/Los Angeles, Univ. of Calif. Press, 1969), pp. 177ff.

[65] See David L. Vierling, "A Conversation with Uwe Brandner," *Kino: German Film,* No. 1 (October 1979), pp. 25-26.

[66] See the script to *In Gefahr und grösster Not bringt der Mittelweg den Tod/In Times of Danger and Greatest Peril, the Path of Compromise Leads to Death,* in *Kursbuch,* No. 41 (September 1975), pp. 41-84. A more recent example of the big city symphony is Alfred Behrens's *Berliner Stadtbahnbilder/Berlin S-Bahn Pictures* (1981). A restored version of Walter Ruttmann's *Berlin, die Sinfonie der Großstadt/Berlin, Symphony of a Big City* (1927) enjoyed a special screening at the 1982 Berlin Film Festival.

[67] See Richard Collins and Vincent Porter, *WDR and the Arbeiterfilm: Fassbinder, Ziewer and Others* (London: British Film Institute, 1981).

[68] Horak (see above) speaks of *Jeder für sich und Gott gegen alle/The Mystery of Kaspar Hauser* (1974) "as a meditation on its subject through a conscious awareness of the classic German film of the Weimar Republic, as presented by Eisner in her seminal history" (p. 223).

[69] See *Ulmer Dramaturgien,* p. 31.

[70] Nigel Andrews, "Dracula in Delft," *American Film,* October 1978, p. 33. Cf. his comments several years earlier in the celebrated interview with Jonathan Cott, "Signs of Life," *Rolling Stone,* 18 Nov. 1976, p. 53: Murnau's *Nosferatu,* claimed Herzog is "the most incredible film ever made in Germany. Once I make a film on that level, I'll be able to step back and be satisfied with my work. But I don't feel any continuity of culture with Murnau—he could have been from Japan or anywhere else..."

[71] We see Achternbusch walk out from under the Valentin memorial in Munich at the beginning of *Der Neger Erwin/Black Erwin* (1980).

[72] Gert played a supporting role in *Der Fangschuss/Coup de Grâce* (1976). Schlöndorff, captivated by the wizened presence, went on to make an hour-long film devoted to her, *Nur zum Spass—nur zum Spiel—Kaleidoskop Valeska Gert/Only for Fun and Games—Kaleidoscope Valeska Gert* (1977), viewing her in John Sandford's words as "a living link with the fabulous Berlin of the twenties, a link with the early German cinema (she had played, for instance, with Greta Garbo in *The Joyless Street,* and in Pabst's *Threepenny Opera*) ..." (p. 45).

[73] One might mention for instance Fassbinder's use of Brigitte Mira, Karlheinz Böhm, and Werner Finck as well as Wenders's casting of Marianne Hoppe in *Wrong Move.*

[74] *Kaspar Hauser* is dedicated to Eisner. Herzog's pilgrimage to her is documented in his book, *Of Walking in Ice* (New York: Tanam, 1980). Saless made a documentary in 1979 entitled *Die langen Ferien der Lotte H. Eisner/The Long Vacation of Lotte H. Eisner.*

[75] Edward Buscombe, "Introduction," *Film Reader 4* (1979), p. 12.

PART TWO
Two Views: Inland and Abroad

"Alle ich bumbum."
—Jorgos, the Greek *Gastarbeiter* in Fassbinder's *Katzelmacher*

Chapter Two

West German Film's Precarious Course in Time: *Misère-en-scène* in the Federal Republic

> *"Either Young German Film in the Federal Republic will become a political, analytical, reflective film —or one not worth talking about."*
> —Wolfram Schütte[1]

> *"The history of West German film from the sixties to the present is basically the history of —to use the jargon of finance ministers —economic growth from* Young Torless *to* The Tin Drum).... *Outside of several necessary minor corrections, everything would seem to be in best order: everywhere you look profits. And what losses stand behind them?"*
> —Klaus Eder[2]

> *"Either one knows that one can make films to please others or one must take up arms."*
> —Vlado Kristl[3]

The Redemption of (West) German Reality

In American estimations, the so-called New German Cinema seems to have risen miraculously out of the postwar shambles. The common explanation tends to run along lines similar to the following depiction in *Time:*

> With little encouragement, less money and no older hands to guide them, a few extraordinary young directors have given birth to a phoenix—the brilliant German cinema of Fritz Lang and Ernst Lubitsch that Hitler had consigned to the ashes 45 years ago. 'We had nothing, and we started with nothing,' says Rainer Werner Fassbinder... 'For a generation nobody made important films in Germany. Until us.'[4]

Etymologies of this nature abound, ones combining facts, truisms, and fictions in a dramatic scenario. While heralding the return of the cinema's prodigal son, such chroniclers conveniently ignore its considerable growing pains. Commentators pay lip service to the problems encountered by West German filmmakers at home, stressing how the directors enjoy a more considerable reputation abroad, and describing with relish the *enfant terrible* status of these brash individuals. One insists this is not a movement or a school, but instead a motley group of creators, "each making films with most distinctive and individual flavours."[5] In an attempt to avoid cubbyholing, one goes to the other extreme and atomizes the filmmakers, denying all but a marginal commonality to them. One rescues the integrity of personal visions at the cost of obscuring a shared historical starting point and an overriding cultural context behind these works. Rarely has one explored in more specific terms the dynamics central to the rise of West German filmmakers since the sixties, seldom have American observers delved into the concrete circumstances shaping the mixed fortunes of *Jungfilmer* in the FRG, and no one thus far has taken a closer look at the critical reception accorded the directors in their homeland.

Before pursuing these questions in the specific terms of Young German Film's development, I need to sketch three larger and related contexts pertinent to cultural production within the postwar FRG. First, West German intellectuals prior to the early sixties had failed to provide any effective opposition to governing constellations, either individually or collectively. The notion of the independent writer *(der freie Schriftsteller)* still held sway as did an attendant reluctance toward group endeavor. The most influential gathering of the country's authors, Group 47, included decidedly critical voices like Heinrich Böll, Günter Grass, and Martin Walser. Still, their protests stemmed from a noncomformism, which, though standing in a broken relationship to present conditions, also stood above them. (Not until the late sixties did each of these figures become prominent in organized politics.) One did not transform dissatisfaction with the *status quo* into concrete political praxis; social criticism assumed above all moralistic tones. Occasional scandals ensued, to be sure. But the most vehement controversy over Grass's ostensible pornography or Böll's attack on the Catholic Church did not stop conservative politicians from using these works in their ideological war against the German Democratic Republic, as proof of the new democracy's pluralistic openness to even its harshest fault-finders.[6] Group 47 presented an example well known to the young filmmakers,[7] a gathering of luminaries ill-disposed to common solutions, a body whose members, at best, could agree on their willingness to disagree with colleagues, an association with little impact on the overall tenor of the Adenauer times. The problems initially encountered by the *Jungfilmer* would in a number of ways replicate these experiences. Interestingly enough, Group 47's final meeting in 1967 would play an integral role in one of the earliest Young German takings of stock, Kluge's *Die Artisten in der Zirkuskuppel: ratlos/The Artists under the Big Top: Perplexed* (1967).

Second, the search of Young German filmmakers for an alternative network of production, distribution, and exhibition possibilities took place within a wider quest of an emerging leftist culture in the FRG for a counter public sphere. As a generation raised in the postwar years came of age, it turned against the mystifications and repressions of its elders' shadowy past, reacting as well to the monopoly over public experience exercised by the government and the establishment media, particularly public television, radio broadcasters, and the bourgeois press. Numerous groups formed themselves to combat the state colonization of everyday experience, seeking to find an outlet and means of expression which took into account a more encompassing view of reality.[8]

Finally, Young German Film arose at a time when intellectual life in the FRG underwent a marked politicization. The generational protest, above all, moved away from the radical hermeticism and existentialism characteristic of discourse in the fifties and turned to the writings of the

Frankfurt School. What came to be known as the *"Neue Linke"* (New Left) ascribed particular importance to analyses of the way in which the dominant order stabilizes and legitimates itself through mass manipulation. Max Horkheimer and Theodor W. Adorno's study of the culture industry provided a basic primer to how cultural manufacturers denigrate the heterogeneity of experience and offer it up in ready-made schemes: "Film, radio and magazines make up a system which is uniform as a whole and in every part."[9] Along with the recognition of the insidiously affirmative quality of such discourse came the call for alternative forms to combat and ultimately replace these mechanisms of social domination. One sought to subvert and restructure *(umfunktionieren)* given forms and replace the old contents. Adorno, whose misgivings about the cinematic medium remain no secret,[10] glimpsed in the first productions of the Young German filmmakers an alternative potential consonant to the critiques offered by himself and his peers:

> In this comparatively awkward and very unprofessional cinema, uncertain of its effects, is inscribed the hope that the so-called mass media might eventually become something qualitatively different. While in autonomous art anything lagging behind the already established technical standards does not rate, vis-à-vis the culture industry—whose standard excludes everything but the predigested and the already integrated, just as the cosmetic trade eliminates facial wrinkles—works which have not completely mastered their technique, conveying as a result something consolingly uncontrolled and accidental, have a liberating quality.[11]

The development of West German film since the early 1960s did not take the form of a continuous and steady evolution nor did it amount to an overnight success story. In retrospect, the most appropriate manner in which to describe this process of two decades involves tropes of combat. The history of West German film reads like a series of explosions, dramatic bursts of creative and critical activity which incited media reaction both at home and abroad, blasts which just as often misfired or were defused by various enemies. A highly volatile atmosphere has prevailed since the meeting at Oberhausen, a shrill exchange of verbal fire between directors and critics, between the youngers and *Papas Kino*. Young German Film initially gained public favor as the hope of the nation, while the press broadcast the return of the country's believed-for-dead cinema. When these high hopes did not find swift fulfillment (as was the case between 1962 and 1966) or when the first successes of 1966 were not immediately followed by yet-larger ones, critical voices in the FRG quickly derided the young filmmakers, repeatedly predicting their imminent demise and taking them to task for their brashness and lack of self-assurance. Yet, on a number of occasions when the end seemed at hand for the tenuous film culture, renewed explosions have surprised and confounded such doomsayers. A highly mercurial dialectic informs the long and circuitous path West German film has trodden since its inception, a road whose critical junctures are 1962, 1966, 1971, 1975, and 1979. What follows is an account of the various strategies employed by the young filmmakers and the particular challenges they encountered at home.

1962: Taking Leave of Yesterday

The Oberhausen Manifesto, the spontaneously drafted document signed at a short-film festival by a group of 26 ambitious youths on February 28, 1962, marked the semi-official birth of the loose collection referred to subsequently as Young German Film. It arose at a time when nearly everyone inside and outside the FRG involved with film concurred that the postwar West German film had reached the end of its creative tether. (It had been a weak link to begin with.) The collapse of *Papas Kino* coincided with the rather ungraceful leave-taking of the Adenauer government. The FRG had come to the end of a reconstruction period, having witnessed the restoration of a capitalist economy under the heading *"Wirtschaftswunder"* ("economic miracle").[12] This wonder had had its price and "the widely deplored low moral and intellectual level of public life in the Bonn Republic"[13] at the start of the sixties made clear just how great the toll of the Adenauer era had been. The infamous *Spiegel*-affair of 1962 sealed the moribund regime's fate. After the government-sanctioned arrest of various *Spiegel* journalists and the confiscation of the magazine's entire archives in the wake of an article critical of the West German army, public disfavor become so prevalent that Adenauer's own party, the CDU, forced him to resign his post within the next year. The event was to be a preview of coming attractions, the first in a series of structural dilemmas and legitimation crises experienced by the young democracy during the coming two decades.

The dire situation within the West German film landscape which brought about the Oberhausen Manifesto has received much commentary, most thoroughly in the studies by Joe Hembus and Klaus Kreimeier (although from very different vantage points).[14] Quite in keeping with the FRG's need to prove itself internationally, West German film creators sought to attract attention. They possessed an undeniable mania for the large and the impressive. Wanting to overwhelm their audiences with lavish production values, filmmakers fashioned a *Zutatenkino*, a cinema of high-cost ingredients, a "construction of value through an accumulation of values."[15] One enlisted expensive stars, spent large sums on extravagant costumes and sets, and turned to well-known literary classics and previously successful formulas (Weimar classics, *Heimatfilme*, serial productions). What was lacking was "the courage to think small,"[16] to face the everyday in all its grittiness, and to deal with the still unconfronted past. So-called *Problemfilme* like Gustav Ucicky's *Bis wir uns wiedersehen/Until We Meet Again* (1952) or Rolf Hansen's *Die grosse Versuchung/The Great Temptation* (1952), examples of a specifically German genre concerned with social dilemmas, rarely managed to place conflicts and contradictions (class-determined or historical ones) into a wider context. They tended to individualize crises as personal troubles and to resolve them with spurious upbeat endings.[17]

Ostensible attempts at confronting the trauma of fascism did little to further the often-called-for project of "coming-to-grips with the past" (*Vergangenheitsbewältigung*). A work like Helmut Käutner's *Des Teufels General/The Devil's General* (1954), for all its stylistic grace and directorial good intentions, never transcended a vague and fatalistic melancholy common to other West German evocations of the Nazi past. Nor did Kurt Hoffmann's celebrated *Wir Wunderkinder/Aren't We Wonderful?* (1958) go beyond an apolitical outrage toward the Third Reich— much less its persistence in the postwar present. Wolfgang Staudte came closest to a convincing understanding of the way in which Nazi Germany had made its dent on the FRG, especially in *Rosen für den Staatsanwalt/Roses for the Prosecutor* (1959) and *Kirmes/Fairground* (1960). These films presented a view of West Germany as a poorly repainted structure, a house that despite all appearances remains brown underneath, thematics to be encountered in numerous Young German films, already in the Böll-adaptations of Jean-Marie Straub and Danièle Huillet, *Machorka-Muff* (1962) and *Nicht versöhnt/Not Reconciled* (1965).

With the bankrupt legacy of *Papas Kino* surrounding them, what influences energized the believers in the new German feature film?

Foreign historians have underestimated at least two points of continuity present at the beginning. First, there did exist a small, but nonetheless significant number of precursors—modest-scale attempts made in the Adenauer years to merge formal experimentation and critical commentary. Herbert Vesely's *nicht mehr fliehen/Stop Running* (1955) posed itself against the dominant escapism and pretentiousness of West German films, offering a Cocteau-like blend of associations, memories, and projections with twelve-tone music, a fragmented narrative, and existentialist contours. The disjunctive documentary style of Ottomar Domnick's *Jonas* (1957) with its distanciated voice-over narration (a mixture of inner speech and ironic commentary) suggests the subsequent work of Kluge, Edgar Reitz, Hans Rolf Strobel, and others. Stylistically, Domnick drew on a series of sources: Hans Richter, Walter Ruttmann, Werner Hochbaum, indeed the arsenal of expressionist effects. Additional ventures into many-levelled discourse and untraditional narratives, works marked as well by a critical resolve and reflexivity atypical of their times, include Vesely's *Das Brot der frühen Jahre/The Bread of the Early Years* and Ferdinand Khittl's *Die Parallelstrasse/The Parallel Street* (both 1961).

Further, there was a circle of concerned critics working to create a progressive film culture. Writing in opposition to the general malaise in the FRG during the restoration period and most emphatically against the kind of quickly-produced throwaway fare which cluttered the country's cinemas, the editors of *Filmkritik* sought to promote an engaged leftist form of criticism. They drew inspiration from foreign models as well as Kracauer's belief in film's ability to disclose the workings of physical reality and to reveal the collective disposition of a nation. Wilfried Berghahn and Enno Patalas outlined their alternative model in the March 1961 issue.[18] Their emphasis—in keeping with Kracauer—remained ardently content-oriented. Nevertheless, they considered form as an integral part of any film's impact. Likewise they stressed the importance of audience appeal and spectator response. Most crucially, Patalas and Berghahn looked forward "to a film conscious of its social function" and advocated a critical praxis that questioned the constellations from which productions stem. Clearly, the links between *Filmkritik* and Young German Film were not as direct as those between *Cahiers du Cinéma* and the *nouvelle vague*. Still, connections did exist. Numerous early and future contributors to the journal would become filmmakers, among others, Hartmut Bitomsky, Hark

Bohm, Alf Brustellin, Harun Farocki, Theodor Kotulla, Gerhard Theuring, Rudolf Thome, and Wim Wenders. And figures like Patalas and Ulrich Gregor did enjoy very close contacts to the young directors. (A perhaps apocryphal story told to me by Frieda Grafe relates that it was Patalas who suggested to Volker Schlöndorff that he make a film based on Robert Musil's *Törless*.)

The young filmmakers' working environment was largely unfriendly to their project and generally sceptical about their abilities. The crisis of West German film, Joe Hembus wrote in his famous squib of 1961,

> is a logical consequence of the vitiated state of German film culture which manifests itself as an indifference toward film, a know-nothingness about film, as a closed-minded intelligentsia that has no relation to film, in the self-understood manner in which the intellectual elite ignores film, and in the reservations with which state, local, and private institutions approach film in their official dealings.[19]

West German films gave little sense of political life and problems of reconstruction in the FRG. The models mentioned by the Oberhausen signatories—at least initially—tended to be foreign ones, in the main the French New Wave and the Italian Neorealists, but also Luis Buñuel, Chris Marker, Robert Bresson, Andrzej Munk, and Stanley Kubrick, because, in Kluge's words of March 1962, "they showed us entirely new possibilities,"[20] something *Papas Kino* decidedly had not.

Still, a denial of *Papas Kino* did not mean abandoning cultural paradigms altogether. The call for "the new German feature film" echoed equally impassioned cries of expressionist pamphleteers earlier in the century for "the new man." A similar desire for a cultural renewal with a younger generation as its driving force was present in Wolfgang Borchert's famous postwar appeal "Das ist unser Manifest"/"This Is Our Manifesto." The first concrete attempt to put the Oberhausen program into practice transpired in Ulm where various signatories founded the *Institut für Filmgestaltung* (Institute for Film Design) in 1962 under the auspices of the *Hochschule für Gestaltung,* a school continuing the work of the *Bauhaus*. Expressly drawing a linkage between their initiative and "the finest tradition of montage in the twenties (Murnau, Richter, Lang, Eisenstein, Vertov, Dovzhenko),"[21] organizers of the *Institut* such as Kluge and Edgar Reitz stated three goals: (1) to educate a new generation of filmmakers in a theoretical center for cinema studies (an idea that came from Fritz Lang who had, at one time, planned on serving as the school's mentor); (2) to seek subsidies for the first feature films, a resolve achieved in the ensuing years; and (3) to insist on "a clear and continuing support of short film production as a constant field of experimentation for film in general."[22] Important components of the curriculum were Critical Theory, an emphasis on the role of montage ("Films were always conceived in terms of editing," claimed Kluge[23]), and an awareness of modern music and contemporary literature. These at any rate were the grand designs. The next years would bring a confrontation between the dreams of the *Oberhausener* and the realities of cultural endeavor within the mainstream of the FRG. After an initial burst of media fanfare, journalists, missing any concrete results, resorted to a wait-and-see attitude. A good while was to pass before the tyros found the wherewithal to deliver on their promises.

1966: First Signs of Life

The Oberhausen Manifesto did not change things overnight nor did it give rise to a wave of new films. Its function was that of a catalyst, one with tangible effects, the beginning of the Ulm *Institut* (an important training and experimentation site for the next two decades) and subsequent film academies in West Berlin (September 1966) and Munich (November 1967) and the establishment in February 1965 of the *Kuratorium junger deutscher Film* (Board of Curators of the Young German Film) being the most significant ones. While the *Jungfilmer*—still lacking a financial base—went on making short films and garnering festival accolades, Alexander Kluge and Norbert Kückelmann (among others) pushed for a funding arrangement, an *Autorenkino* that would allow for the "freedom from the conventions of the industry and from commercial interference from the establishment" outlined in the Manifesto. (Kluge no doubt remembered watching Fritz Lang suffer under the petty likes of the producer Artur Brauner in a Berlin studio.) Lobbyists for Young German Film fought for structures that would allow individual autonomy, seeking to liberate directors from "economic and dramaturgical rules" and "established forms of cinematic aesthetics" so that they might produce "personal testimonies, structures of ideas, chains of associations, reflections of feelings" (Ulrich Gregor).[24] This special notion of authorship took on much more radical contours than the French *politique des auteurs* in that it stressed the importance of having the artist enjoy absolute financial and creative control over a given film.[25] Bound up in a spirit of protest, *Autorenkino* was meant as a provocation posed

> against all know-it-alls, salesmen, show business trend-setters, against producers, distributors, dramaturgists, exhibitors, profiteers, careerists, theoreticians, critics, talent scouts, patrons of the arts, academics, against studios, against makeup, against the star system, against the cultural establishment, against the dependence on other art forms like literature and theater, against genres, bags of tricks, seasonal trends; in short, against all of those things that control film, that treat it like a child, suppress it, constrain it, use and abuse it (Edgar Reitz).[26]

The stress on subjective expression, however, and the simultaneous reliance on government (and later public) funding to support such artistic freedom would lead to a number of problems. *Autorenkino* in essence institutionalized directorial autonomy. It would also give rise to intense competition among individual *Autoren,* to ruthless vying for pieces of the subsidy pie. Likewise it would put the creators at the beck and call of the very institutions so much of their work aimed to call into question.

The *Kuratorium* had immediate consequences. Funded by the Ministry of the Interior, the body provided up to 300,000 DM for each work it subsidized. It would support some twenty films in the next three years, enough to give Young German Film the initial boost it needed—and dramatically alter the West German film landscape. Meanwhile the same dreary fare adorned cinema screens: Harald Reinl's Karl May-westerns (*Winnetou I* in 1963 was followed by two sequels), bastardizations of Weimar classics (Reinl's *Die Nibelungen I & II,* 1966), a spate of Edgar Wallace thrillers, *Schlagerfilme* (pop music films), and diluted—and deluded—adaptations of Thomas Mann stories by the would-be stylist Rolf Thiele (*Tonio Kröger* and *Wälsungenblut/Blood of the Walsungs,* both 1964). *Papas Kino* was not dead, though its continued output remained as moribund as ever. Even conservative critics bemoaned the lack of reality in West German films: "The penchant for the exotic, the desire for the fragrance of the wide world," claimed a *Spiegel* article late in 1964, "has become predominant in recent German film productions and has led to a phenomenon without parallel: the disappearance of German people and German settings from German films."[27]

Four films, all funded by the *Kuratorium,* generated much discussion in 1966 and caused numerous people to rhapsodize over Young German Film's turn to West German problems, over a new cinema bound up in the past and present of the FRG. As we shall see, this enthusiasm would pass quickly and even the initial response was anything but wholeheartedly approving. Ulrich Schamoni's *Es/It* and Volker Schlöndorff's *Young Törless* represented the FRG at Cannes that year where the latter received the International Critics Prize. Peter Schamoni's *Schonzeit für Füchse/Closed Season on Fox Hunting* won a Silver Bear at the Berlin festival a few months later and Kluge's *Abschied von gestern/Yesterday Girl* gained a Silver Lion after its Venice screening.[28] These works abound with a sullen anger, a brooding sense of bottled-up aggression. A generation disfranchised by the medium suddenly could express its own aspirations and disappointments on film—hence the very apt designation *Young* German Film.

All four debut efforts reflect the pre-1968 atmosphere, sketching private rebellions of alienated youths with few ties. The protagonists inhabit harsh and uninviting spaces: the frozen fields and rigid structures in *Törless,* the equally unappealing ruins and postwar buildings in the West Berlin of *It,* the mean streets in *Yesterday Girl,* and the sterile Düsseldorf night spots in *Closed Season.* The initiates have a hard time imagining themselves fitting into the world of their parents (whom they scorn with silence or mock), and yet, outside of a few vague ideas and an unchannelled energy, they lack any definite direction—and the world in which they move surely has no guideposts worth heeding. In *Yesterday Girl,* Anita G.'s interviews with a host of responsible but unresponsive officials only confuse her. Törless's teachers cannot answer his questions. Victor *(Closed Season)* disdains his elders' empty rituals and disenchanted lives. In the end, though, we watch the less-and-less confident young hero descend the stairs of a train station with his pregnant lover, disappearing into the moot dark of a conformist future. Anita G., a Jewish refugee from the GDR, tells a judge that she freezes even in summer. She wants to better herself, an inter-title informs us, but meets only cold efficiency and stultifying narrowness no matter where she turns. Moments one does not forget: Törless's retreat to his mother's lap at the close of Schlöndorff's debut; the silence that shrieks as Bruno and Hilke face each other at the end of *It;* Anita G.'s plaintive stare in the last seconds of *Yesterday Girl,* a close-up with all the haunting resonance of a frozen-framed Antoine Doinel in the final shot of Francois Trauffaut's *The 400 Blows*. The films conclude tenuously, denying spectators spurious harmonies, insisting on the possible while showing the negatively real. The sad face in Kluge's film is followed by a title, a quotation from *Crime and Punishment:* "Everyone is responsible for everything; if everyone knew this we would have paradise on earth."

Formally, these films have a rough edge to them. Limited budgets fostered the integrity of hands perforce dirtied by the everyday. Commentators praised the starkness of Ulrich Schamoni's Berlin city scapes and Kluge's explorations of the structures of public experience. Whether or not the works displayed a knowledge of a "new film language" called for in the Manifesto remained a matter of contention, the majority opinion being that most directors used an idiom more determined by socio-critical intentions than radical formal experimentation with the medium.[29] All of the works—save Schlöndorff's which bore solid evidence of the director's apprenticeship with various French filmmakers—had an elliptical and often jerky quality in which staged fiction and found reality frequently came together. A documentary mode dominated, a narrative discourse punctuated— especially in the work of Kluge and Reitz—by calmly intonated protocols, quotations, authentic documents, photographs, fantasy sequences, intertitles, voice-overs, and nursery rhymes. In *Not Reconciled,* Straub/Huillet exercised an uncompromising minimalism, rarely moving their camera or interrupting long takes, avoiding spectacle and undercutting audience identification—in all, offering a narrative intransitivity that stood as Young German Film's most extreme post-Brechtian challenge to conventional cinema. Vlado Kristl, an anarchistic bohemian, constituted the outer fringe of the ambitious counter-cinema with an unabashed resolve to subvert viewer expectations. *Der Brief/The Letter* (1966) was made, claimed its creator, for the blind—a typical statement from a director who felt most pleased when audiences squirmed or fled theaters. To re-create cinema, Kristl submitted, one must destroy it. On the one hand, Kluge, Straub/Huillet, and Kristl; on the other, Schlöndorff and some more accessible peers who placed radical contents in attractive and well-crafted containers. (Many, like the Schamonis, would soon revert to blatantly commercial patterns.) In the years to come the disparity paradigmatically embodied by *Yesterday Girl* and *Törless* would become even more apparent.

For all the initial laudations, press attention, and—to a certain degree—box-office success these films generated, one finds more misgiving than praise in the responses of West German film critics and historians. Repeatedly, commentators noted a strained seriousness, a stylistic earnestness inappropriate to the subject matter at hand. More irksome, though, was these films' fraudulent claim to verisimilitude and spontaneity; in fact, they started with a finished analysis before proceeding to reality, using actors and milieux to demonstrate theses. The Schamonis, in particular, had a reputation for heavy-handedness.[30] *It* and *Closed Season* only dabbled with surface appearances and reproduced social stereotypes, argued many. Schlöndorff's frames all too often contained a tension between open and closed style, between attention to milieu and formal control.[31] From the point of view of most progressive critics writing in 1966, Kluge, Kristl, and Straub/Huillet presented the hope for the new German film. (Among more conservative circles, these filmmakers enjoyed at best cautious respect, at worst downright disfavor.) The films of the Schamonis, Christian Rischert, Edgar Reitz, Haro Senft, Johannes Schaaf, and other first-wave productions, for all their different styles and varying quality, still added up in the minds of most critics to little more than affirmative culture garbed in radical veneers. "They repeat," submitted Urs Jenny, "popular notions of love, marriage, daily life and its problems; they reproduce popular modes of social criticism." More than anything else, Jenny noted, these films "attest to their directors' ambitiousness."[32]

1971: The Second Awakening of Young German Film

Young German Film's first productions created a great stir at a time when audiences were particularly responsive to alternative endeavors and politically-engaged art. With the fragmentation and ultimate collapse of the student movement in the early seventies followed the frustration borne of lapsed collectivity and a skepticism toward group endeavor. Further disappointment came with the new Social Democratic government's failure to effect the structural changes and liberalization one had hoped for when Willi Brandt became chancellor in 1969. A decided shift in the political wind became evident, a *Tendenzwende* many explained as a backlash against the activism and radical challenges of the student movement. Less and less the bickering *Jungfilmer*—they had squabbled from the start—could find moments of concord where they were able to speak as a "we." While they fought among each other and with the powers-that-be, West German cinemas continued to screen the increasingly egregious and still dominant speculations of the older branch (now referred to pejoratively as *Opas Kino,* i.e. Grandpa's Cinema). Nearly half of the FRG's productions consisted of *Pornofilme,* many of which posed as sexual enlightenment exercises replete with voice-over commentary and statistics, indications that the elders had even managed to mainstream the documentary trend. Weepies *(Schnulzen)* and schoolroom comedies *(Pauker-* and *Lümmelfilme)* also filled out film programs.

Young German filmmakers could not form a united front. Elsewhere in the fledgling film culture, one found numerous examples of infighting. Factions of the avantgarde clashed in the *"Coop-Krach"* of 1970, a battle between alternative cooperatives over the distribution of independent films. (The heyday of *das andere Kino,* West Germany's underground cinema, was over; a highly organized network of experimental adherents collapsed.) A falling-out between leftists and sensibilists on the *Filmkritik* staff caused seven co-workers to resign and brought a decisive change in the journal's editorial policy, a move away from its sociological emphasis in the direction of a more aestheticized discourse.[33]

Put perhaps too simply, the choice for Young German filmmakers seemed to be either sell out or stand steady, i.e. to conform to market realities and be able to make films or to make do defiantly as best as possible whatever the consequences. The *Arbeitsgemeinschaft neuer deutscher Spielfilmproduzenten* (Syndicate of New German Film Producers) had been formed in November 1966 to ensure more effective political representation as *Kuratorium* funds ran out and the *Filmförderungsgesetz* (FFG or Film Subsidies Bill) took shape. In the scramble among competing lobbyist factions, the *Jungfilmer* were outmaneuvered by the established old guard who succeeded in putting through a support model based solely on economic (not artistic) criteria.[34] The FFG, passed in 1967, placed filmmakers in a Catch-22 dilemma aptly described by Thomas Elsaesser:

> One had to have made a film (the so-called *Referenzfilm*) before applying to the Board, since the bill did not initially provide for subsidies on scripts or script-outlines, as in the case of the Kuratorium. Once the reference film was made, it needed a distributor. Production was again at the mercy of the prevailing distribution system...Were a

distributor found, financial success still depended on the amount of publicity he was prepared to invest in.[35]

A number of *Jungfilmer,* foresaking the Oberhausen design, made a commercial go of it. (This highly visible faction usually goes unmentioned in American considerations.[36]) Most clearly, not all the new filmmakers shared the ideals of Kluge or Straub/Huillet. Eckhart Schmidt's comments spoke for a collection of Schwabing dandies eager to make marketable movies:

> Crude reality does not interest me nor do dirty apartments nor pimply-faced people. When I watch films I like to look at attractive people and environments.... I think you can more readily show how things are by looking at the rich and the successful. Of course I can describe the dilemma of the person who goes to the factory or the office every day, but that does not interest me personally nor do I think it interests people in general.[37]

Marran Gosov, Roger Fritz, and Michael Verhoeven, in the wake of the popular wave of sex films, produced erotic comedies. Schlöndorff attempted to make a commercial success directed at a teenage audience. *Mord und Totschlag/A Degree of Murder* (1967), claimed the director, was for "15 to 17-year-olds! A film for Barbarella!"[38] *Michael Kohlhaas—Der Rebell* (1969) may have started with newsreel images of the 1968 street fights, but the rest of the large-budget international coproduction had little to do with topical issues.

Straub/Huillet in the meanwhile had moved to Rome and Kristl had become even more vehement. (After 1971 he would all but disappear from the film scene, retreating to shorts shot in super-eight.) Kluge's *The Artists under the Big Top: Perplexed* is a key work during this phase, a meta-film that analyzed—and embodied in its form—the problems facing filmmakers who cared about the cinema as a social institution, people who wanted to open audiences to the richness of experience and not close off the human senses. Leni Peickert, Kluge's ambitious entrepeneuse, sets out to establish a reform circus, one in which animals will be shown authentically, a circus worthy of the art form's long history. But Leni's idealistic plans never come to fruition even after she gains the necessary financial means; her theoretical concept is clear, but she still does not know for whom the circus is to be staged. Kluge's associative montage, essayistic discursiveness, and intellectual rigor likewise appealed to only a very small audience; his reform cinema was having every bit as hard a time of it as Leni's *Reformzirkus*. Young German filmmakers were being pushed into a commercial corner by the new subsidy system. Their films gained production funding, but still were not finding their way into cinemas. Distributors had lost interest in directors they derided as *Obermünchhausener* and cinema owners remained loath to exhibit films they considered to be box-office poison.

In April 1970 it was reported that nineteen Young German films could not find a distributor. The gap between *Kunst und Kommerz,* art and commerce, seemed unbridgeable: *Kunst* had in a number of cases gone over to *Kommerz* and the remaining truly independent artists suffered under the dictates of a commercially-based system. The central metaphor of Werner Schroeter's *Der Tod der Maria Malibran/The Death of Maria Malibran* (1971) posed the alternative: the creator must allow himself to be blinded in exchange for something to eat. A crisis both creative and economic faced the Young German Film, which above all needed a reliable means of getting its films into theaters. In 1971 as the Syndicate of New German Film Producers split over the issue of representation on the Film Subsidy Board (*Filmförderungsanstalt* or FFA), a new collective constituted itself as a self-help organization for filmmakers. The *Filmverlag der Autoren,* which included Uwe Brandner, Hark Bohm, Hans W. Geissendörfer, Peter Lilienthal, Thomas Schamoni, and Wim Wenders, was conceived as an independent production company, but soon turned to matters of distribution, a task assumed by the enterprising business manager, Laurens Straub. The *Filmverlag* did not mean an immediate end to the ills of the Young German Film. Nonetheless, at a time when the pursuit of film subsidies forced filmmakers into commercial deadends or competitive cut-throatishness, the alternative strategy provided hope for new solidarity among the *Jungfilmer.*

In 1971 a younger generation of directors came into the forefront of attention. After his underground dalliances, exercises in a number of genres and with models ranging from Hollywood gangster films to Godard and Straub/Huillet, Rainer Werner Fassbinder began to come into his own. *Warnung vor einer heiligen Nutte/Beware of a Holy Whore* (1970) summed up the beginner's earliest throw-away efforts, providing a self- criticism of what Fassbinder later described as his elitism and insularity. *Der Händler der vier Jahreszeiten/The Merchant of Four Seasons* came after Fassbinder's discovery of the work of Douglas Sirk and a visit with the director. It was to be his first film meant for a more general audience—not just his friends and admirers—and would mingle a consummate formalism with a sympathy for his object. A new project brewed in the mind of Werner Herzog, a talent still known at that time primarily as a maker of eccentric items, experimental documentaries (*Fata Morgana,* 1970), and gripping shorts. He planned a feature about an ill-fated search for El Dorado in the Amazon wilds, a mission commandered by a madman who harkened back to the tyrants of the Caligari-to-Hitler epoch.[39] The final product, *Aguirre, der Zorn Gottes/Aguirre, the Wrath of God* (1972) demonstrated the narrative disjunction between an official chronicler writing in diary form and a reality that can only be fully grasped with images—a situation one remembers from F.W. Murnau's *Nosferatu* (1921).[40] *Aguirre,* though not an immediate success, would mark a turning point in Herzog's career and later gain him international accolades.

Wim Wenders, the first noteworthy graduate of one of the film academies, made his commercial debut in 1971 after a number of student shorts and a long final project *(Summer in the City,* 1970). The important experience he underwent while doing an adaptation of Peter Handke's *Die Angst des Tormanns beim Elfmeter/The Goalie's Anxiety at the Penalty Kick*—a film that blended Hollywood grammar with a narrative intransitivity full of elliptical leaps, lacking transition shots, and missing motivations—was one the director described in an interview:

> I can see now what I did unconsciously: and the mixture exactly reflects the situation of someone who has inherited something, like the American cinema, but doesn't have an American mind. I realised while I was shooting *The Goalie* that I wasn't an American director; that although I loved the American cinema's way of showing things, I wasn't able to recreate it, because I had a different grammar in my mind.[41]

Fassbinder's mixture of Sirkian melodrama, social commentary, and formal deconstruction, Herzog's zeal for undisclosed states of mind and unexplored terrains, Wenders's synthesis of traditional narrative codes and ploys of the counter-cinema: these young West German directors clearly were coming out of an insular phase, formulating strategies that merged conventional and subversive elements, not forsaking a quest for alternative images—and still bearing a larger audience in mind. This amalgam, if anything, would bring the New German Cinema its international reputation in years to come.

Clearly one cannot ignore the many foreign influences that shaped the development of Young German Film, especially the role of Hollywood and Godard. And critics—foreign and domestic—have not. What has gone for the most unnoticed is the way in which Young German Film gradually found its way back to German film history: Fassbinder's recourse to Sirk and the tradition the master had brought with him to Hollywood from Germany, Herzog's turn—even though he has often denied it in interviews—to the expressionist models of the twenties, and Wenders's awareness of a hidden grammar every bit as much a part of him as the American one he unsuccessfully tried to emulate. In 1971, Niklaus Schilling made *Nachtschatten/Night Shadows,* yet another example of Young German Film's revisitaton of a cinematic legacy, a still unappreciated effort that abounds in *Stimmung* and exudes the atmospheric fascination of Carl Dreyer's *Vampyr* (1932) and early Murnau, besides its references to *Heimatfilme* of the Nazi era and the fifties.[42] Other filmmakers rethought German film history while revamping the *Heimatfilm,* imparting a less sanguine and simplistic view of provincial life than Bavarian cottage industry productions had during the Adenauer years. Other film activists, especially in West Berlin, reestablished the *Arbeiterfilm,* the worker film, a for-the-most-forgotten heritage from the Weimar Republic. Directors like Theo Gallehr and Rolf Schübel *(Rote Fahnen sieht man besser/Red Flags Can Be Seen Better)* were among the first to give expression to an important sector of West German daily life, one unexplored in previous postwar films. The genre would continue well into the seventies.[43]

Young German Film did not have many supporters at home during these years. Journalists enthusiastically and maliciously pointed out the splits within the *Jungfilmer,* sketching detailed and derisive typologies of the different camps.[44] Even sympathetic and intelligent defenders like Wolfram Schütte launched charges of capitulation in the face of pressing reality after the commercial wave of 1967 and spoke of "leftist resignation" when the *Anti-Heimatfilme* came out in 1971. None of the young directors, Schütte wrote, had made the dent on public life which Rolf Hochhuth achieved with *Der Stellvertreter/The Deputy* or had caused the necessary controversy that Günter Walraff's undercover explorations of West German institutions stimulated. This proved, maintained Schütte, just "how far away the young film is from a true critique of our society."[45] A continuing gap between films made for a small group of cineastes and ones produced for popular audiences characterized in most conservative critics' estimation the situation.[46]

The *Jungfilmer* had their heads in the clouds—meanwhile, *Opas Kino* dragged its feet in the dirt. The years of apprenticeship *(Lehrjahre)* reached an end in 1971. From here on out one tended to speak of the "New German Film" when discussing the *Jungfilmer.* (One did so not always sensitive to how the term replicated a certain Cold War mind set, the assumption that one could say "German" when one meant *West* German, acting as if the GDR did not exist.) Many indications of a renewed critical and creative energy emerged in 1971: a new hope for solidarity with the *Filmverlag* collective, an alternative distribution plan, the establishment of the first communal cinema in Frankfurt (the model for a non-commercial exhibition network of locally-supported houses),[47] and a growing awareness of one's own film history. Still, West German films remained an insider tip at festivals, unsuccessful in their quest for a home audience. Scorned, ridiculed, and ignored in the FRG, West German directors embarked on their years of wayfaring, their *Wanderjahre,* seeking abroad what they could not find inland.

1975: West German Film in the Cities

While international cineastes warmed up to a "German New Wave," audiences in the FRG continued to give West German filmmakers the cold shoulder. Paid admissions dropped from 136 million tickets sold in 1974 to 127 million during the next year for *all* films screened in West Germany, of which 80 percent were imports, American titles alone accounting for one-third. New German Film enjoyed a pauper's share of the ailing homemarket; between the years 1971-1974, its box-office successes can be counted on one hand. Many critics claimed the not-so Young German Film had simply run out of excuses. In recent years, argued Wilfried Wiegand, theories of Young German Film's failure had become more numerous than the films themselves. Perhaps it was time to blame the filmmakers for their troubles, especially when after substantial government funding and television cooperation the gap between West German films and their audiences remained larger than ever.[48] "When the German film-going public talks about movies," reasoned another unsympathetic reviewer, the bitter ex-*Jungfilmer* Eckhart Schmidt, "it doesn't think about German films (which are synonymous with sex, garbage, weepies, and *Jungfilmer* convulsions); it thinks about foreign films."[49] Schmidt was completely correct at least in one respect: the wave of *Pornofilme* continued to dominate cinema programs. (Of the 72 works produced in the FRG during 1973, 39 of them were sex films.) By 1975 a series of very lucrative "schoolgirl reports" *(Schulmädchenreport)* had enjoyed its eighth installment; more would follow.[50] And Schmidt likewise did have a point regarding the relative lack of stature enjoyed by independent directors at home. Little had changed.

With the collapse of *Film* (1970) and Kraft Wetzel's *Kino* (1974), accompanied by the increasingly obscure and random contents of each number of *Filmkritik* (the closest thing to a mouthpiece the young directors had had), no journal served as a sympathetic organ for the West German film culture. Filmmakers stood on dangerous ground where it was—to use the phrase Herzog lifted from Roger Corman's *The Trip*—"every man for himself." Lest the last sentence be misunderstood as a carelessly sexist one which forgets the female directors working at the time in the FRG, be it said that they still remained for the most ghettoized and ignored by the mainstream of West Germany's paltry film culture well into the mid-seventies. In 1974 Helke Sander and others established the journal *Frauen und Film,* a key step in the feminist filmmakers' attempts to create their own organizational structures.

New German filmmakers operated out of a pressure zone, "a field of force...made up of the German film industry, the hegemony of Hollywood over Europe, and the media policy of the Federal German government."[51] And this pressure zone had already stifled a great part of West Germany's most independent film activity. By 1975 many of the significant avant-garde and documentary directors had moved elsewhere or ceased to work in the film medium. Peter Nestler now lived in Sweden, Klaus Wyborny in New York, Straub/Huillet in Rome. Vlado Kristl mainly painted and wrote poetry, Hellmuth Costard made TV films for children, and Werner Schroeter spent most of his time staging plays.[52] The WDR *(Westdeutscher Rundfunk),* the country's important producer of television films, one guided through the early seventies by the FRG's most liberal programming policy, had come under much fire from conservative politicians and as a result stopped its series of progressive *Arbeiterfilme.*[53]

Ironically enough, at the same time a small number of West German directors triumphed abroad, a development that caused much irritation and confusion among domestic critics. What Americans spoke of as the "New German Cinema" virtually occupied the 1975 New York Film Festival. Fassbinder, increasingly shunned at home, where one depicted him as "a tired *Wunderknabe*" and a misanthrope,[54] discovered solace in an International Critics Prize at Cannes in 1974 for *Angst essen Seele auf/Ali: Fear Eats the Soul.* This came after an "Hommage à Fassbinder" in Paris and a work retrospective at the London National Film Theatre in 1972. Herzog's *Aguirre,* at best a cult film in the FRG known to a very few admirers, had transfixed international enthusiasts after showings in Mexico, Switzerland, Italy, and France. During the fall of 1974, *Jeder für sich und Gott gegen alle/The Mystery of Kaspar Hauser* played in West German cinemas and disappeared within weeks. Next spring at Cannes it won the Ecumenical Prize, the Special Jury Prize, and International Critics Award. British dailies raved about West Germany's new productions that dominated attention at the London Film Festival in 1975.[55]

Even if West German films had become important cultural representatives for the FRG abroad, critics at home remained unswayed in their low opinions, not understanding all this fanfare and casting the enthusiasms off as a fluke and a passing fancy.[56] A sympathetic voice like Wolf Donner's was rare indeed. He heralded the new cinema's undying energies and staying power despite imposing odds. "It's not the way films are being made in Germany today which is provincial," he maintained. "It's the way they're being treated."[57] For several months in 1975 some optimism did reign about a rise in attendance figures. By year's end, however, only several films (Schlöndorff/von Trotta's *Die verlorene Ehre der Katharina Blum/The Lost Honor of Katharina Blum* and Alf Brustellin/Bernhard Sinkel's *Lina Braake* and *Berlinger*) had managed to score at the box-office.

But more weighty considerations than the problems of the film industry came into play. A tense backdrop posed itself: professional proscription *(Berufsverbot),* state measures against potential dissidents in the form of a radical decree and massive government security checks, media hysteria that equated critics of the establishment with enemies of the state, and large-scale campaigns against the country's small group of terrorists as well as suspected "sympathizers." The shrill atmosphere fostered intense attacks on independent thinkers and alternative groups, who in popular representations became the real spawners of the criminal acts perpetrated by the *Rote Armee Fraktion* (Red Army Fraction or RAF, commonly referred to in the Springer press as the "Baader-Meinhof Gang"). In hindsight, the swing to the right characteristic of the mid-seventies in the FRG takes the appearance of a paranoid attempt to eradicate all challenges from left of center and "to prevent the emergence of emancipatory forms of civil cooperation and democratic self-determination,"[58] a reaction in sum against all signs of alternative and progressive thinking, a situation not without precedents in German history.[59] West German filmmakers—bound to a complex of government subsidy and public networks, instances very responsive to the whims of political fortune—reflected the tenuous constellations in a series of works focussing on victims captured by circumstances beyond their control. Quite understandably, more incisively topical films, ones concerned directly with the present and its consequences, did not get made.

In general one used oblique strategies to portray the FRG of the mid-seventies, flashing back to the turn-of-the-century in Alsace-Lorraine to show what happens to a radical civil servant in a small town (Peter Lilienthal's *Hauptlehrer Hofer/Schoolmaster Hofer*) or depicting government prying into the most intimate spheres of citizens' lives in a Weimar Republic setting (Ottokar Runze's *Verlorenes Leben/A Life in Vain*). West German film's protagonists were frightened housewives (Fassbinder's *Angst vor der Angst/Fear of Fear*), inhabitants of a fascist regime (Lilienthal's *Es herrscht Ruhe im Land/Calm Prevails over the Country*), and frenzied spirits eager to flee Bavaria (Herbert Achternbusch's *Die Atlantikschwimmer/The Atlantic Swimmers*). Pent-up individuals live in these frames, people wanting to transcend the constraints that fetter them, but not quite knowing how. Images of containment abound: John (in Ulf Miehe's *John Glückstadt*) peers out of a cell window, gazing into the distance with vague hopes, his face lit by a few rays of sun which pass through the bars. Wilhelm (in Wenders's *Falsche Bewegung/Wrong Move*) sullenly storms through his narrow room; his stereo blares as he too looks out of a window onto a near-empty town square. In a silent rage he shatters the pane with his bare fist. Herzog's Kaspar Hauser unknowingly fidgets with a toy horse, growling occasionally in a straw-covered dungeon before his master, a gigantic man shrouded in black, drags the innocent out into the world. Rieche (in Kluge's *Der starke Ferdinand/Strong Man Ferdinand*) sits uneasily in vague surroundings whose outlines we can only sense in the film's first shot. The indistinct background quickly becomes concrete; Ferdinand (a police officer soon to be a security expert) dwells in a smugly complacent country where economic prosperity is no longer so much a matter of miracles as it is a fact of life. Most people believe in the normal state of affairs. "Rieche," Kluge's off-camera voice relates, "believes just as strongly in emergency."

So too did most West German filmmakers, even if Volker Schlöndorff and Margarethe von Trotta remained the only ones to succeed in expressing it in direct terms. Fear and loathing in the Federal Republic: no movie measured the pulse of a frantic nation anno 1975 better than *The Lost Honor of Katharina Blum*. Scenes from a hunt in North Rhine-Westphalia, the film chronicles "how violence develops and where it leads," the subtitle to the Böll textual basis. While bystanders drunkenly celebrate carnival, police officials encircle buildings, break down apartment doors, plant bugs, and collaborate with yellow journalists. A repellent reporter from the scandal sheet *The News* (a fictional counterpart to the *Bild-Zeitung*, the FRG's most widely-read newspaper), playing on the atmosphere of suspicion and fear, destroys lives and careers for a sensational story. Again and again we glimpse headlines that twist facts; photographs in the tabloid distort Katharina so that she appears as a beast. Schlöndorff and von Trotta confronted and analyzed media abuse as a crucial factor in the ambience of government witchhunting. One might argue that they combatted the fustian of the *Bild* with bombast of their own, replicating in their approach the tactics the film as a whole meant to criticize. This becomes a very viable critique when one compares the film's shrillness with the relative soberness of Böll's narrative or when one looks at the one-dimensional characterization of Tötges, the unscrupulous journalist. Such judgments, though, overlook the contextual exigencies that made this kind of overstatement inevitable. Schlöndorff would suffer the political consequences of the film for a long while; he would be defamed as a sympathizer and subjected to vehement public attacks. For a number of years critics would gauge the political climate by determining whether or not another *Katharina Blum* could be made in it.

The question remained: how far could West German filmmakers go in criticizing the public and state institutions to which they ultimately were beholden? Looking at the films made between 1975 and 1977, not very far. This concern became particularly pressing after the signing of a cooperative agreement between the FFA and broadcasting networks in the form of the *Film/Fernsehen Abkommen* on November 4, 1974. During the next four years, public stations would invest 34 million DM in films co-produced for later TV airing. Directors ceased fears that early TV screenings might ruin a film's box-office potential, for the agreement stipulated that movies would not be broadcast until two years after production. Likewise, provisions were made for presale of high quality titles for future television exposure.[60] TV became "the patron saint of the new independent feature," functioning for the filmmakers in the seventies every bit as crucially as the *Kuratorium* had for them in the mid-sixties.[61] The *Film/Fernsehen Abkommen* brought additional support, though it further dramatized just how inexorably the would-be critical cinema was trapped in a labyrinth of institutional channels. Commentators like Hans C. Blumenberg would argue that West German filmmakers trying to make political works tended to confuse realism with understatement, exactness with a fetish for detail, the result being what the critic called "a cinema of zombies."[62] This kind of rhetoric, which came from one of the few interested and basically sympathetic commentators in the FRG, indicated how readily one tended to overlook the way in which many directors—unlike Schlöndorff and von Trotta—made films marked by obliqueness, indirection, and more subtle subversion.

1979: Coming of Age

The jubilant optimism expressed by West German filmmakers during the Hamburg *Filmfest* in September 1979 issued as a celebration of vicissitudes overcome. The years 1976 and 1977 saw the near collapse of the *Filmverlag* (saved only at the last hour by the intervention of Rudolf Augstein), even more virulent public and government suspicion toward progressive or freespirited activity, and threats of emigration by West Germany's most prominent directors. The summer of 1976 brought box-office disaster as film business hit a nadir. West German films slumped to a 12 percent share of the domestic market. While enthusiasm for the New German Cinema steadily grew abroad, representatives from the West German film scene gathered in Frankfurt to discuss the crisis situation. Subsidy boards and TV stations studiously avoided controversy or incisive social criticism, preferring instead to toe a line more in keeping with the conservative trend. A wave of bland literary adaptations resulted, turgid efforts like Heidi Genée's *Grete Minde,* Alexander Petrović's *Gruppenbild mit Dame/Group Portrait with Lady,* and Helma Sanders-Brahms's Kleist-biography *Heinrich*.

Past beneficiaries of the subsidy and TV cooperation system grew impatient with its red tape and soft stepping. At the 1977 Berlin Film Festival, Fassbinder announced his imminent departure for the United States. He despised the "mediocre picture books, lacking both imagination and courage" which had represented the FRG at Cannes that year and had received state film prizes.⁶³ Herzog intimated in the fall of 1976 he might move to Ireland, Werner Schroeter spoke of resetting in Mexico, and Kluge—frustrated by the indifferent response to *Strong Man Ferdinand*—retreated to his writing.⁶⁴ Syberberg claimed the West German critics had shunned his *Hitler*-film at Cannes and penned a passionate letter of farewell to a country he felt failed to honor his work, a land he denounced as moribund and sterile.⁶⁵ *Servus Bayern/Bye Bye, Bavaria* found Achternbusch's hero exchanging the spiritual wasteland of Bavaria with the icy scapes of Greenland and experiencing little difference: "In Greenland there's a lot more ice, but not as much as here by us." A number of other characters left home in films thematicizing emigration such as Herzog's *Stroszek*, Ingemo Engström/Gerhard Theuring's *Fluchtweg nach Marseille/Escape Route to Marseilles,* and Fassbinder's *Eine Reise ins Licht/Despair.* Everywhere one looked, signs of retreat: from all ties to others into a solitary state (Peter Handke's *Die linkshändige Frau/The Left-Handed Woman*), from job and responsibility to the margins of society (Uwe Brandner's *halbe-halbe/Fifty-Fifty*), and from one's *Kiosk* cubbyhole to the streets of Manhattan (Walter Bockmayer/Rolf Bührmann's *Flammende Herzen/Flaming Hearts*). West German films had taken flight—and numerous directors seemed on the verge of picking up and relocating.

For all their histrionics and protestations, West German filmmakers did not leave. Their threats did indicate a new confidence, though, one borne of their triumphs abroad. One could now say that one after all had alternatives. The ultimate answer remained staying put and witnessing the final acts of West Germany's most serious postwar crisis, the fall of 1977 with its abduction of the industrial leader Hanns-Martin Schleyer and the ensuing state-wide search for his kidnappers, events that paralyzed the left even further and found the right leading a witch hunt to "drain the swamp of terrorist sympathizers." Gerhard Zwerenz, in a provocative paper delivered at the 1977 Römerberg-conference in Frankfurt, asked why the FRG had produced so few political films based on West German realities, counterparts to American movies like *All the President's Men* and *Network.* "What is wrong with us? Are we lackeys? Blind? Or just too careful? Or maybe corrupt? Or simply cowards? Or perhaps under-financed?"⁶⁶ *Deutschland im Herbst/Germany in Autumn,* an independently-produced project (no state or TV funds were involved) of a filmmaker collective, endeavored to understand the public and private ramifications of the traumatic period. It served as the best possible answer to Zwerenz's probing questions and provided the most conspicuous demonstration of filmmaker solidarity and critical resolve since the Oberhausen declaration.

The film festival in Hamburg, staged by the directors themselves after a comedy of errors with the original planners of the event in Munich, came as a further sign of the filmmakers' sense that—as Herzog put it—"We are the German film."[67] The sixty filmmakers who gathered in Hamburg during the days in September 1979 signed a new declaration, a document charged with their newly-gained confidence. The text of the so-called *"Hamburger Erklärung"* (Hamburg Declaration) proclaimed:

> On the occasion of the Hamburg Film Festival we German filmmakers have come together. Seventeen years after Oberhausen we have taken stock.
>
> The strength of German film is its variety. In three months the eighties will begin.
>
> Imagination does not allow itself to be governed. Committee heads cannot decide what the productive film should do. The German film of the eighties can no longer be governed by outside forces like committees, institutions, and interest groups as it has been in the past.
>
> Above all:
>
> We will not allow ourselves to be divided
> —the feature film from the documentary film,
> —experienced filmmakers from newcomers,
> —films that reflect on the medium (in a practical way as experiments) from the narrative and commercial film.
>
> We have proven our professionalism. That does not mean we have to see ourselves as a guild. We have learned that our only allies can be the spectators:
>
> That means the people who work, who have wishes, dreams, and desires, that means the people who go to the movies and who do not, and that also means people who can imagine a totally different kind of film.
>
> We must get on the ball:
>
>   Hamburg 9 September 1979

The declaration summarizes in important ways the historical experience behind the rise of Young German Film to its more mature extension. The style and approach of the statement bear the stamp of Alexander Kluge, West German film's most significant public defender and spokesman since the sixties. The process of taking stock as a group involves the filmmakers' collective awareness of a common history, a shared continuity of concern over the years despite all their individual differences. West German filmmakers have in fact produced a number of works which seen together serve as a running self-reflection. In what other national cinema does one encounter the consistent and persistent meta-films which one finds in the FRG? The long series includes, among others:

—Franz Josef Spieker's *Wilder Reiter Gmbh./Wild Rider, Inc.* (1966): Young German Film and its inherent ambitiousness behind all the counter-culture bravado, the mercenary character of numerous go-getters posing as *enfants terribles;*

—Kluge's *The Artists under the Big Top: Perplexed* (1967): Young German Film with its lofty dreams and its difficulty finding people who would understand much less share these hopes;

—Fassbinder's *Beware of a Holy Whore* (1970): the *Autorenfilm* as a passion play wherein the director appears alternately as *deus ex machina*, petty tyrant, exploiter, and victim;

—Wenders's *Im Lauf der Zeit/Kings of the Road* (1976): a national film tradition without cinemas to show its films, a legacy symbolized by an emigrant film history incarnate, Fritz Lang;

—Reitz's *Der Schneider von Ulm/The Tailor of Ulm* (1978): an allegory depicting the experiences of the Ulm *Institut* project and its utopian designs in an historical setting.

One quite justifiably drew attention to West Germany's diversity, a fact often obscured at home and more often than not abroad. As the seventies ended, West German film had its prominent few and its unnoticed many. And the successes of Fassbinder, Herzog, Wenders, and others did not seem to arouse curiosity or receptivity for their less well-known peers. As a rule the most provocative rough edges of the national cinema were usually sanded off when one spoke of "New German Film" in the public sphere. The Hamburg document pointed in the direction of self-determination and freedom from outside pressures, reiterating the premises of *Autorenkino* yet again. But the necessity to restate the often-made points indicated how much outside pressure still loomed as a reality limiting creativity. (Only the most successful directors could on occasion—e.g. Fassbinder in *Die dritte Generation/The Third Generation* [1979]—finance their own radical undertakings.) Filmmakers, though, managed to form larger and politically more effective representation groups in the late seventies. The *Bundesvereinigung des deutschen Films* (The Federal Association of German Film) combined all of the individual interest groups within the wider whole of West German film culture under a collective rubric. As the subsidy system grew to include local and regional (Berlin, Hamburg, North Rhine-Westphalia, Bavaria) operations, filmmakers found themselves with even more possibilities. Detractors of course would argue that the system has spawned an overly subsidized cinema, giving rise to abuse of such funding by opportunistic producers and inept novices.

The insistence on a united front ("We will not allow ourselves to be divided") reflected the very real desire for solidarity and the equally real splits among individuals and groups. Documentary filmmakers criticized the topical pretensions of various directors, claiming that the feature films knew more of romantic irony than they did of the real world. Newcomers resented established elders as much as the *Jungfilmer* once scorned *Papas Kino*. And experimental filmmakers *did* exist apart from other sectors of the film culture, so much so that residents of Hamburg, one of the most important centers of West Germany's film avant-garde, were for the most unrepresented in the Hamburg *Filmfest* program. And a division not even broached by the declaration was that between the male mainstream and the extremely active feminist film culture, which still remained marginalized in the overall scheme. The cine-feminists continued to encounter a host of problems within the male-dominated film political establishment.[68]

The appeal to the spectator as the ultimate addressee of any film is of course a thought often uttered by Kluge. Not all of Kluge's peers, however, carried the thought to such radical consequences. The split, present already in the first batch of feature films after Oberhausen, that between *Törless* and *Yesterday Girl,* between a conventional notion of cinematic realism and a more radical one, found its continuation in 1979 in the different approaches of *Die Blechtrommel/The Tin Drum* and *Die Patriotin/The Patriot,* two films bound up in an exploration of German history. One received an Oscar and proved to be a box-office hit at home and abroad, the other remains still undistributed in the US and is very rarely shown in the FRG. Two very different senses of the past inhere in the films: Schlöndorff presents history as a set of completed events and shows how a larger socio-political backdrop shapes individual lives. Kluge sees history as something not simply given, as a sequence of events fixed for all time, but rather as something that must be reflected upon and confronted in the present if the future is to look any different. In one view the subject becomes the relatively powerless object conditioned by forces larger than itself; in the other, the subject, realizing its relative insignificance in the inhuman constellations of modernity, still recognizes that its efforts pose the only chance of ever changing the state of emergency in which it lives.

"We must get on the ball." Entering the eighties, West German film remains viable and multifaceted, a product of unrelenting tensions and impulses fostered by the clash between independent aspirations and public institutions, between the fatal continuities inherent in German history and attempts to break out of them. Its strength is its variety, but historically the most radical expressions of this variety have had the hardest time making their presence known. And if the words "tenuous" and "precarious" often come to mind when describing the evolution from Oberhausen to Hamburg, then the terms particularly apply in the case of the FRG's most innovative and difficult talents. What happened to Vlado Kristl? Why did Werner Schroeter remain on the periphery for as long as he did? Why do feminist filmmakers receive, at best, patronizing pats on the back, but little serious discussion? Retracing the path of the Young German Film, one finds a number of detours, wrong movements in the direction of the blatantly commercial cinema eschewed by the Oberhausen signatories. (Not only linguistic rules explain the shift from *Es* to *Das Boot*.) Along the way one encounters many exits: alternative filmmakers leaving Germany or the cinematic medium. There is the high road of the established international art film, the *Romantische Strasse* of New German Cinema. And there is a relatively undeveloped low road of popular film, a narrow thoroughfare that increasing and seemingly inevitable commercialization may very well widen in the eighties (without necessarily enhancing the overall network).

West German film has become famous abroad, a frequent box-office success at home, and the key hope in Europe's quest for a revival of its long-sagging film economy. The actual *practice,* though, of West German filmmakers has been more often than not—to use the phrase again—precarious, as their *reception* abroad has been, a fact one tends to obscure on this side of the Atlantic amidst the general excitement about New German Cinema.[69] Both of these considerations will receive further exploration as we retread various paths of the West German film since 1962 more carefully.

NOTES

Portions of this chapter appeared as "Critical Junctures Since Oberhausen: West German Film in the Course of Time," in *Quarterly Review of Film Studies,* Spring 1980, pp. 141-56.

[1] "Für eine rationale Phantasie im Kino. Darstellung gesellschaftlicher Wirklichkeit: Einige Bemerkungen zum jungen Film in der Bundesrepublik," *Frankfurter Rundschau,* 18 Nov. 1967.

[2] Klaus Eder and Alexander Kluge, *Ulmer Dramaturgien. Reibungsverluste* (Munich: Hanser, 1980), p. 85.

[3] Quoted in Heinz Ungureit, "Der junge deutsche Film—eine Bilanz," in *Neuer deutscher Film: Eine Dokumentation* (Mannheim: Verband der deutschen Filmklubs, 1967), p. 15.

[4] Gerald Clarke, "Seeking Planets That Do Not Exist: The new German cinema is the liveliest in Europe," *Time,* 20 March 1978, p. 51.

[5] John Sandford, *The New German Cinema* (Totowa, N.J.: Barnes & Noble, 1980), p. 6.

[6] See Heinz-B. Heller's analysis, "Literatur in der Bundesrepublik: Literatur im Zeichen der Rezession, Neuen Linken und 'Tendenzwende,' " in *Sozialgeschichte der deutschen Literatur von 1918 bis zur Gegenwart* (Frankfurt: Fischer, 1981), pp. 645-765.

[7] The Oberhausen signatories in fact met with the Group 47 during 1962, an event contemplated with much anticipation which ended in a total fiasco, each side in no way understanding the other.

[8] Literary life found a renewed interest for problems of the working world. Collections like the Dortmund Group 61 and the *Werkkreis Literatur der Arbeitswelt* (Circle for Literature of the Working World) posed themselves as alternatives to the bourgeois productions of the Group 47, taking recourse to a tradition of proletarian literature ignored by the cultural establishment.

[9] "The Culture Industry: Enlightenment as Mass Deception," in *Dialectic of Enlightenment,* trans. John Cumming (New York: Seabury, 1972), p. 120.

[10] See Diane Waldman, "Critical Theory and Film: Adorno and 'The Culture Industry' Revisited," *New German Critique,* No. 12 (Fall 1977), pp. 39-60; for a more differentiated account, see Miriam B. Hansen, "Introduction to Adorno, 'Transparencies on Film' (1966)," *New German Critique,* No. 24-25 (Fall/Winter 1981-2), pp. 186-98.

[11] "Transparencies on Film," trans. Thomas Y. Levin, *New German Critique,* No. 24-25 (Fall/Winter 1981-2), p. 199.

[12] Heller, p. 646.

[13] Koppel S. Pinson and Klaus Epstein, *Modern Germany: Its History and Civilization,* 2nd rev. ed. (New York: MacMillan, 1966), p. 588.

[14] Hembus, *Der deutsche Film kann gar nicht besser sein: Ein Pamphlet von gestern. Eine Abrechnung von heute* (Munich: Rogner & Bernhard, 1981) and Kreimeier, *Kino und Filmindustrie in der BRD: Ideologieproduktion und Klassenwirklichkeit nach 1945* (Kronberg: Scriptor, 1973).

[15] Hembus, p. 95.

[16] Ibid., pp. 85ff.
[17] Kreimeier, p. 160.
[18] "Gibt es eine linke Kritik?" *Filmkritik,* March 1961, pp. 131-35.
[19] *Der deutsche Film kann gar nicht besser sein,* p. 143.
[20] " 'Wir wollen den neuen deutschen Film machen': Zehn junge Regisseure legen ihre Absichten und Pläne dar/Eine *SZ*-Umfrage," *Süddeutsche Zeitung,* 10 March 1962.
[21] *Ulmer Dramaturgien,* p. 5.
[22] Ibid., p. 31.
[23] Ibid., p. 34.
[24] Quoted in Sheila Johnston, "The Author as Public Institution: The 'New' Cinema in the Federal Republic of Germany," *Screen Education,* Nos. 32/33 (Autumn-Winter 1979/80), p. 72.
[25] Johnston points to the decisive variance between the French and West German understandings of authorship: "In contrast to this project [the *politique des auteurs*] of showing that artistic self-expression *was* possible even in an industrial system like Hollywood, the West German directors, writers and administrators were arguing that the *Autor* film could only be made under conditions which assured the director-producer absolute financial and artistic control" (p. 70).
[26] "Das Kino der Autoren lebt!: Gegen die Verkäufer, Rezeptbäcker und Profiteure," *Medium,* May 1980, p. 32.
[27] "Flucht nach Teneriffa," *Spiegel,* 18 Nov. 1964.
[28] Karsten Peters, "1966—das erfolgreiche Jahr," in *Der junge deutsche Film: Dokumentation zu einer Ausstellung der Constantin-Film* (Munich: Constantin-Film, 1967), pp. 40-41.
[29] Hans Günther Pflaum and Hans Helmut Prinzler, *Film in der Bundesrepublik Deutschland* (Munich: Hanser, 1979), pp. 12-13. For variations on this theme, see the articles in *Neuer deutscher Film: Eine Dokumentation* (Mannheim: Verband der deutschen Filmclubs, 1967).
[30] See the critiques of *It* and *Closed Season* in *Neuer deutscher Film.*
[31] Peter M. Ladiges in *Filmkritik,* July 1966, pp. 397-98.
[32] "Der junge deutsche Film—eine Bilanz," in *Neuer deutscher Film,* p. 5.
[33] See Heinz Ungureit, "Kann die Filmkritik noch parieren?," *Kirche und Film,* May 1969, pp. 2-4.
[34] For a detailed account of the young filmmakers' experiences as lobbyists and politicians, see Jan Dawson, "A Labyrinth of Subsidies: The Origins of New German Cinema," *Sight & Sound,* Winter 1980/81, pp. 14-20.
[35] "The Postwar German Cinema," in *Fassbinder,* ed. Tony Rayns, 2nd rev. ed. (London: British Film Institute, 1979), pp. 9-10.
[36] The only account of any length is a translation of an article from *Spiegel* which appeared as "Young German Film" in *Film Comment,* Spring 1970, pp. 32-45.
[37] Quoted in Helmut Schmerber, "Kleine Privatrebellionen: Junge deutsche Regisseure filmen ihre Generation, Zwischen Widerstand und Anpassung," *Sonntagsblatt* (Hamburg), 9 June 1968.

[38] Quoted in Hembus, p. 245.
[39] This linkage has become even clearer with Herzog's own *Nosferatu* (1978) and *Fitzcarraldo* (1982). The term "tyrant film" of course is one taken from Siegfried Kracauer's *From Caligari to Hitler: A Psychological History of the German Film* (Princeton: Princeton U.P., 1947), pp. 77ff. See esp. p. 79 where Kracauer describes Nosferatu as a "scourge of God."
[40] The chronicle of Johann Cavallius can no more account for the plague in Bremen than can the diary entries of Gaspar de Carvajal explain the catastrophic journey.
[41] Jan Dawson, *Wim Wenders* (Toronto: Festival of Festivals, 1976), p. 9.
[42] See Daniel Dohter, "Der deutsche Heimatfilm: Ein Versuch," *Film-Korrespondenz,* September 1972, p. 20.
[43] See Richard Collins and Vincent Porter, *WDR and the Arbeiterfilm: Fassbinder, Ziewer and others* (London: British Film Institute, 1981).
[44] Kurt Joachim Fischer, "Bestiarium des Films," *Die Welt,* 24 July 1968.
[45] "Für eine rationale Phantasie im Kino," op. cit. His attack on the *Anti-Heimatfilm* appeared as "Linke Flucht in rechte Vergangenheit," *Frankfurter Rundschau,* 19 May 1971.
[46] See for instance Uta Gote, "Kunst, Kommerz—oder beides? Das Kino und sein Publikum—Zur Situation des jungen westdeutschen Films," *Die Welt,* 26 Nov. 1970.
[47] For a detailed analysis of the growth of communal cinemas in the FRG, see Dierk Joachim and Peter Nowotny, *Kommunale Kinos in der BRD* (Münster: Arbeitshefte zur Medientheorie und Medienpraxis, 1978).
[48] "Am Publikum vorbei," *Frankfurter Allgemeine Zeitung,* 4 Feb. 1975.
[49] "Das Kino hat uns wieder," *Deutsche Zeitung,* 27 Dec. 1974.
[50] See Henryk M. Broder, "Unterm Dirndl wird gekurbelt," *Die Zeit,* 17 Jan. 1975.
[51] Thomas Elsaesser, "The Postwar German Cinema," p. 1.
[52] See Dietmar Schmidt, "Werner Nekes über das 'andere Kino': Ausradierte Hoffnungen," *Rheinische Post* (Düsseldorf), 19 April 1975.
[53] Porter/Collins, pp. 104ff.
[54] See Benjamin Heinrichs, "Müder Wunderknabe. Rainer Werner Fassbinder: Von der Theaterkommune zur Kunstfabrik," *Zeit-Magazin,* 8 June 1973; and Hans C. Blumenberg, "Lüstern und sadistisch," *Die Zeit,* 31 May 1974.
[55] See Karl Heinz Bohrer, "Das Triumvirat des neuen Films: Späte Begeisterung in England," *Frankfurter Allgemeine Zeitung*, 15 Nov. 1975.
[56] The *Frankfurter Allgemeine* devoted an entire page to the reception of West German film abroad in the fall of 1975 with reports from correspondents in France, the U.S., and England, each of which registered distinct signs of incredulity and skepticism. See "Bilder einer gigantischen Selbstentblössung," 15 Nov. 1975.
[57] "Die Deutschen kommen: Warum der neue bundesrepublikanische Film im Ausland schafft, was ihm zu Hause nur mühsam gelingt," *Die Zeit*, 21 Nov. 1975.

[58] Jack Zipes, "From *Berufsverbot* to Terrorism," *Telos,* No. 34 (Winter 1977-78), p. 137.

[59] See Oskar Negt, "The Misery of Bourgeois Democracy in Germany," *Telos,* No. 34 (Winter 1977-78), pp. 123-35.

[60] See Pflaum/Prinzler, op. cit., pp. 90-91.

[61] Elsaesser, p. 14.

[62] "Politik der kleinen Spuren," *Die Zeit,* 28 March 1975.

[63] Quoted in Hans C. Blumenberg, "Das Jahr des Teufels," 8 July 1977.

[64] Peter Buchka, " 'Wir leben in einem toten Land': Haben die deutschen Filmemacher nur noch die Wahl zwischen äusserer und innerer Emigration?," *Süddeutsche Zeitung,* 20 August 1977.

[65] Syberberg's open letter bore the title "Wir leben in einem toten Land" and was dated June 20, 1977.

[66] "Die falschen Stoffe: Anmerkungen zu den Themen deutscher Filmemacher," reprinted in *Jahrbuch Film 77/78*, ed. Hans Günther Pflaum (Munich: Hanser, 1977), p. 43.

[67] " 'Wir sind nicht mehr der Jungfilm': *Spiegel*-Interview mit den Regisseuren Herzog, Brandner, Bohm, Hauff," *Spiegel,* 18 June 1979, p. 181.

[68] The dilemmas at hand in this tension have been documented over the years in the publication *Frauen und Film*.

[69] Cf. Kluge, "On Film and the Public Sphere," trans. Thomas Y. Levin and Miriam B. Hansen, *New German Critique,* No. 24-25 (Fall/Winter 1981-2), p. 207, under the heading "The Critical Measure of Production: What Is Left Out": "These days German cinema is becoming famous abroad. The actual practice of German filmmakers, however, is precarious. 'When skating on thin ice, the only way to keep from breaking through is to move as fast as possible.' "

Chapter Three

American Friends and the New German Cinema: Patterns of Reception

> —*Leopards break into the temple and drink to the dregs what is in the sacrificial pitchers; this is repeated over and over again; finally it can be calculated in advance, and it becomes a part of the ceremony.*"
> —Franz Kafka[1]

> "*We American critics are largely to blame for predetermining the categories within which foreign films are permitted to enrich our cultural diet.*"
> —Andrew Sarris[2]

From Young German Film to New German Cinema

The making of the New German Cinema to a great extent took place in the United States. Previously ignored, indeed neglected, West German directors gained much from the accolades accorded them by American cineastes; lacking a receptive audience inland, they turned abroad to find one. In the process, though, much went by the wayside. Young German Film—a product of the sixties' ferment and the revolt of a generation disenchanted with its elders' abuse of the cinematic medium—became transformed into an arthouse commodity, a hot item circulating in the seventies under the rubric "New German Cinema." This recognition had many consequences. American critics obscured the long years of struggle, the fierce battles waged to gain film and television subsidies, the intense debates about the problematic nature of Germany's broken film history, and focussed instead on the scintillating personalities and the remarkable visions presented by these madmen from across the water. One mythologized, writing of geniuses and brash *Wunderkinder* from abroad.[3] Tabloid tastemakers succeeded for the most in housebreaking the Young German Film, at least in American eyes, once again demonstrating the mass media's persistent and resourceful manner of turning radical challenges into pleasing—and ultimately harmless—entertainments.[4] Popular journalists and bourgeois film critics defused what began as a counter-cinema dedicated to alternative modes of representation, to views of the present not found in the established media, a cinema appealing to a younger generation previously ignored by German filmmakers, a cinema that angered, provoked, scolded, and challenged its audiences, demanding that spectators think along instead of succumbing to seductive images and narrative persuasions. Avant-garde attacks were channelled into the mainstream—and in the process, once-radical filmmakers (in some cases politically, in others formally, in a few both), thriving in the false aura created around them, found access to large budgets, international coproductions, star casts, and wide distribution networks. The making of New German Cinema in some ways has meant the undoing of the hopes espoused by the Oberhausen signatories and the utopian designs articulated over the years by Alexander Kluge. Young German Film and its American friends: the tale warrants telling.

West German Film at Home and on the Road

Moments out of time as an enthusiasm grows: during the spring of 1972, the New York Museum of Modern Art presented a series of recent films from the FRG, some twelve features and seventeen shorts. The initial response was one of discovery: "The current cycle at the MOMA," reported Jonas Mekas, "suggests that the new German cinema may be the most exciting new cinema outside of that of the American avant garde."[5] Amos Vogel indicated a month later just how lingering an impression these films had left. Post-Oberhausen output was "finally beginning to assume the proportions of a movement," even if its effect on the home market remained negligible and its successes in the main were limited to festivals and retrospectives.[6] Firmly established as a regular guest at each year's New York Film Festival (NYFF), the "movement" soon took on more conspicuous dimensions in American eyes. After the 1974 festival, Richard Koszarski remarked: "While a taste for Fassbinder, Herzog, et al. is by no means universal, they can no longer be ignored."[7] The message spread.

Late in 1976, Andrew Sarris wrote how New German Cinema (now written large) had

> inspired a growing body of serious film criticism... Cult followings have been developed by screenings at the New York Film Festival, the Carnegie Hall and Bleecker Street cinemas, the Film Forum, Goethe House, and comparable enclaves in Boston, Chicago, Washington, Berkeley, Los Angeles, and on innumerable campuses from coast to coast.[8]

1977 brought a lengthy "Fassbinder Festival" to the New Yorker Theater and later a New German Cinema retrospective to the Cinema Studio. Vincent Canby, the influential head critic of the *New York Times*, passed judgment:

> Of all the national film movements that have surfaced in Europe since the end of World War II, none has exhibited the consistent ferocity of the half-dozen German directors whose work now more or less defines—for us on this side of the Atlantic—the long-awaited renaissance of the German film.[9]

In a garishly illustrated article, *Time* declared a few months later that "as far as foreign films are concerned, the '70s belong to the Germans.... The Germans are now producing the most original films outside America."[10] Critical clamor reached a crescendo. Early in 1980, a headline in *Variety* announced an initial triumph on the American commercial market by Fassbinder and Schlöndorff films: "German Pix U.S. 'Breakthrough' Paced by *Maria Braun;* Seen Near $1,000,000; *Drum* heard."[11]

Young German Film made its first appearance late in the sixties at the NYFF as an esoteric bit of exotica, a ripple amidst the ebbing tides of Czech and French new waves. At first of interest to a small circle of film buffs, it gradually gained increased exposure, critical plaudits, and eventual commercial distribution. By the end of the seventies, New German Cinema had found a considerable audience in the United

States—and clearly its largest and most devoted following anywhere in the world. Its key figures took up residence as Valhalla directors, while auteurists refurbished their critical pantheons. Fassbinder was hailed as "the most original talent since Godard"[12]; Herzog enjoyed billing as a priestly visionary, a "seer, speaking the language of dreams, ravens, dwarfs, roosters, prophets."[13] Adulation for Wenders came a bit later, but after *Der amerikanische Freund/The American Friend* surfaced in the fall of 1977, commentators noted the rise of a Wenders cult.[14]

These high opinions and bounteous hymns of praise contrasted sharply with the moderate, often skeptical, indeed more-than-occasionally harsh appraisals Young German directors had received from their native public. Unlike their *nouvelle vague* counterparts, the Young Germans initially had no well-developed film culture out of which to work, no widespread network of film clubs, no *Cahiers du Cinéma*. The major West German film periodical of the late fifties and sixties, *Filmkritik*, concentrated more on foreign productions and did not speak of domestic activity at any great length.[15] The new generation had no critical identification figure like André Bazin, no dedicated protector of its film heritage like Henri Langlois, no accepted master like Jean Renoir. Siegfried Kracauer had fled to New York, Lotte Eisner to Paris, both many years before. The country's film legacy was spread all over the world, dispersed—what was left of it, at any rate, after two world wars—in a number of private collections and poorly-subsidized public institutions. The grand master of German film history, Fritz Lang, returned from exile after the war, a director who, for all his accomplishments, still enjoyed a much stabler and more considerable reputation outside his homeland.

Within the mainstream cultural establishment in the Federal Republic, film assumed a pariah status, taking up little space in *Feuilleton* sections, and receiving only a miniscule fraction of the public subsidies granted to the other arts. Young German Film, to be sure, had its small circle of aficionados, a marginal sub-culture at best, insular and incestuous; for the most, though, West German film critics writing for the big circulation daily newspapers and weekly magazines took on a rather haughty and, in some cases, blatantly hostile relation to the tyros. Domestic audiences showed *Jungfilmer* a cold shoulder from the start and the film branch (represented by the *Spitzenorganisation der Filmwirtschaft* or SPIO, the Head Organization of the Film Economy) actively militated against what it perceived to be a challenge to its position on the home market, a vendetta graphically documented over the years in its official organ, *Film-Echo/Filmwoche*.[16] Faced with a home audience ill-disposed to their sincere quest for new images, alternative narrative strategies, and political effectiveness, the Young German filmmakers had to search abroad for a counter public sphere. They found one eventually, in Cannes, London, Paris—and New York, San Francisco, Los Angeles, and Chicago. The tale of Young German Film on its way to recognition runs like a road movie full of halting starts and quick stops; there was no sudden fame for the once-poor filmmakers of Germany. Acknowledgment by filmgoers came in a number of foreign settings, at festivals, retrospectives, and homages, not overnight, but in the course of time. Without these accolades found in transit, it seems likely that the Young German Film would have died an obscure death at home, unmourned and quickly forgotten.

The divergent reception of West German filmmakers in the Federal Republic and the United States stems in part from two completely different critical climates. Many West German film critics still stand very much under the influence of Siegfried Kracauer, or at least a watered-down version of the premier German film historian and theoretician.[17] Following Kracauer's claim of 1930 that "the good film critic can only be thought of as a social critic,"[18] commentators in the FRG scrutinize the medium in terms of its manifest content, political message, and ideological assumptions. Clearly, notable exceptions to the rule do exist, individuals whose writing possesses a regard for film as both a social document and an artistic form, journalists whose output displays a stylistic flair and historical perspective characteristic of the best *Feuilleton* prose. One might point out Peter Buchka, Wolf Donner, Peter Jansen, Gertrud Koch, Enno Patalas, Wolfram Schütte, and Karsten Witte as significant exceptions to the rule in West German.[19] In general, though, a less careful and perceptive mode prevails, a tendency to reduce a film's worth down to its social use value: film criticism as political trend analysis.

The principal forums granted to film criticism in West Germany are:

1. **The bourgeois media:** daily newspapers (the conservative *Die Welt* and *Frankfurter Allgemeine Zeitung,* the more liberal *Süddeutsche Zeitung* and *Frankfurter Rundschau*), weekly large-circulation magazines (news digests like *Der Spiegel,* glossy journals such as *Stern,* and cultural readers like *Die Zeit*), or television and radio programs (film festival coverage, regular shows like *Aspekte* and *Apropos Film*);

2. **Film journals,** ranging from the blatantly commercial likes of *Cinema* to the widely-read *TIP-magazin,* as well as titles with more specialized readerships: *Filmkritik* (film esthetes), *Frauen und Film* (feminist film culture), *Filmfaust* (newcomers to the West German film scene), *Medium* (communications experts), besides no longer existent periodicals like *Kino* (West Berlin), *Film, Filmstudio,* and *Filmforum.* The most consistent emphasis on West German film was found in *Filme;* the most comprehensive and well-edited film journals in the FRG are the ever reliable press services, *Film-Korrespondenz* and *Kirche und Film;*

3. **Film books,** found mainly in the programs of several larger publishing houses (e.g. Hanser, Fischer, Rowohlt) as well as in occasional efforts by smaller firms. As the eighties commenced, though, the boom in serious film literature seemed to be over, as more popular titles such as the superficial *Heyne Filmbibliothek* hogged the market;

4. **Literary, cultural, and alternative journals** with occasional articles on film (*Frankfurter Hefte,*[20] *Ästhetik und Kommunikation, Merkur, Courage,* to name only some representative possibilities in this wide category).[21]

Few critics demonstrate more than passing interest for matters of cinematic form and visual/aural realization. Thumbing through the articles devoted to film in *Spiegel, Stern,* and dailies like *Die Welt, Deutsche Zeitung,* or a host of smaller provincial newspapers, one notes a distinct haughtiness toward the cinematic medium. Indeed, Hans-Jürgen Syberberg's continual indictment of the film critical establishment in the FRG, for all the sour-grapes thinking behind the attack, does contain some objective truth: there is very little sensitive writing on film being done in West German today. (That Syberberg's tantrum directs itself at exactly some of the most concerned and capable critics — ones whose major crime seems to have been not taking the director seriously enough — warrants mention.) The vast majority of West German film critics come from academic backgrounds, mostly literature, not film — no wonder in a country with next to no opportunities to study cinema systematically.[22] It comes as no surprise that a good number of directors and several critics spent time in Paris learning about and watching films. A film's impact on German public spheres, be they mainstream or progressive, bourgeois or alternative, depends for the most on its social relevance. An English observer of the German film scene in the seventies wrote:

> Despite the legacies of Brecht and occasional lip-service to more organic theories of political cinema, the dominant assumption behind most critical... practice in the Federal Republic is that the message is the medium; that style... is something slightly suspect, a kind of undemocratic aberration; and that form is merely the never-to-be questioned democratic framework within which information is sifted, analyzed, regurgitated.[23]

In the minds of even its most painstaking chroniclers (Hans Günther Pflaum and Hans Helmut Prinzler), Young German Film has been decidedly deficient in its attempts to reflect German realities, past and present; as a political program, the Oberhausen Manifesto did not live up to its promise.[24]

For all the liveliness and methodological multiplicity in American film discourse (something definitely lacking in the FRG) and despite numerous persuasive attacks on the auteurist position, the reception accorded Young German directors in the United States proves, if anything, that the authorship bias still exercises a very crucial influence on this country's film criticism.[25] In West Germany, one concentrates on the totality from which a film issues and measures a film's success in terms of its ability to reflect a larger social context. American commentators tend not to care how true-to-life Young German films have been. They focus instead on the unique world and singular vision presented by these individual directors. As a collective body more formative and—for better and worse—less materialist in their assumptions, American film critics (and not only popular ones) have emphasized the striking images, the deconstructed narratives, and the willful on- and off-screen eccentricities of the New German filmmakers. Typically, one lauds the idiosyncratic way in which these *enfants terribles* construct fictional spaces, praising them for their personal cinema bound in "a very glossy visual style." One applauds German directors for being concerned "not so much with facts and plots in their films as with subtleties and relationships": Fassbinder and peers "focus not on what happens, but how it happens, how life keeps changing, shearing off bits of our consciousness along the way."[26]

The majority of West German film critics are divided from their American counterparts by a critical praxis that conceives of cinema as a *mirror,* as a reflector of social experience and everyday reality, as opposed to a praxis that thinks of cinema as a *window,* as an opening onto worlds the viewer would otherwise never see. German critics have consistently since the mid-sixties berated the Young German Film for its failure to mirror contemporary West Germany. The Americans recognize the important and continuing contribution German filmmakers have made toward universal notions of the possibilities of filmic expression, in terms of form and style. What Kracauer overlooked, argues Sarris,

> was the pervasive influence of German cinema on our very notion of what constitutes a movie.... The inner space of the psyche, the sense of life as a labyrinth to be explored by the individual as part of a very private rendezvous with death, the breaking away from the arbitrary frames of the film image with the aid of the mysteriously moving camera so that the world is seen unambiguously as a unified cosmos rather than inferred ideologically from a series of carefully composed ideograms: this is the artistic heritage imparted to us in the masterworks of F.W. Murnau, Fritz Lang, and G.W. Pabst among many others.[27]

In this sense, the New German Cinema—as the heir of the Weimar classics—has advanced a singular world view.

German film journalists have voiced no small amount of skepticism about these accolades from abroad. They have been quick to point out reasons for misgiving regarding the fanfare, noting with gusto exceptions to the enthusiastic rule, chortling in some corners over American indulgence of directorial flamboyance, and registering more than a modicum of incredulity about the phenomenon in general.[28] If one cannot ignore the raves, one at least tries to put them in proportion. And to be sure, such second thoughts have some due justification. A number of factors indicate that the acclaim New German Cinema has found in America is not as whole-hearted, all-encompassing, or well-founded as a first impression gained from the media hurrahs might suggest. First of all, New German films enjoy only a limited amount of cinema play. Dan Talbot, head of New Yorker Films, the most significant distributor of West German titles in the country, estimates that of the 30,000 movie screens in America, "only 200 play foreign films at least 40 percent of the year." And, of these, "there are only 15 outside New York that are Michelin four-star theatres."[29] New German Cinema inhabits arthouses on the two U.S. coasts (thus the epithet *Küstenfilme* [coastal films], common parlance among skeptics in the FRG) and wends its way from campus to campus on the college circuit. Second, the approval German filmmakers have encountered abroad was a long time in coming and even today is anything but unanimous. New German Cinema has its passionate advocates; it also has vehement adversaries and scornful debunkers, individuals like Jay Cocks (former critic for *Time*), Pauline Kael *(The New Yorker),* Elliott Stein *(Film Comment),* and most definitively, John Simon *(New York).* "Pity the national cinema," the self-styled curmudgeon and derailer of pretentiousness claimed in an article entitled "German Measliness," "whose summit achievements are the films of R.W. Fassbinder and Werner Herzog (to say nothing of a Straub and Schlöndorff)!"[30]

Beyond this, American observers suffer all the tribulations of foreigners trying to keep up with a lively and diverse film culture from afar. *Aus der Ferne sehe ich dieses Land/From the Distance I See This Country:* the title of Christian Ziewer's 1978 film aptly states the dilemma. Only a very slight percent of West German output reaches America (for festival showings and Goethe Institute packages); even less will find a commercial distributor, a situation that has become increasingly acute since 1979, despite continuing attempts on the part of lesser-known directors to break into exhibition circuits. Vincent Canby describes the problem:

> Trying to get a fix on the state of German film art—and on the state of Germany—from the vantage point of New York is like studying a star 2,000 light years away. One can't be sure that the star we're seeing still exists. When we describe the star, we're talking history.[31]

To continue the trope: American audiences have gazed upon a small number of stars without much sense of how they fit into the vast space from which they originate. Even in the case of more well-known bodies, one has only a vague notion of the constellations to which they belong. Fassbinder's work, for instance, has graced the marquées of many cinemas,[32] but the films have been released and exhibited in no particular chronological order. Titles show up a year or more after their overseas runs. Other crucial productions still remain all but unviewed in the U.S. (e.g. the TV-films *Acht Stunden sind kein Tag/Eight Hours Don't Make a Day* [1972], *Martha* [1973], *Welt am Draht/World on a Wire* [1973], *Frauen in New York/Women in New York* [1977], and *Berlin Alexanderplatz).* [33] "The time machine is all askew" for American critics who perforce speak of Fassbinder "in the perpetual present with no clear sense of his stylistic evolution."[34] One considers West German cinema as a whole even though one only has access to a few bits and pieces; unfortunately, American critics generalize from very limited information, and these summary accounts are repeated in subsequent descriptions.

One must bear these factors in mind when discussing the foreign successes of New German Cinema. Nonetheless, one cannot so readily overlook the American effusions. For they represent a further compelling chapter in a half-century's tale of interactions between American friends and German cinema. As Hans C. Blumenberg once said: "A close tie always linked Hollywood and German film: not always a felicitous one, but one important for all concerned. American cinema would be unthinkable without the Germans [who worked] in Hollywood."[35] American studios virtually assimilated the entire mainstream of the Weimar Republic's film culture. German filmmakers like Ernst Lubitsch, E.A. Dupont, Paul Leni, F.W. Murnau, Karl Freund moved, or—in the case of individuals like Fritz Lang—fled to the U.S. and made an indelible mark on Hollywood productions. After World War II, Allied occupiers glutted German movie houses with American-made films that considerably shaped German post-1945 dreams, desires, and illusions.[36] American interests to this day maintain a strangle-hold on the German film economy, especially on distribution. One commentator recently provided a striking example of the hegemony exercised by the U.S. on the German market: "Before the viewer catches a glimpse of the major German film event of 1979, *The Tin Drum,* winner of the Cannes and German State prizes, 'United Artists—A Transamerica Company' flashes across the screen."[37]

It remains to be seen whether the key figures of yet another generation of German film talent will be appropriated by the American film industry. Despite much controversy regarding a possible arrangement with Hollywood, Fassbinder never made the move. He did, though, find his way to international coproductions (e.g. *Eine Reise ins Licht/ Despair* [1977], made in part with tax-shelter monies, scripted by Tom Stoppard, cast with European stars). His last films were too expensive for New Yorker Films to distribute in the US; they were handled by United Artists Classics, a further indication of an advance toward wider markets. Twentieth-Century Fox promoted Werner Herzog's *Nosferatu* (1978) and his latest film *Fitzcarraldo* (1982) originally was to feature an array of international stars. (Jason Robards and Mick Jagger, however, did not appear in the final version.) Wenders, the first Young German to move to Hollywood, went through countless scripts, much hardship, and five years to complete the lensing of Joe Gores's *Hammett,* a production screened at the 1982 Cannes Festival.[38] The director's excruciating experiences with an American studio and its overbearing producer have provided the background for Wenders's *Der Stand der Dinge/The State of Things* (1982). A planned production with MGM *(The Trap Door)* recently fell through. Although Wenders continues to maintain a permanent residence in Manhattan, he seems unlikely to become an American director.

Other West German filmmakers have succeeded in turning out commercially calculated and economically prosperous productions targeted for the export market as well as domestic circuits. Wolfgang Petersen's mammoth work, *Das Boot* (1981) and Ulrich Edel's *Christiane F. —Wir Kinder vom Bahnhof Zoo/Christiane F.* (1980) played to general audiences in America in both subtitled and (after the lucrative first runs in arthouses) dubbed versions (for wider release). No one thus far, though, seems likely to establish himself in Hollywood, although numerous German directors readily model themselves along such lines. Especially since the start of the eighties, there has been a spate of commercial activity in the FRG, so much so that one does not have to be a cynic to see links between these works and the output of *Papas Kino* two decades ago. Recent examples of such mercenary designs include: Klaus Lemke's cycle of hick-from-the-sticks-in-the-big-city films, Eckhart Schmidt's *Der Fan/The Fan* (1981), and Christian Rateuke and Hartmann Schmige's *Der Mann im Pyjama/The Man in Pyjamas* (1981).

The American reception of Young German filmmakers has brought them into the public eye, caused the making of at least modest fortunes—and whetted appetites for larger ones. Once independent denizens of the underground have collaborated with key members of *Papas Kino:* Fassbinder's *Lili Marleen* (1980) was scripted by Manfred Purzer and produced by Luggi Waldleitner, two of the *Jungfilmer*'s most vocal adversaries. Walter Bockmayer and Rolf Bührmann's *Looping* (1981), a film distributed by United Artists which recently surfaced on American cable TV, stars Shelley Winters and Sydney Rome, and is set in an obscure carnival background half German and half American. This work—meant to capitalize on the release of Winters's memoirs—is a far cry from the direct and naive flair of the directors' super-eight productions of the early seventies or their previous feature films.

Young German Film has come of age: not too long ago Canby dubbed the seventies the decade of New German Cinema. Much has been gained, but more has been lost. American hymns of praise to West

German films have had discernible consequences: the singling out of a trio of star directors, critical emphasis on a very small number of films, and the resultant neglect of the many other equally noteworthy factors that constitute the West German film scene.

Once Every Year at Lincoln Center

A closer examination of the rise of New German Cinema best begins with the New York Film Festival, for it offered the Oberhausen directors and their successors the first continuing forum outside of Europe. What started as a novelty—and in some minds, an irritation—on each year's program, one dominated by French titles, soon became a focal point every autumn in Lincoln Center. The following films enjoyed American premieres at the NYFF:

1967: *Abschied von gestern/Yesterday Girl; Der junge Törless/Young Törless*

1968: *Die Artisten in der Zirkuskuppel:ratlos/The Artists under the Big Top: Perplexed; Die Chronik der Anna Magdalena Bach/The Chronicle of Anna Magdalena Bach; Lebenszeichen/Signs of Life*

1970: *Auch Zwerge haben klein angefangen/Even Dwarfs Started Small; Othon*

1971: *Fata Morgana; Pionere in Ingolstadt/Pioneers in Ingolstadt*

1972: *Der Händler der vier Jahreszeiten/The Merchant of Four Seasons*

1973: *Die bitteren Tränen der Petra von Kant/The Bitter Tears of Petra von Kant; Land des Schweigens und der Dunkelheit/Land of Silence and Darkness; Geschichtsunterricht/History Lessons*

1974: *Alice in den Städten/Alice in the Cities; Angst essen Seele auf/Ali: Fear Eats the Soul; Gelegenheitsarbeit einer Sklavin/Part-Time Work of a Domestic Slave*

1975: *Faustrecht der Freiheit/Fox and His Friends; Jeder für sich und Gott gegen alle/The Mystery of Kaspar Hauser; Moses und Aron/Moses and Aaron; Die verlorene Ehre der Katharina Blum/The Lost Honor of Katharina Blum*

1976: *Angst vor der Angst/Fear of Fear; Im Lauf der Zeit/Kings of the Road; Die Marquise von O***; Der starke Ferdinand/Strong Man Ferdinand*

1977: *Der amerikanische Freund/The American Friend; Herz aus Glas/ Heart of Glass; La Soufrière*

1978: *Eine Reise ins Licht/Despair; Die linkshändige Frau/The Left-Handed Woman*

1979: *Die Ehe der Maria Braun/The Marriage of Maria Braun; In einem Jahr mit 13 Monden/In a Year of 13 Moons; Nosferatu*

1980: no German selection

1981: *Lightning over Water; Taxi zum Klo/Taxi to the Loo*

1982: *Bolwieser/The Stationmaster's Wife; Fitzcarraldo; Parsifal; Die Sehnsucht der Veronika Voss/Veronika Voss.*

Three steps mark the rise of New German Cinema in the United States:

(1) From 1967-1972, critics realized the post-war German film *misère* no longer completely obtained, that a generation of young directors had set about changing their country's film fortunes in a brash and ambitious way. Still, despite their respect for this enterprise, American commentators had a hard time with these works. As perceptive a critic as Sarris, hardly a stranger to Godard's cinema of deconstruction, could not grasp the distanciated discourse of Alexander Kluge's *Yesterday Girl:* clearly the director was "trying to say something about Germany today, but he gets lost in a scenario hopelessly alienated from itself."[39] Paul D. Zimmerman, summing up the 1971 NYFF, spoke for most American reviewers at that point who simply had little patience with the outlandish visions of the still adventurous *Jungfilmer:*

> There have been the usual disasters, such as German director Werner Herzog's meaningless meanderings around junk piles in the Sahara, *Fata Morgana*.... Another German film, *Pioneers in Ingolstadt,* may be the clumsiest, most mannered movie ever made about soldiers and their girls.[40]

(2) Two events deepened American appreciation of Young German Film in 1972: the spring MOMA series and fall premiere of *The Merchant of Four Seasons.* Independent image-makers like Dore O., Werner Schroeter, Hellmuth Costard, Birgit and Wilhelm Hein, Rosa von Praunheim, Ula Stöckl, and Werner Nekes received enthusiastic praise for their work and its "subtle and exciting 'decadence,' " its "intelligence, sophistication, subtlety, and daring." Jonas Mekas recognized

what would later prove to be a major staying power of the less cooptable fringes of Young German Film, a trait that spared these recalcitrant souls the early death of other "new cinemas": "The new German cinema is not restricting its researches and its creation to the narrow narrative film but is going into both extremes of cinema, the narrative and the non-narrative."[41] Both Mekas and Amos Vogel glimpsed an attempt to transcend traditional as well as avant-garde strategies and to shape novel critical and reflexive forms. Despite their intellectual rigor and sense of shell-shock, these films were not—as some complained— cold and unapproachable. They eschewed outdated illusion-making, to be sure:

> Time and time again, we are—by dialogue, editing, camera movement—pulled back from old-fashioned 'involvement' with individual characters, and instead exposed to the steely, ice-cold humanism of the '70s, set in a universe of chance, and hence, paradoxically, even greater human responsibility.[42]

A lingering awareness of the manipulative potential in the celluloid medium had fostered a cinema that refused to pander to audiences. Fassbinder's *The Merchant of Four Seasons,* shown later that year, characterized the socially-minded and post-Brechtian mode of filmmaking Mekas and Vogel hailed, a mode appealing both to emotions and minds. Response to *Merchant* was hardly uniformly positive (Nora Sayre's *New York Times* notice billed it as "a real loser"[43]), but it did cause ripples of excitement among some people discovering Fassbinder's "wonderfully idiomatic way to make movies." Roger Greenspun found the young Bavarian's work "neither easy nor ingratiating"; still he could not resist its galvanizing effect.[44] Sarris ventured so far as to claim that *Merchant* "may be the most exquisite achievement to reach these shores since the Golden Age of Murnau, Lang, Pabst, et al." For all that, he had to allow how Fassbinder's notoriety rested solely on the NYFF. Had it not been for Richard Roud's "predilection for Fassbinder, Straub, and Herzog, the contemporary German cinema would be completely unknown in these precincts."[45]

(3) West German directors virtually took the 1975 NYFF by storm, laying claim to the majority of critical fervor generated by the year's gathering. Mekas and Vogel had stressed the historical conjunctions out of which new German films appeared; they had vested hopes in the blend of traditional and avant-garde elements found in these works

while marvelling at the variety of possibilities. All of this was obscured in 1975 as stars were born. Fassbinder had become a taste many had taken the time to acquire. He was seen as a provocative eclectic, someone who fashioned images of a kaput modernity, retaining Hollywood conventions (the arsenal of the cinema of identification) while destroying filmic illusions with his hardly affirmative narrative strategies.[46] *The Mystery of Kaspar Hauser* helped revise many previous negative assessments of Herzog. (In 1970, New York spectators had reacted violently to *Even Dwarfs Started Small,* decrying its director as an exploiter and a misanthrope.) The Kaspar Hauser-film had received awards in the spring at Cannes—as Fassbinder's *Ali: Fear Eats the Soul* had the year before—for its stunning visuals and moving thematics, virtues commentators at the 1975 NYFF reiterated: "... The awkward framing, unpredictable camera positions, the flow of light that meanders in and out of the frame—is the droll, zestful, looming work of a filmmaker still on the prowl, making an exploratory work each time out."[47] *Moses and Aaron* was accompanied by the customary controversy attending screenings of Straub/Huillet's work. Schlöndorff and von Trotta's *The Lost Honor of Katharina Blum* proved to be more of a crowd- than a critic-pleaser.[48] In short, though, the long-anticipated breakthrough had come to pass. "The Germans are coming! The Germans are coming!" resounded as a refrain in a host of longer articles heralding the return of the cinema's prodigal son. Even if there remained a fair number of dissenting opinions, the majority concurred with Sarris's finding: "...Between them, Herzog, Fassbinder, and Straub make us rethink many of our most cherished notions about cinema."[49]

Products, Texts, and Stars: The Packaging of New German Cinema

Up until this point, only a relatively meager circle of filmgoers and critics had partaken of the new German films. That would soon change when many of the titles came into distribution (mainly through New Yorker, but also New Line Cinema, Liberty Films [previously known as Bauer-16], Cinema 5, and Gray City Inc., to name the more important commercial sources[50]), to be shown in arthouses and university communities. The summary appraisals and flip judgments passed in the pages of large-circulation newspapers and magazines soon gave way to more in-depth specialized articles in film periodicals. Cinema instructors and German professors started using the films in their classrooms[51]; and in subsequent years, more scholarly inquiries scrutinized the work of the *Jungfilmer*.[52]

Thus far, we have traced the evolving regard granted to West German films in America with an eye to immediate responses. Given the vagaries of foreign film distribution in the U.S., New German Cinema had first to become a media event (big write-ups in *Time* and *Newsweek*, rave notices in the *New York Times*, continuing attention in the *Village Voice*)[53] before it enjoyed the exposure that would guarantee its continuing presence on American screens. Film journalists secured West German directors widespread acclaim. Much curiosity came of the many laudations written about New German Cinema, a designation soon to become as familiar as *nouvelle vague*. As these films underwent closer scholarly examination, a dimension of discourse all but lacking in the FRG, it become clear how the media images that fostered the New German Cinema continued to persist in American representations, even in articles by more discerning and well-informed observers. Three crucial accents in the main govern the large amount of literature devoted to New German Cinema, accents gained from the media's making of the phenomenon.

(1) *A stress on the finished product and a relative disregard for the process.* Very few Americans—unlike their British colleagues[54]—demonstrate much understanding for the precarious dynamics behind the German film subsidy system or the tenuous socio-political climate in the FRG. Even would-be dispellers of critical clichés have promulgated further misinformation. In March 1978, Rob Baker, a critic generally sympathetic to West German filmmakers, penned an article attempting to counter the misconceptions and "self-perpetuating mythmaking" in American discussions of New German Cinema.[55] Seeking to clear the air, Baker only added to the media muddle. He seriously glossed over the question of the freedom of expression under the existing subsidy and television coproduction arrangements. Most of the West German directors, Baker submitted, are politically liberal and skeptical about the capitalist order. (A host of Berlin directors, as well as Fassbinder, Kluge, von Praunheim, Schroeter, and numerous other West German filmmakers would hardly accept the designation "liberal" as a compliment—nor would they be likely to concur with its appropriateness.)

> They are permitted to express their doubts and concerns openly in their films (there seems to be little censorship); and probably as a

> result of that freedom, their films steer clear of anti-government rabble-rousing and sophomoric rhetoric...[56]

The conclusions hardly correspond to West German realities. Anyone close to the vicissitudes of filmmakers in the FRG, especially at the critical juncture from which Baker's article issued, could only view the comments as utterly cynical—or simply mistaken. A few months before the essay appeared, major representatives of the film scene in the FRG gathered in Frankfurt for a symposium entitled "Sie schlagen uns das Kino tot" ("They Are Dealing Our Cinema a Death Blow"), so dire did the crisis seem.[57] The conservative climate of the years 1976 and 1977, a period where rather circumspect cultural politics guided film project commissions and television stations, will be dealt with in more detail later. Suffice to say that the support systems squelched undertakings with critical or controversial subjects, backing off from topical or incisively realistic glimpses at the socio-political workings of the FRG.

One encounters a similar misapprehension in Charles Eidsvik's introduction to a special number of *Literature/Film Quarterly* devoted to "New German Cinema," a piece meant as a guide through the larger context in the FRG:

> Because funding is allocated directly to filmmakers on the basis of scripts submitted to granting agencies, filmmakers have a great deal of authorial freedom in making their films once they are granted...[58]

In one regard Eidsvik is simply mistaken: West German filmmakers have not always enjoyed a high degree of autonomy in shaping films after approval of their scripts.[59] In fact, as Kluge's experience with *Part-Time Work of a Domestic Slave* showed, directors who deviate from the letter of a scenario can face disastrous consequences. At one point, Kluge was told he would have to repay his government subsidy because his finished film did not accord to expectations raised by the submitted script. More than one person suggested that the move was merely an official attempt to censure Kluge for the critical stance he expressed in the film toward existing abortion statutes.[60]

In another respect Eidsvik overlooks the problematic drawback to a subsidy system that demands finished scripts as the basis for its deliberations, in essence bureaucratizing creative activity. Hellmuth Costard's *Der kleine Godard an das Kuratorium junger deutscher Film/The Little Godard* (1978) trenchantly illustrates just how utterly the procedure can stifle image-makers:

The projects which gain official blessings are those which fit most tidily into the complex bureaucratic schemes for their administration: even an open-minded experiment must be squeezed into the requirements of the official forms. Thus Costard finds himself, from the moment he sets pen to paper, in a false position: obliged to draft what amounts virtually to a script for what he hopes will be an unscripted project; obliged to use words to try to convince a committee that it is time to liberate film from the heavy-handed tyranny of the written word.[61]

Government funding agencies and the subsidy system as a whole have provided support for independent filmmakers as well as subdued more outspoken and alternative impulses. This dilemma takes on particularly virulent proportions in the case of feminist directors, victims of both political and sexual discrimination, as Helke Sander has persuasively argued.[62]

The ability of a democracy to tolerate—and indeed support—criticism of its institutions remains the ultimate acid test of its viability. Contrary to the misleading descriptions supplied by observers like Baker and Eidsvik, critical filmmakers in the FRG have not always enjoyed ideal working conditions, no matter how utopian the German subsidy system might appear at first glance to foreign eyes. And one dare not forget the other pitfalls to be encountered once a film is finished: relatively limited exhibition possibilities, few reliable distributors, rating boards, and hostile critics. Clearly, such matters demand closer observation than text-bound American commentators have heretofore granted them.

(2) *Concentration on the formal attributes of films without taking into account the socio-historical setting they reflect or issue from: the primacy of text over context.* When American journalists and even scholars broach the issue of the politics espoused by exponents of New German Cinema, they invariably resort to broad and general locutions. Canby, for instance, pays lip service to the social-mindedness of "the German renaissance," claiming its members "have as their only easily defined common denominator the humanist's outrage with the quality of life in West Germany today..."[63] General terms forestall any critical appraisal. Likewise, one finds references to the strained contemporary situation in the FRG, obligatory mention of professional proscription and terrorism, but rarely any specific discussion of the events that framed the formation and evolution of Young German Film (the student move-

ment, the economic crisis of 1966-67, the conservative swing of the SPD after it assumed power in 1969) or influenced its continued activity (the turn of the political climate, the recession of 1974-75, stricter laws regarding political opposition, the fall of 1977). A film like *Deutschland im Herbst/Germany in Autumn* (1978), one so deeply rooted in recent West German history, had little success in America, a country otherwise so smitten by the work of Fassbinder and Schlöndorff, two of its many collaborators. U.S. distributors have resolutely steered clear of more incisively political films (something not always the case with other national cinemas[64]) such as the work of the virtually unknown Berlin School, feminist directors, and a host of unrecognized documentary filmmakers.[65] American critics prefer to deal with individual films, stressing the visual and narrative virtues of single texts while only vaguely attending to the context from which these works stem.

This approach has its problematic contours, especially when one deals with a body of films so distinctly grounded in a national experience. The relatively warm commentaries devoted to Fassbinder's *Lili Marleen* (1980) upon its American premiere, for example, talk about the film as if it only related to American traditions, to Hollywood musicals of the 1940s, to Douglas Sirk's Universal Studio love stories of the 1950s.[66] In their catalogues of stylistic precursors, American critics fail to mention a decisive influence, the UFA *Revuefilm* from the Nazi era,[67] a legacy Fassbinder draws from in the biopic. His stylistic indulgences here have given rise to the hardly-complimentary designation "*Lili Marleen*-Effekt," a mixture of show business, infamy, and swastika-pomp.[68] West German audiences who have been served a large amount of Nazi nostalgia in recent years, stage extravagances in brown by Boy Gobert and Peter Zadek,[69] clearly harbor a much more broken relation to Fassbinder's appropriation of the *Revuefilm* and the bankrupt aesthetics numerous performance scenes celebrate. In his positive review of the film, Sarris claimed "there is something intuitively eccentric in the conception and execution of *Lili Marleen*,"[70] a judgment one readily accepts—without sharing Sarris's enthusiasm.

Another case in point: Manny Farber and Patricia Patterson wrote one of the first insightful appreciations of Fassbinder's visual style. In their influential *Film Comment* homage, they detailed Fassbinder's "ritualized syntax" and commented on the stylistic dynamics of various key films, including *The Merchant of Four Seasons:* "It's not the sodden story of a downtrodden, henpecked husband but a hard portrait of middle-class ritual, circa 1972."[71] In actuality, *Merchant* quite fastidiously reconstructs the Adenauer era, not Germany of the seventies. An average German spectator readily recognizes the epoch's ambience in the clothing, hair styles, furniture, and kitchen décor, not to mention the many anachronisms, which (as Wilhelm Roth has pointed out) reach back to the Third Reich: Hans's sister's hairdo and white dress, the names Epp and von Schirach (those of important Nazi officials). Together with the modern license plates and telephones, Fassbinder established a linkage between three points in time: the Nazi past, the filmic setting in the fifties, and the spectator's present.[72] To locate the film's action in 1972 (it was made in 1971!) is to obscure the complex historical continuity set up by Fassbinder. At such a juncture, the limits of auteurist and formalist praxis (still inordinately dominant in American film punditry, despite advances made among academics by semiotics, post-structuralism, phenomenology, feminism, and psychoanalysis) become strikingly manifest.

(3) *The enshrinement of a few privileged directors in the auteurist pantheon, thus fostering an extremely narrow view of West German cinema as a whole as well as an often inaccurate image of the canonized luminaries.* During the mid-seventies, Fassbinder, Herzog, and Wenders took their places in a triumvirate that become synonymous with New German Cinema in American representations. The three dominated the media fanfare hailing the renascence of German film; a few others at best received some notice.[73] This factor, encouraged by the choices of the NYFF selection committee and film distributors, has made for a lively continuing discussion of the star directors' work. It has also promoted a rather limited view of what is arguably Europe's most dynamic and versatile national cinema. For all the care and close attention paid to the heralded trio's work, there exist crucial reasons for misgiving: critical adulation has given way on the one hand to cult worship and its attendant mythologizing. On the other hand, it has produced a number of clichés and misconceptions which gloss over or misconstrue some of the finer and subtler contours of these works, not to mention their more problematic aspects. This particularly applies to Fassbinder and Herzog, less in the case of Wenders.

Two related *idées fixes* characterize the large spectrum of Fassbinder literature, from more popular articles to recent scholarly treatments.[74] First, Fassbinder is viewed as a true inheritor of the early Andy Warhol and his films as a whole are seen as being "mainly sprung out of a camp sensibility."[75] These "camp" elements include a penchant "for the outlandish, vulgar, and banal in matters of taste, the use of old movie conventions, a no-sweat approach to making movies, moving easily from one media [sic] to another, the element of facetiousness and play in terms of style..."[76] Style—the ultimate criterion of excellence in the auteurist critical lexicon—thus forms the basis of Fassbinder's world view. Clearly, the director's concentrated and controlled use of artifice, the second-hand character of many of his narratives ("Camp sees everything in quotation marks"[77]) and his mannerism: these are all in accord with Susan Sontag's definition of the "camp" sensibility. But camp also involves

> a certain mode of artistic aestheticism. It is *one* way of seeing the world as an aesthetic phenomenon.... It goes without saying that the Camp sensibility is disengaged, depoliticized—or at least apolitical.[78]

It equally goes without saying that Fassbinder's films are anything but disengaged, depoliticized, or apolitical. "I don't make any films which aren't political,"[79] the director once said. Regardless of whether his work always delivers on its ambitious political resolve, and despite Fassbinder's dramatic efforts to promote his work before his untimely death in June 1982, one still has to admit his status as *the* great epic filmmaker of postwar Germany.

Taken as a body, his films serve as a psychological history of the Federal Republic from Adenauer to Schmidt, an undertaking embodied by the negative images at the end of *The Marriage of Maria Braun* and his often-mentioned plans to make a nine-part series of interrelated films depicting the history of West Germany.[80] Hardly one to use the past as a mere trapping for nostalgic evocation, Fassbinder envisioned his life's work as eventually leading to a sweeping chronicle depicting the German middle-class from 1848 to the present.[81] Fassbinder consistently focussed on the nature of the everyday in the FRG and its least attractive aspects: terrorism and state violence, intolerance toward unwanted but necessary foreign workers, the pressures of the workaday world and consumer society, and the battleground of sexual politics, among many other primary social concerns central to Fassbinder's *oeuvre*.

A political impulse is evident in his films, both in the choice of contents as well as the forms in which he couched them. His appropriation of the melodrama and its codes (expressive lighting, theatrical tableaux, garish décor within narrow interiors, mirror reflections, heavily enunciated music at crucial junctures) and his indebtedness to the work of Douglas Sirk have—especially since his homage to Sirk was translated into English[82]—received extensive commentary and analysis. If Fassbinder the "camp" director is one persistent misapprehension of his work, then Fassbinder the "Sirkian" filmmaker is another. Almost every discussion of his post-1971 work has attempted to cast him in a Sirkian mold. The fact is—as Tony Rayns has pointed out—that Fassbinder's major lesson from Sirk was one of strategy, not of style.[83] From films like *All That Heaven Allows* and *Written on the Wind* he learned how a popular form could be recast to appeal to audience expectations while simultaneously subverting them, calling movie-derived reactions into question as well as the social structures traditional narratives have reaffirmed. In recycling the ingredients for a potboiler, Fassbinder cooked up a different concoction altogether. (*Satansbraten* indeed.)

To label Fassbinder a "Sirkian" director is to diminish his singular voice and to overemphasize one influence among many in the work of someone who was a highly eclectic talent. Claude Chabrol, Werner Schroeter, Luchino Visconti, Robert Bresson, Alfred Döblin[84]: all of these forces figure crucially in his later films, just as the pre-1968 Godard continued to play a role in works like *Die dritte Generation/The Third Generation* (1979). "...This is what is disconcerting about Fassbinder," an American critic lamented, "he seems to be much more than the sum of his influences."[85] A critical view that simply sees his work as variations on Warholian or Sirkian themes cannot account for the continuing challenges posed by Rainer Werner Fassbinder.

An even more problematic tenor has governed American responses to Werner Herzog. This can to a great extent be traced back to Jonathan Cott's *Rolling Stone* panegyric to the director. Cott proclaimed Herzog to be a latter-day poet-priest, someone within "the mystical tradition of Master Eckhart and Jacob Boehme, as well as of the *Märchen*, supernatural fairy tale, tradition of the German Romantic poet Novalis."[86] Cott recorded the numerous tales of adventure and peril encountered in the making of Herzog's films, tales that in subsequent yeas have formed a *mythos* of sorts, an epic in which Herzog takes on all the qualities of a romantic hero-director. Herzog became in the seventies what Hermann Hesse was to the flower children of the sixties. "One considers him," Gideon Bachmann admitted, "without wanting to, as a sort of prophet."[87]

Several very uncritical and questionable assumptions are inherent in much of the American writing on Herzog. First, a cult of genius has evolved. Observers have accepted Herzog's self-characterization as someone standing beyond time and tradition. His works are seen as the symbolic expressions of a singular aesthetic experience, unmediated by historical or socio-political concerns. Herzog, as a host of faithful American interviewers have recounted, does not consider himself a Romantic or an Expressionist. He is not a typical 19th-century artist and he does not have much in common with other New German directors. If one must cubby-hole him at all, Herzog would rather have himself numbered among those visionaries who stood apart from the times in which they lived and yet saw through to the deeper realities of their day, figures like Heinrich von Kleist, Freidrich Hölderlin, Georg Büchner, and Franz Kafka. In this light, perhaps no single director has so clearly illustrated the romantic worship of the artist inherent in auteurism: one grants the creator a right of exception as an individual living outside of the restrictions binding others and apart from the temporal problems shared by most mortals.

A related perception insists that Herzog's images speak stronger than words. One takes the narrator's statement in *Fata Morgana* at face value: "There are landscapes without deeper meaning." "Film is not the art of scholars, but of illiterates," argues Herzog,[88] implicitly censuring those who would closely scrutinize his images and attempt to explain them. Discursive language only impoverishes the ineffable richness of the perceived image. Herzog, as one worshipper described him on the set,

> violently refuses interpretation...Any type of psychologically or metaphysically charged discussion is strictly forbidden. 'We must not talk about this,' he will say, and wander off.... One has no choice but to surrender to Herzog's vision, and though this is sometimes infuriating, it also has a dangerous appeal.[89]

Few filmmakers have so resolutely endeavored to control all aspects of a film, ranging from its creation (through directing landscapes and hypnotizing actors) to its reception (by extensive interviews meant to preform a viewer's experience and mold impressions afterwards). Clearly, not everyone has fallen sway to Herzog's guru-like charms. Elliott Stein, for instance, described a press conference attended by the director after a screening of *Nosferatu:* "...The air was thick with *Hoch Herzogian Anmasslichkeit* [sic!]: 'A necessity higher than our professional existences made us do this film.' You don't *really*," Stein commented, "have to sound like Moses coming down from the Mountain to make a good vampire film."[90] Such derision justifiably deflates unnecessary bravado. It does little, though, to further serious discussion about a director whose work poses a distinct challenge: how does one confront films bound up in a virulent fatalism without, on the one hand, succumbing to such an undialectical world view or, on the other hand, without rejecting Herzog's clearly singular and haunting images of violated innocents, suffering outsiders, and border situations? Thus far America critics have, by and large, not found a way out of this hermeneutical impasse–nor have they begun to perceive it as a problem worth their attention.

Wenders did not join Fassbinder and Herzog in the new pantheon until relatively late. Various factors have ensured his receiving a more moderated and less codified critical treatment. First, given the abounding American influences in his work ("The Yanks have colonized our unconscious," Robert says at one point to Bruno during *Kings of the Road*), Wenders's films have not appeared as exotic as Herzog's (thus requiring a rarified terminology to deal with them) or as esoteric as Fassbinder's (therefore demanding American analogues—Warhol and Sirk—to approach them). Second, Wenders's public persona has tended to be much more relaxed and modest than those of his intense, histrionic, and media-conscious colleagues. There is very little of the *poseur* in Wenders (he does not advertise his private life or make dramatic pronouncements) for the press to latch onto. Beyond that, Wenders has been less in the public eye than his extremely active counterparts. In fact, after the 1977 NYFF showing of *The American Friend* and subsequent repertory release of *Falsche Bewegung/Wrong Move* (1974), Wenders all but remained invisible as he grappled with the American production of *Hammett* (finally premiered at Cannes in 1982), and in between lensed a documentary homage to Nicholas Ray, *Lightning over Water,* and another film in Europe.

Two critical clichés have nevertheless surfaced in American treatments of Wenders. The director's introspective works are often perceived as having a frosty, dispassionate, and sometimes numbing quality. *Wrong Move,* according to Canby, is "too chilly to be very involving." The movie, much like its protagonist, attends to the details of haptic experience and ignores the feelings and sensitivities of other characters.[91] Pauline Kael sensed in *The American Friend* turgid "poetic urban masochism" so extremely overbearing as to be "indistinguishable from the heavygoing German films of the Emil Jannings period.... By the time it grinds to a halt, you feel your mind is clouded."[92] Kael and others have likewise taken Wenders to task for a second reason, namely his convoluted narratives: "...though Wenders is attracted to the idea of telling a story he can't quite keep his mind on it."[93] Clearly Canby's and Kael's traditional expectations (fully-rounded characters and transparent narratives) shipwreck on Wenders's brand of filmmaking. They fault him for what other discerning viewers regard as his strengths. By limiting the narrative perspective in *Wrong Move* to a solipsistic hero, Wenders in fact attempted to show the debilitating effects of such unmediated selfishness, quite fitting for a film whose journey in space proves to be a series of wrong moves because no corresponding interior change accompanies them. The final product thus stands as a decisive reckoning with the German equivalent of the "Me Generation," the so-called *Neue Innerlichkeit,* a phenomenon to be pursued later in this book. If one—as Kael—demands of films the linear clarity of classical American cinema, one will clearly be bothered by Wenders's refusal to cater to structures audiences have internalized.

No film reflects so vividly the love-hatred of American culture essential to Wenders's directorial vision as *The American Friend*. Timothy Corrigan has persuasively argued in fact that nearly every scene and shot of the film contain an ambivalence, a simultaneous respect for the technical precision of American cinema as well as a distrust of its often manipulative illusion-making.[94] The historical nexus (a postwar Germany ready to accept the U.S. colonization of its fantasies as a way to escape its own haunting images from a troubled past) and social process (growing up listening to the Armed Forces Network, watching Hollywood films, and partaking of the consumer ideals and popular culture of a foreign country) behind such celluloid experiences demand more consideration than commentators in America thus far have allowed or exercised. They would do well to attend to the larger picture, the one beyond the filmic texts of the few directors to whom they—reviewers, critics, and scholars alike—have in the past remained so beholden. Until serious scholars can combine their manifest visual sensitivity and formal incisiveness with equally perspicacious scrutiny of these other factors, they stand open to a criticism Kracauer once articulated:

> Much as been written about the German cinema in a continual attempt to analyze its exceptional qualities...But this literature, essentially aesthetic, deals with films as if they were autonomous structures.[95]

New German Cinema: Auteurism's Last Stand?

Contemporary West German film, more so than the nation's art, literature, or theater, has played a seminal role in shaping American images of the FRG, just as American perceptions of the New German Cinema have helped much to bring about its international successes. American friends have fostered a foreign cinema that had floundered at home. And these enthusiasms have impressed even dour German politicians: the New German Cinema has become a crucial ambassador for the FRG, one viewed by conservative officials as a valuable cultural asset. The international resonance found by West German directors clearly has helped their lot at home (despite continual disclaimers by domestic film pundits): increased local and federal film subsidies, readiness on even the part of previously unwilling producers to back filmmakers (a situation not without its problems), and more favorable distribution and exhibition conditions.[96] In this regard Thomas Elsaesser has a point when he speaks of the foreign successes of New German Cinema as a case of a "productive misreading."[97]

Tom Ripley's fascination for Jonathan Zimmermann's work (in *The American Friend*) comes of the craftsman's painstaking creation of frames around images, a trade Zimmermann the independent worker performs with pride and integrity. American critics likewise have greeted these meticulously-shaped frames, images, and narratives from the Federal Republic with an incredibly high level of interest. The response has had a remarkably *aesthetic* tenor; one sings praises of certain directors and their extraordinary visions. American effusions have produced a small number of superstars (hence the ubiquitous phrases *"Wunderkinder,"* "genius," "visionary," etc.). The most flamboyant figures have found the largest acclaim, individuals like Fassbinder, Herzog, and most recently Syberberg, a self-advertiser *par excellence* and romantic martyr, eager to disclose his sufferings, who seems to have found compliant listeners on this side of the Atlantic.[98]

Unfortunately, the fixation on a few celebrities in an already marginal foreign film market has led to a situation where only the canonized triumvirate and a privileged few others (Hauff, Schlöndorff, Syberberg, von Trotta, and to a lesser degree Kluge and Straub/Huillet) enjoy the public exposure likely to motivate commercial distributors and cinema owners to forget their traditional prejudices (especially since World War II) about German films. A more differentiated, well-considered, and complex notion of West German cinema seems unlikely to develop in the U.S. as long as American viewers have such limited access to the veritable riches lying in the FRG, in archives, television stations, distributor warehouses, and filmmakers' apartments. Current ideas about "New German Cinema" know very little about so much. The following sectors of FRG output remain all but unexplored by American friends:

- documentaries by the likes of Günther Hörmann, Klaus Wildenhahn, Eberhard Fechner, Peter Nestler, and others;[99]
- a large number of feature films *(Spielfilme)* screened only on West German TV *(Das kleine Fernsehspiel* in ZDF[100], serials like Hans W. Geissendörfer's *Theodor Chindler* [1979] and Fassbinder's *Berlin Alexanderplatz* [1980]);
- feminist productions, especially the considerable activity of cinefeminists in West Berlin (at present Margarethe von Trotta seems to serve the function of a token figure at best);[101]
- the avant-garde, which besides being one of the world's most important continuing sources of experimental cinema, also has had a decisive impact on more recognized directors (e.g. Werner Schroeter's influence on Fassbinder and Syberberg,[102] Klaus Wyborny's work on Herzog's *The Mystery of Kaspar Hauser*);[103]
- a large number of mainstream West German directors whose work awaits more thorough-going exposure in the U.S., above and beyond festival screenings, occasional German film weeks, and Goethe Institute presentations (e.g. Herbert Achternbusch, Edgar Reitz, Ottokar Runze, Helma Sanders-Brahms, Rudolf Thome, among others, not to forget the many talented foreigners based in the FRG like Erwin Keusch, Niklaus Schilling, and Sohrab Shahid Saless).

Why has the reception of West German film followed these patterns in the United States? One can at best speculate. In popular representations one often resorts to such explanations for the phenomenon:

After Vietnam and Watergate, it's understandable that Americans should begin to wonder if morally we are any different from the Germans, and experience a psychological rapprochement—a new closeness to directors who dredge around in guilt. With nihilism in the air here, the extreme moralism of the Germans may be appealingly exotic.[104]

Is New German Cinema therapy for American viewers still suffering from post-Vietnam fallout, finding little interest in their native dream factory to deal with the national trauma? Or perhaps one relives the major catastrophe of the past century, the horrors of the Nazi era and its effects so grippingly depicted in New German film's revisitations of that epoch, aware of the presentiment of future cataclysm, cognizant of the looming potential for nuclear catastrophe. (This might explain as well the conspicuous number of recent American TV movies dealing with the Third Reich.) Another reason suggested in the above quote and elsewhere is the "exoticism thesis," the persuasion that West German filmmakers appeal so much because of their unrelentingly bizarre indulgences, their virulent fatalism, and nightmarish whimsy, penchants very much in keeping with a current climate of opinion hardly prone to understatement. This generalization captures the inherently romantic terms of much American regard for the New German Cinema. Popular and—for the most—critical discussions thus far have ignored the "peculiar historical inscriptions" of these films and instead underlined stylistic and formal eccentricities (something for everybody, auteurists and deconstructionists alike), while simultaneously erecting cults around their creators.[105] If anything, New German Cinema has helped many to keep the notion of the author a very real consideration.

West Germany, for all the drawbacks in its subsidy systems and television coproduction arrangements, still has provided conditions that have allowed directors to fashion a body of work with stylistic continuity and distinct visual flair. At a time when mavericks find it impossible to deal with the machinery of the American movie industry (the fate of the independent is paradigmatically embodied by Nicholas Ray), where individual visions less and less find their way intact through script re-writes, post-production editing, and the exigencies of marketing campaigns, West German filmmakers still operate within structures that much more readily allow one to continue using the auteurist critical lexicon. (At least for now; this could very well change with larger budgets and increasing internationalization, trends very present at the start of the eighties.) How can one talk about individual style and persistence of personal vision when the majority of films made in Hollywood today comes from first-time directors or ones under the tutelage of corporations?

It is obvious that this discourse has left much unsaid and in a great way only begins to account for West German cinema's undeniable hold on the imagination. The loss of a common world, a universal sense of displacement, the inability to identify with a shared past, the search for enchantment in a world increasingly devoid of amenities, a desire to create images that do not denigrate the given or reaffirm an unbearable *status quo,* a pause to consider the question of sexual difference: much remains to be said about such matters in the light of recent West German films. Besides dealing with concrete films and individual directors, one needs to come to grips with the socio-political factors under which films have been made in West Germany, the cultural traditions out of which they arise and to which they often take exception, as well as the question of how final products have been regarded by critical and popular audiences, inland and abroad. For, as we have seen, the manner in which a nation's films are received can have a lot to do with the formation of present images—and the making of future ones.

NOTES

An earlier version of this chapter appeared in *New German Critique,* No. 24-25 (Fall/Winter 1981-2), pp. 7-35.

[1] "Leopards in the Temple," in *Parables and Paradoxes* (New York: Schocken, 1961), p. 93.

[2] "Viva l'Italia!," *Village Voice (VV),* 7. Jan. 1981, p. 37.

[3] Max Horkheimer and Theodor W. Adorno's analysis of the "Culture Industry" applies here. See *Dialectic of Enlightenment,* trans. John Cumming (New York: Seabury, 1971), pp. 120-67.

[4] Cf. Irving Howe, *Literary Modernism* (Greenwich, Conn.: Fawcett, 1967), p. 24. The insight comes from Benjamin's "The Author as Producer," in *Reflections,* ed. Peter Demetz (New York/London: Harcourt Brace Jovanovich, 1978), p. 229: "For we are faced with the fact...that the bourgeois apparatus of production and publication can assimilate astonishing qualities of revolutionary themes, indeed, can propagate them without calling its own existence, and the existence of the class that owns it, seriously into question."

[5] "Movie Journal," *VV,* 13 April 1972, p. 77.

[6] "A nation comes out of shell-shock," *VV,* 4 May 1972, p. 87.

[7] "New York Film Festival Reviews," *Film Comment,* Nov./Dec. 1974, p. 36.

[8] "Can Fassbinder Break the Box-Office Barrier?," *VV,* 22 Nov. 1976, p. 57.

[9] "The German Renaissance—No Room for Laughter or Love," *New York Times (NYT),* 11 Dec. 1977.

[10] Gerald Clarke, "Seeking Planets That Do Not Exist," *Time,* 20 March 1978, p. 51.

[11] Ronald Holloway, *Variety,* 23 Jan. 1980, p. 4.

[12] Vincent Canby, "Rainer Fassbinder—The Most Original Talent Since Godard," *NYT,* 6 March 1977.

[13] Jonathan Cott, "Signs of Life," *Rolling Stone,* 18 Nov. 1976, p. 49.

[14] Terry Curtis Fox, "Wenders Crosses the Border," *VV,* 3 Oct. 1977, p. 42.

[15] Also important during this period were *Film* and the Frankfurt student quarterly *Filmstudio.* By the early seventies, though, both journals had folded.

[16] See Jan Dawson, "A Labyrinth of Subsidies: The Origins of the New German Cinema," *Sight & Sound,* Winter 1980-81, pp. 14-20.

[17] Kracauer, for all the often-noted stress on the primacy he placed on content, nevertheless demonstrated in his own film criticism considerable understanding for cinematic form and style. Not all West German critics have reduced his lessons down to such monolithic terms, e.g. Karsten Witte, "Visual Pleasure Inhibited: Aspects of the German Revue Film," Trans. J.D. Steakley and Gabriele Hoover, *New German Critique,* No. 24-25 (Fall/Winter 1981-2), pp. 238-63. A crucial statement in the reception of Kracauerian aesthetics by West German film critics is Enno Patalas's "Plädoyer für die ästhetische Linke. Zum Selbstverständnis der *Filmkritik,*" *Filmkritik,* July 1966. See also Frieda Grafe, "Doktor Caligari gegen Doktor Kracauer oder Die Errettung der ästhetischen Realität," *Süddeutsche Zeitung,* 25 Feb. 1970; reprinted in *Filmkritik,* May 1970.

[18] "Über die Aufgabe des Filmkritikers," in Siegfried Kracauer, *Kino: Essays, Studien, Glossen zum Film,* ed. Karsten Witte (Frankfurt: Suhrkamp, 1974), p. 11. The passage continues: "His mission is to ferret out the hidden social contents and ideologies in film offerings and through such revelations to diminish the influence of these films."

[19] The split between leftist critics and so-called *Sensibilisten* in the editorial ranks of *Filmkritik* which occurred in 1969 still has its consequences for present-day praxis. *Sensibilismus* developed in Munich during the sixties within a circle of critics and film students (including Wenders). It stresses the role of an individual's personal relationship to a film, insisting on the subjective nature of the in-the-dark experience. As a rule such criticism tends to be very descriptive in nature: one recounts privileged moments, relives certain scenes, producing a sort of discourse which a less sympathetic observer might label as poetic empiricism. The periodical *Filme,* founded in 1980 and discontinued in 1982, contained much writing in the sensibilist vein, despite its pluralistic editorial policy. Norbert Jochum and Norbert Grob, two of the journal's editors and consistent practitioners of this approach, also wrote regularly in *Die Zeit* during the early eighties.

[20] Especially during the fifties, the *Frankfurter Hefte* printed some key socio-historical studies on German film, e.g. Enno Patalas, "Autorität und Revolte im deutschen Film: Nationale Leitbilder von Caligari bis Canaris," Jan. 1956.

[21] Between the categories there exists much overlap. The same individual for instance wrote notices for the *Süddeutsche Zeitung* and *Die Zeit,* edited *Filmkritik,* and had published previously in the *Frankfurter Hefte.* (The critic in question is Enno Patalas during the sixties.) This overlap if anything attests to the very limited number of practicing film critics in the FRG, as well as the relatively closed nature of the institution. With the presence of film critics on film subsidy boards in recent years, a host of new problems has come to the fore. For an overview of film journalism in the FRG, see *Seminar: Filmkritik. Protokolle einer Veranstaltung der Arbeitsgemeinschaft der Filmjournalisten in Frankfurt am Main 1978,* ed. Gertrud Koch and Karsten Witte (Frankfurt: Arbeitsgemeinschaft der Filmjournalisten, 1978).

[22] For compilations of the inroads made by cinema studies into university curricula in West Germany, see the various installments of *Film und Fernsehen in Forschung und Lehre* (Berlin: Stiftung Deutsche Kinemathek, 1978ff.).

[23] Jan Dawson, "*Germany in Autumn* and *Eine Kleine Godard* [sic]," *Take One,* Nov. 1978, p. 14.

[24] *Film in der Bundesrepublik Deutschland* (Munich: Hanser, 1979), pp. 12, 20, 22, 77.

[25] This is not to underestimate the considerable gains made by semiotics, post-structuralism, feminism, and other methodologies in the past decade, only to note their relative isolation and nonacceptance among most practicing popular film critics. For an overview of the problem of authorship in film studies, see *Theories of Authorship,* ed. John Caughie (Boston/London: Routledge & Kegan Paul, in association with the British Film Institute, 1981).

[26] All three quotes in Rob Baker, " 'New German Cinema': A Fistful of Myths," *Soho Weekly News,* 23 March 1978, p. 22.

[27] "The Germanic Factor: Taking Hitler Out of Caligari," *VV,* 1 Oct. 1979. p. 49.

[28] See Peter Figlestahler, "Viel gelobt, aber wenig angeschaut: Das Kritikerecho in America," *Frankfurter Allgemeine Zeitung,* 15 Nov. 1975. A more sympathetic appraisal is found in H.G. Pflaum's "Nachrichten vom 'German Film Boom': Deutsche Filme stossen in New York auf zunehmendes Interesse," *Süddeutsche Zeitung,* 18 Oct. 1979.

[29] As reported in Stuart Byron, "Rules of the Game," *VV,* 14 Jan. 1980, p. 43. Attempts of a "German Film Tour" during 1979 and 1980 to break into the commercial market within the United States met with at best mixed success. The main problem remains the reluctance on the part of film subsidy agencies to support such wider distribution. As the eighties commenced, a continuing topic of conversation was a German Film Office in New York.

[30] *New York,* 5 Sept. 1977, p. 70. See also Simon's "Cinematic Illiterates," *New York,* 20 Oct. 1975, pp. 86-87.

[31] "The German Renaissance," op. cit.

[32] Yet another major Fassbinder Retrospective ran during the fall months of 1981 in New York City at the Film Forum 2.

[33] For descriptions of several previously lesser-known Fassbinder works, see George Morris, "Fassbinder X 5," *Film Comment,* Sept./Oct. 1981, pp. 59-65.

[34] Andrew Sarris, "Can Fassbinder Break the Box-Office Barrier?," *VV,* 22 Nov. 1976, p. 57. American critics likewise have not enjoyed access to his numerous newspaper articles, interviews, and television appearances, much less his work for the theater, as actor and director.

[35] "Von Caligari bis Coppola: Junge deutsche Filmemacher in Hollywood auf den Spuren von Lubitsch, Murnau und Lang," *Die Zeit,* 22 Feb. 1980. The work of German directors in exile remains a phenomenon yet to be considered at any length in terms of its relation to German film history. During the fall of 1979, the Goethe House in New York offered an impressive program of films and lectures as well as an exhibit devoted to "German Film Directors in Hollywood."

[36] Wim Wenders speaks of this as a form of escapism, a way of circumventing any confrontation with one's own historical dilemma. See Jan Dawson, *Wim Wenders* (Toronto: Festival of Festivals, 1976), p. 7: "The most dominant effect was the tendency to stick to other histories or to become involved in other cultures. In the early fifties or even the sixties, it was American culture. In other words, the need to forget 20 years created a hole, and people tried to cover this...in both senses...by assimilating American culture..."

[37] Hans-Bernhard Moeller, "New German Cinema and Its Precarious Subsidy and Finance System," *Quarterly Review of Film Studies (QRFS),* Spring 1980, p. 162.

[38] Wenders set up his own production and distribution company in New York City during the early eighties under the name Gray City Films. See

Lawrence Cohn, "Gray City Films As Wim Wenders' N.Y. Distribution & Production Base," *Variety,* 30 Sept. 1981, pp. 6, 38.

[39] "Festival Round-Up," *VV,* 12 Oct. 1967, p. 31.

[40] "Movies in the Round," *Newsweek,* 18 Oct. 1971, p. 108.

[41] "Movie Journal," *VV,* 13 April 1972, p. 77.

[42] Amos Vogel, "A nation comes out of shell-shock," *VV,* 4 May 1972, p. 87.

[43] "Screen: A Real Loser," *NYT,* 17 Nov. 1973.

[44] "Film Festival: *Merchant of Four Seasons,*" *NYT,* 9 Oct. 1972.

[45] "Lost love, found despair," *VV,* 22 Nov. 1973, pp. 77-78.

[46] Cf. Stuart Byron, *"The Merchant of Four Seasons," Real Paper* (Boston), 9 Jan. 1974. The editors of *Film Comment* devoted a large part of the Nov./Dec. 1975 issue to a special section on Fassbinder. The director, claimed the editors, "is more concerned with the carcass of traditional narrative, attacking old stories with an iconographic thrust home that results in political superrealism" (p. 4).

[47] Manny Farber and Patricia Patterson, "New York Film Festival Review: Breaking Rules at the Roulette Table," *Film Comment,* Nov./Dec. 1975, p. 33.

[48] See Elliott Stein, "New York Film Festival Review: Kitsch 'n Synch," *Film Comment,* Nov./Dec. 1975, p. 36: *Katharina Blum* was for Stein "the most obnoxious entry this year. Volker Schlöndorff is a coarse director... His new work is another exercise in mindless Manichaeism—the new German cinema's *plat du jour* these days.... Scholöndorff's [sic] firecracker is wet."

[49] "The Germans Are Coming! The Germans Are Coming!," *VV,* 27 Oct. 1975, p. 139. For less enthusiastic press echoes, see Stein's comments on other German entries at the 1975 NYFF (see note 48); Pauline Kael, "Metaphysical Tarzan" (review of *Kaspar Hauser*), *New Yorker,* 20 Oct. 1975, pp. 142-49; and Jay Cocks, "Grave New World: *Every Man for Himself and God against All,*" *Time,* 3 Nov. 1975, p. 72.

[50] As of fall 1981, Gray City Films took over American distribution of Wim Wenders's films.

[51] See "German Film Courses and Resources: A Special Survey," *Monatshefte,* Fall 1977, pp. 305-19.

[52] Among the increasing number of scholarly inquiries devoted to West German films, see the following: "Special Issue: New German Cinema," *Literature/Film Quarterly,* Vol. 7, No. 3 (1979); "New German Cinema," *Wide Angle,* Vol. 3, No. 4 (1980); "West German Film in the 1970s," *QRFS,* Spring 1980; and "Special Double Issue on New German Cinema," *New German Critique,* No. 24-25 (Fall/Winter 1981-2).

[53] See Carter Wiseman and others, "The German Film Renaissance," *Newsweek,* 2 Feb. 1976 (cover story of the international edition); Gerald Clarke, "Seeking Planets That Do Not Exist," *Time,* 20 March 1978, pp. 51-53; and Vincent Canby, "The German Renaissance—No Room for Laughter or Love," *NYT,* 11 Dec. 1977. Also: Diane Jacobs, "Hitler's Ungrateful Grandchildren: Today's German Filmmakers," *American Film,* May 1980, pp. 34-40; and Peter Gambaccini, "The New German Film Makers," *Horizon,* June 1980, pp. 22-33 (cover story).

[54] These critics include Richard Collins, Jan Dawson, Thomas Elsaesser, Sheila Johnston, Vincent Porter, and Tony Rayns.

[55] "A Fistful of Myths," op. cit., p. 22. The "myths" he catalogues reveal themselves as over-simplifications that only vaguely correspond to what had been written. Contrary to Baker, next to no one had claimed that New German Cinema was a box-office hit and practically everyone had taken pains to group the young directors in a differentiated way, making apparent the stylistic and thematic divergencies.

[56] Baker, p. 22.

[57] See Gerhard Zwerenz, "Die falschen Stoffe: Anmerkungen zu den Themen deutscher Filmemacher," in *Jahrbuch Film 77/78*, ed. Hans Günther Pflaum (Munich: Hanser, 1977), pp. 41-49.

[58] "Behind the Crest of the Wave: An Overview of the New German Cinema," *Literature/Film Quarterly*, Vol. 7. No. 3 (1979), pp. 167-68.

[59] And on a number of occasions in recent years, *completed* films scheduled for television screenings have been withdrawn at the last minute, or changed to a regional sender, or in some cases, deferred to a less popular hour—out of fear regarding possible scandal, controversy, or public outcry. There have also been cases where certain passages of completed films have been purged before screening.

[60] See Charlotte Kerr, "Das Drehbuch ist kein Evangelium: Ein Gespräch mit dem Filmemacher Alexander Kluge," *Süddeutsche Zeitung*, 17 May 1974.

[61] Jan Dawson, *The Films of Hellmuth Costard* (London: Riverside Studios, 1979), p. 7.

[62] "sexismus in den massenmedien," *Frauen und Film*, No. 1 (1974), p. 12.

[63] "German Renaissance," op. cit.

[64] Unifilm (formerly Tricontinental) carries a wide selection of political films from the Third World countries, especially Latin American ones, but recently backed away from a deal involving a package of West German films.

[65] Useful studies of the *Arbeiterfilm* in English are an article and a book by Richard Collins and Vincent Porter: "*Westdeutscher Rundfunk* and the *Arbeiterfilm* (1967-1977)," *QRFS*, Spring 1980, pp. 233-51; and *WDR and the Arbeiterfilm: Fassbinder, Ziewer and others* (London: British Film Institute, 1981). For introductions and overviews of feminist filmmaking in the FRG, see Marc Silberman, "Cine-Feminists in West Berlin," *QRFS*, Spring 1980, pp. 217-32, and "Woman Filmmakers Working in West Germany: A Catalog," *camera obscura*, No. 6 (1980), pp. 122-52. See also Claudia Lenssen's brochure written for a recent package of feminist films for the Goethe Institute, *Women's Cinema in Germany* (Munich: Goethe Institute, 1980). On documentary filmmakers in the FRG, see Wilhelm Roth's brochure, *The Federal Republic of Germany as Reflected in its Documentary Films* (Munich: Goethe Institute, 1980). Roth recently completed a lengthy study in German on the documentary film.

[66] See Andrew Sarris, "Is History Merely an Old Movie?," *VV*, 8 July 1981, p. 33; also, Richard T. Jameson, "West Germany's Fassbinder Goes Hollywood," *The Weekly* (Seattle), 5 Aug. 1981, pp. 22, 24.

[67] See *Wir tanzen um die Welt: Deutsche Revuefilme 1933-1945*, ed. Helga Belach (Munich: Hanser, 1979); also, Hans C. Blumenberg, "Wie lustig ist die Tyrannei?: Fassbinders *Lili Marleen*," *Die Zeit*, 16 Jan. 1981.

[68] "Tanz auf dem Vulkan," *Der Spiegel,* 5 Oct. 1981, p. 228 (unsigned).
[69] Cf. "Frühling für Hitler and Lili Marleen," *Der Spiegel,* 19 Jan. 1981, pp. 168-76 (unsigned).
[70] Sarris, "Is History Merely an Old Movie?," p. 33.
[71] "Fassbinder," *Film Comment,* Nov./Dec. 1975, p. 6.
[72] *Rainer Werner Fassbinder,* ed. Peter W. Jansen and Wolfram Schütte, 3rd rev. ed. (Munich: Hanser, 1979), pp. 123-24.
[73] Straub/Huillet have never really emerged from the underground; only a small fraction of Kluge's output has come into commercial distribution. Schlöndorff and von Trotta seem likely to receive increased notice during the eighties as does Syberberg.
[74] More differentiated and methodologically sophisticated exceptions to this rule include Judith Mayne, "Fassbinder and Spectatorship," *New German Critique,* No. 12 (Fall 1977), pp. 61-74; and Catherine Johnson, "The Imaginary and *The Bitter Tears of Petra von Kant,*" *Wide Angle,* Vol. 3, No. 4 (1980), pp. 20-25.
[75] Farber and Patterson, "Fassbinder," p. 5.
[76] Ibid., pp. 5-6. One finds the same misapprehension almost four years later in Frank Rich's review of *The Marriage of Maria Braun,* "High Camp," *Time,* 22 Oct. 1979, p. 85: "Increasingly, he [Fassbinder] seems to be the '70s heir to such past camp masters as the '50s Hollywood director Douglas Sirk...and the '60s Warhol disciple Paul Morrissey..."
[77] Susan Sontag, "Notes on 'Camp,'" in *Against Interpretation and Other Essays* (New York: Delta, 1966), p. 280.
[78] Ibid., p. 277.
[79] "A New Realism: Fassbinder Interviewed by John Hughes and Brooks Riley," *Film Comment,* Nov./Dec. 1975, p. 14.
[80] *Lola* (1981) and *Veronika Voss* (1982) were further installments in the FRG-project of which *The Marriage of Maria Braun* was the first part.
[81] Fassbinder articulated these plans in an interview with Helmut Schmitz, "Die Lage war keineswegs so ernst: Mit Fassbinder in die 50er Jahre: *Lola,*" *Frankfurter Rundschau,* 21 Aug. 1981.
[82] "Fassbinder on Sirk," trans. Thomas Elsaesser, *Film Comment,* Nov./Dec. 1975, pp. 22-24.
[83] "Notes on Form and Syntax," in *Fassbinder,* ed. Tony Rayns (London: British Film Institute, 1976), p. 43.
[84] For Fassbinder on Chabrol, see "Insects in a Glass Cage: random thoughts on the films of Claude Chabrol," *Sight & Sound,* Autumn 1976, pp. 205-06, 252. The stylistic and thematic nearness of the more abrasive Chabrol (e.g. *Les Noces rouges* [1972] and *Docteur Popaul* [1972]) to the two 1976 productions *(Satansbraten/Satan's Brew* and *Chinesisches Roulette/Chinese Roulette)* received little mention. Fassbinder's Chabrol-essay contains numerous criticisms of the French director's practice, ones that often apply to the films Fassbinder made shortly after writing the article in 1975. For Schroeter's influence, see Fassbinder's tribute, "Klimmzug, Handstand, Salto mortale— sicher gestanden. Über den Filmregisseur Werner Schroeter, dem gelang, was

kaum je gelingt—anlässlich seiner *Neapolitanischen Geschwister,*" *Frankfurter Rundschau,* 24 Feb. 1979. Regarding Visconti, Fassbinder maintained he had seen *La Caduta degli Dei/The Damned* (1969) thirty times, in "Nur so entsehen bei uns Filme: indem man sie ohne Rücksicht auf Verluste macht': Aus einem Gespräch mit Rainer Werner Fassbinder über unsere Filmsituation, seine jüngsten Filme, das 'Modell Deutschland' und über das, was ihn ermutigt," *Frankfurter Rundschau,* 20 Feb. 1979. Fassbinder spoke up for Bresson on numerous occasions; he quoted from *Le Diable probablement* (1976) early in *The Third Generation.* For Fassbinder's very personal homage to Döblin, see his essay, "Die Städte des Menschen und seine Seele: Einige ungeordnete Gedanken zu Alfred Döblins Roman *Berlin Alexanderplatz,*" *Die Zeit,* 14 March 1980.

[85] Andrew Sarris, "Can Fassbinder Break the Box-Office Barrier?," *VV,* 22 Nov. 1976, p. 57.

[86] "Signs of Life," *Rolling Stone,* 18 Nov. 1976, p. 50.

[87] "The Man on the Volcano: A Portrait of Werner Herzog," *Film Quarterly,* Fall 1977, p. 4. See also *"Images at the Horizon,"* ed. Gene Walsh (Chicago: Facets Multimedia, 1979).

[88] Quoted in Alan Greenberg's hagiographical tribute to of Herzog working on a film, *Heart of Glass* (Munich: Skellig, 1976), p. 174.

[89] Beverly Walker, "Werner Herzog's *Nosferatu,*" *Sight & Sound,* Autumn 1978, p. 204.

[90] "Reports from the New York Film Festival," *Film Comment,* Nov./Dec. 1979, p. 68.

[91] "Screen: Wenders's *The Wrong Move," NYT,* 25 Jan. 1980.

[92] "Heart/Soul," *New Yorker,* 17 Oct. 1977, p. 179.

[93] Ibid., p. 178.

[94] "The Realist Gesture in the Films of Wim Wenders: Hollywood and the New German Cinema," *QRFS,* Spring 1980, pp. 205-16.

[95] *From Caligari to Hitler: A Psychological History of the German Film* (Princeton: Princeton U.P., 1947), p. 4.

[96] A good number of new-comers (*Nachwuchsfilmer*) and other independents still have yet to benefit from new opportunities mainly open to established *Jungfilmer.*

[97] "Primary Identification and the Historical Subject: Fassbinder and Germany," *Ciné-Tracts,* No. 11 (1980), p. 52.

[98] See *Hans-Jürgen Syberberg's Our Hitler: A Film from Germany: A Documentation,* compiled by Ingrid Scheib-Rothbart (New York: Goethe House, 1980). A brave dissenting voice among wide-spread American yea-saying is that of Henry Pachter, "Our Hitler, or His?," *Cineaste,* Spring 1980, pp. 25-27.

[99] For literature on West German documentaries, see note 65 above.

[100] See *A Tribute to Das Kleine Fernsehspiel/ZDF: Alternative Filmmaking in Television* (Berkeley/San Francisco: University Art Museum, Pacific Film Archive, Goethe Institute San Francisco, and KQED-TV, 1979).

[101] For a superficial introduction, see Renate Möhrmann, *Die Frau mit der Kamera: Filmemacherinnnen in der Bundesrepublik Deutschland* (Munich: Hanser, 1980). The book was greeted with considerable dissatisfaction and anger among West Germany's active feminist film critics and filmmakers.

[102] See Timothy Corrigan, "Werner Schroeter's Cinematic Opera," *Discourse,* No. 3 (1981), pp. 46-59.
[103] Wyborny contributed the dream sequences, ones numerous critics generally attribute to Herzog, lauding the director for his visionary powers.
[104] Pauline Kael, "Heart/Soul," *New Yorker,* 17 Oct. 1977, p. 178.
[105] Elsaesser, "Fassbinder and Germany," p. 52.

PART THREE
Texts and Contexts, *Auteurs* and Others: Three Challenges

"It's really difficult to render German history in a patriotic version."
—Gabi Teichert in Alexander Kluge's *Die Patriotin*

"Art is free. What happens, though, when artists are not?"
—Gerhard Zwerenz

"The contradictions are the hope!"
—The motto to Bertolt Brecht's *Der Dreigroschenprozess*

Chapter Four

Calamity Prevails over the Country: Young German Filmmakers Revisit the Homeland

> "In our German culture there is hardly a more ambivalent feeling, hardly a more painful mixture of happiness and bitterness than the experience vested in the word 'Heimat' [homeland]. Throughout the history of German culture one has been continually plagued by this feeling."
> —Edgar Reitz[1]

The Illusory Idyll

A still-life of a country house with a few people gathered around it, snow on the ground: this is what the viewer sees at the start of Reinhard Hauff's *Mathias Kneissl*. The credits for Volker Schlöndorff's *Der plötzliche Reichtum der armen Leute von Kombach/The Sudden Wealth of the Poor People of Kombach* flash over a drawing of a German village, a sketch with the direct appeal of naive art. Uwe Brandner's *Ich liebe dich, ich töte dich/ I Love You, I Kill You* commences with a series of landscape images: open fields, tree-covered hillsides, the housetops of a sleepy burg where church bells chime. Calm prevails over the country—or does it? All three examples from the 1971 renaissance of the *Heimatfilm* begin with quiet, composed pictures, scenes from an idyll—an idyll that swiftly proves to be illusory. In Hauff's film, we cut to a family bidding farewell to a member who leaves the homeland forever. Schlöndorff moves from the static sketch to frenzied tracking shots of desperate peasants hurrying through a forest. Brandner's postcard panoramas very quickly elicit a sense of foreboding. In one of the earliest shots we glimpse a green meadow in extreme longshot; all is not so tranquil, though, as we hear thunder and see ominously dark clouds hanging over the fields. A seeming calm in all three cases will shift to its opposite; the apparent peacefulness only momentarily conceals an abiding unrest and anxiety. Signs of a timeless bucolic simplicity will give way to the not-so-simple facts of life ordering those who inhabit these landscapes. From the very outset, these films demonstrate an unsettling intention. With the zeal of Gabi Teichert, Alexander Kluge's indefatigable patriot, the *Anti-Heimatfilme* aim to correct the falsifications of official German history. Exploding stereotypes, they deconstruct false images of the past while fashioning new ones addressed to the present.

It is often maintained how the Young German Film had to start from ground zero. In the face of a bankrupt national cinema, it is commonly claimed, the new directors had to begin again.[2] This cliché, however, will not bear up under closer scrutiny. Among numerous points of continuity linking films after 1962 with German tradition, one heritage stands out conspicuously: the *Heimatfilm*. As powerful a force in the popular imagination as the Western in America, the Samurai-film in Japan, and the partisan epic in Yugoslavia,[3] the *Heimatfilm,* by dint of its persistence throughout the entire span of German film history, acts as a seismograph, one that allows us to gauge enduring presences as they have evolved over the last eighty years. Although I intend to concentrate on the critical *Heimatfilm* of the early seventies, I must first back up—true to the spirit of Kluge's energetic school teacher in her search "for the foundations of German history"—and trace its development. Only then can I sketch the subversive earmarks—both thematic and formal—found in the three examples above. Lastly, I will discuss how the *Anti-Heimatfilm* continued throughout the seventies and abides now as one of the central contributions of West German filmmakers since the Oberhausen Manifesto.

Origins and Development of the *Heimatfilm*

One can trace the literary precursors of the traditional *Heimatfilm* back to the mid-19th century as the word *Heimat* takes on an emotional connotation:[4] greater mobility becomes possible, the Industrial Revolution starts to take its toll on nature, and urbanization leads to an increasing rationalization and transformation of human relations. It is only after *Heimat* ceases to be taken for granted that the notion is articulated.[5] Rural landscapes and peasant life serve as the raw material for the idealized images in the emerging *Heimat*-literature, a body of writing glorifying the simplicity and stability of the countryside. More often than not, the idyllic harmony lauded in such outpourings rested not so much on nature untouched by human institutions, but rather on a feudal order harking back to Romantic projections of the Middle Ages like Novalis's *Christendom or Europe* (1799).

Two literary genres feed directly into the *Heimatfilm*: the *Dorfgeschichte* (village tale) and the *Volksschauspiel* (folk drama).[6] The village tales of Jeremias Gotthelf, Berthold Auerbach, Josef Rank, and Karl Immermann presented an unravaged countryside and unspoiled nature, factors held up as a moral alternative to the artificial ways of the city. Emotional tonalities—indeed at times a pantheistic fervor—govern these works, ones written by authors who do not always demonstrate first-hand knowledge of the milieu and people they extol. Ludwig Ganghofer, the most successful popularizer of this tradition who would produce dozens of novels well into the 20th century, continually resorted to overwrought phrases in his sentimental evocation of the country and its inhabitants. "What is very decidedly missing is the real state of affairs," Irmgard Hermanns argued in her study of Ganghofer's stories. "These *are not* farmers, but rather middle-class *projections* of farmers from the turn of the century."[7] Such false images will prove paradigmatic for the later celluloid renderings of *Heimat*-novels.

The *Volksschauspiel*[8] flourished in the last quarter of the 19th century. Records indicate that during the period over 600 *Volkstheater* operated, particularly in Southern Germany and Austria. This rural tradition later provided *Heimatfilme* with textual sources and stylistic influences, as well as authors and actors. Many *Heimatfilme* used the province theaters as sets and studios.[9] The proliferation of these peasant and folk theaters did not simply stem from civic pride; the rise of tourism and its attendant economic advantages played no small role. The *Volksschau-*

spiele had a limited number of themes, operating within highly circumscribed conventions and well-known topoi, presenting scenic confrontations between stock figures in modern-day morality plays, where good invariably won out. For all their earthy humor, dialect, and local color, the dramas rarely transcended universal stereotypes of village life. Characters bowed to the dictates of an omnipotent Fate in the plays. While ostensibly sympathizing with the simple people, these works, in fact, lent credence to a class hierarchy with its privileged few and its oppressed many.

Even a German critic writing during the Third Reich could not escape mentioning the ideological assumptions of such seemingly innocuous plays. Describing a popular sub-genre, namely the *Ritterdrama* (plays centered around the adventures of knights), Hans Moser claimed in an essay of 1935:

> The simple man, subjected to a life full of toil and work in a world of the harshest social inequity, heard from the mouths of all these figures [in the *Ritterdrama*] and learned from their actions again and again the same lesson: that all finery, all power, everything beyond his grasp, were false and deceptive, and in the face of God and Fate meant nothing, whereas a pure heart and good will meant everything.[10]

Schlöndorff's *Kombach* analyzes the dynamics by which a moribund feudal regime keeps its subjects docile, showing how certain oppressive mechanisms become so internalized that only minimal official force is needed to maintain order. The peasant Heinrich Geiz remains the only character in the entire film to see through the insidious web fettering his every move. "This is how they finish me off bit by bit," he says shortly before his public execution. The point of view—with few notable exceptions—stands as one foreign to the village tale and the *Volksschauspiel*, works that in their tranfiguration of milieu and cavalier attitude toward history left the *status quo* unquestioned.

Some of the first German films featured spectacular views of mountain panoramas. Even the emerging medium's most vehement adversaries could find virtue in its depiction of "the landscapes of the German fatherland, the characteristic beauty of the *Heimat*."[11] As early as 1919, Peter Ostermayr made arrangements to produce a lengthy series of Ganghofer adaptations. Later to be heralded as "the grand master of the *Heimatfilm*," Ostermayr had already made scenic documentaries in 1907 and would continue drawing on Ganghofer's novels until his death in 1967. During the teens, the *Wiener Kunstfilmgesellschaft* (Viennese Art

Film Company) produced numerous novels by Ludwig Anzengruber, works that gained the designation *Heimatschnulzen* (homeland weepies) and *Volksfilme*.[12]

Inextricably bound to the *Heimat*-output were the *Bergfilme* (mountain films) of the twenties and early thirties, melodramatic affairs played out on the peaks of imposing alpine settings. Siegfried Kracauer quite correctly spoke of the genre's problematic ideological implications, viewing in the *Bergfilm* a cultish enthusiasm for adventure and heroic ideals, a blend of "sparkling ice-axes and inflated sentiments."[13] Both the early *Heimatfilm* as well as the *Bergfilm* fed the latent irrationalism in the late Weimar years and fueled the subsequent *Blut und Boden* (blood and soil) productions of the Nazi era. In the words of a critic writing in 1935:

> The feature film of the Third Reich takes advantage of every single possibility to show us the grandness and beauty of nature, its mountains and forests, and to awaken our respect for the peculiarities of farmers and village dwellers far removed from the tempo and the heart of the big city.[14]

The personnel of the *Bergfilme* would greatly influence Nazi film culture—as well as postwar movie productions. A direct line links Leni Riefenstahl's *Das blaue Licht/The Blue Light* (1932) with *Tiefland* (1954) or Luis Trenker's mountain epics of the thirties with those of his attempted comeback in the fifties. "The German people, the German song in the German landscape," announced Fritz Stege in 1935, "achieving this trinity should remain the overall artistic resolve of the German sound film."[15] To a large degree, this remained the case for the next quarter-century.

There was no *Nullpunkt* (zero point) in postwar West German film. After a series of *Trümmerfilme* (rubble films)—works exceedingly dependent on Expressionism for their formal as well as thematic impetus—producers reverted to past models: to costume epics, to literary adaptations of canonized bourgeois classics, to exotic escapist fare, and, of course, to the *Heimatfilm*. Virtually no break in the tradition took place; the same directors who made blood and soil films under Goebbels found steady work after 1945 in what would become the Federal Republic. (These include Hans Deppe, Joe Stöckel, Erich Waschnek, the infamous Veit Harlan, among others.) Over thirty *Heimatfilme* done during the Third Reich were remade between 1947 and 1960, in one case by the same director.[16] The question remains: why the sudden rebirth of a tried-and-true but nonetheless timeworn genre? The answer is clear. In a Federal Republic burdened with an unassimilated war guilt and still in the process of rebuilding itself, the felicities of a fantasy countryside devoid of rubble and Allied occupation troops allowed audiences to dream of a simpler primeval Germany. Instead of ruined cities, one contemplated untouched nature; in the midst of widespread homelessness, one reveled in a world where people had roots; and above all, one replaced a presentiment of existential devastation with more comforting notions of a timeless and harmonious reality. One retreated from the exigencies of the present into the insulated sanctuary of such films as *Schwarzwaldmädel/Black Forest Girl* (Hans Deppe, 1950), *Grün ist die Heide/Green Is the Heather* (Hans Deppe, 1951), *Die Fischerin vom Bodensee/The Fisherwoman from Lake Constance* (Harald Reinl, 1956), and *Schloss Hubertus/Hubertus Palace* (Helmut Weiss, 1954) — to name only a few of the more than 300 *Heimatfilme* made between 1947 and 1960, one-fifth of the entire West German film production.

For all the diatribes launched by contemporary critics against such vacations from history, these movies had audiences flocking to the cinema in droves.[17] A disoriented and insecure public found in these quickly-made films a temporary domicile; in a certain sense, the *Heimatfilme* served a function analogous to the one played by the *Neubauten* (new buildings) that rose out of the postwar ruins.[18] "The greatest fear of the era is homelessness," submitted Ulrich Kurowski.[19] The *Heimatfilm* both reflected and encouraged a drawing back into the private realm of marriage, family, and home life. It reduced all conflicts to domestic ones and imparted an abiding trust in the benevolent hand of Fate. "We can't do anything," says a character in *Zugvögel/Migrating Birds* (Rolf Meyer, 1947), "things just simply happen to us." One did not need a propaganda ministry with movies like these exercising such a powerful hold on the popular imagination, preaching a message of quietism and accession to the powers that be.[20]

By the end of the fifties, a saturation point was finally reached. The *Heimatfilm* lost its hold on the masses and the German film industry reached a dead end. Enno Patalas took stock of a cinematic wasteland, a national film output that knew little of reflection or critique, one for the most devoid of any alternative incentives, one that demonstrated little distance or irony.[21] It would take a new generation of filmmakers and a different aesthetic to change this.

The Rise of the Critical *Heimatfilm*

The *Heimatfilm* resurfaced during the late sixties in two guises. The first aligned itself with a spate of domestic sex comedies, rechanneling the wave of porno films to countryside settings to produce throw-away fare like *Pudelnackt in Oberbayern/Stark Naked in Upper Bavaria* (Hans Albin, 1968), *Unterm Dirndl wird gejodelt/Someone's Yodeling under My Dirndl* (Alois Brummer, 1973), and *Urlaubsgrüsse aus dem Unterhöschen/ Vacation Greetings from the Lower Reaches* (Walter Boos, 1973). These purely commercial speculations proved at best how *Papas Kino* was not dead, just desperate. Needless to say, the trend enjoyed no more than passing success. The second and more significant reincarnation came with Peter Fleischmann's adaptation of Martin Sperr's drama *Jagdszenen aus Niederbayern/Hunting Scenes from Lower Bavaria* (1968). It flourished in 1971 when *Mathias Kneissl, The Sudden Wealth of the Poor People of Kombach, I Love You, I Kill You* premiered along with Volker Vogeler's *Jaider—der einsame Jäger/Jaider—The Lonely Hunter*. The bourgeois press heralded a "critical" or "leftist" *Heimatfilm* that offered audiences revisionist views of their own history, unique glimpses at a milieu and time falsified or neglected in earlier efforts in the genre.[22] Commentators readily pointed out the main impulses at work here:

> These films all shared a provincial landscape for their setting, the use of motifs from the traditional *Heimatfilm* as well as dialect and a lack of overt references to the present. By dint of their historical settings (Uwe Brandner is in this regard an exception in that he used the near future for his story) these films took on the character of a parable; the social criticism voiced by the directors clearly applied to the present as well.[23]

Such a representative description contains numerous truisms, to be sure, but it leaves much to be elucidated. What indeed stood behind the revamped *Heimatfilm?* What in particular distinguished it from previous exercises in the genre? And how specifically did its appeal to the past—in Brandner's case the future—bear on the present?

Three major influences stood behind the *Anti-Heimatfilm:* (1) the critical *Volksstück,* (2) the Italo-Western, and (3) Young German Film's own grappling with its cinematic heritage and its growing awareness of a cultural mission. German writers had not left the conservative legacy of *Heimatliteratur* untouched. Especially during the Weimar Republic, a tradition of critical *Volksstücke* offered more incisive glimpses at provincial life, alternative views of peasants and workers. For the most part, though, these works remained dust-covered until the mid-sixties, when Ödön von Horváth's plays found their way into even middle-of-the-road repertoires. These dramas from the thirties were designed to refurbish the old *Volksstück* by doing away with its kitschy *Gemütlichkeit* and dealing with the real problems of simple people from a point of view sympathetic to them—one that used their often faltering language.[24] Marieluise Fleisser also underwent a rediscovery; her *Dramen der Betroffenheit* (dramas of social concern) portrayed smalltown dwellers unable to grasp the mechanisms that beat them into passivity or drove them to fits of aggression.[25] At the same time, Georg Büchner's 19th-century play *Woyzeck* took on a seminal importance for a new generation of dramatists.

One need not dig deeply for evidence linking Horváth and Fleisser with the younger writers Sperr, Fassbinder, and Franz Xaver Kroetz. The direct debt owed to the renewers of the *Volksstück* has been forthrightly acknowledged. Kroetz extolled his elders' insight into the plight of the lower classes in an essay "Horváth von heute für heute"/ "Horváth from Today for Today" (1971).[26] Elsewhere he lauded Fleisser's concern for—in Horváth's words—"those who count":

> Fleisser showed us that stupidity is not a basic human weakness, but rather that a social process controlled by people seeking power and profit needs to have its 'ignorant' many and its 'clever' few, and thus lets things develop this way, in a ruthless and criminal manner.[27]

The trio Sperr, Fassbinder, and Kroetz were quite appropriately referred to in media representations as the disciples of Marieluise Fleisser.[28]

Equally direct links connect the radical *Volksstücke* of the late sixties and the *Anti-Heimatfilm*. Sperr provided the script for *Hunting Scenes from Lower Bavaria;* he also collaborated with Hauff on the scenario for *Mathias Kneissl.*[29] *Hunting Scenes*—the first part of the *Bayrische Trilogie/Bavarian Trilogy*—contains a structure paradigmatic for the new *Heimatfilm,* one still functioning in Josef Rödl's *Albert—warum/ Albert—Why?* (1978). Untrusting townspeople mistreat an outsider, passing rumors about him, and tormenting him with their insinuations and blatant cruelty. In the end, the newcomer vents his anger on someone weaker than himself, knifing—in a scene reminiscent of *Woyzeck*—the farm girl who claims to be carrying his child. He flees to the woods, the eager villagers track him down, and the police take him away. An eerie and disquieting long shot of a peaceful burg ends the film. Calamity—and not calm—prevails over the country.

Kroetz's drama *Wildwechsel/Wild Game Crossing* become a controversial film directed by Fassbinder in 1972, one ultimately disowned by the author.[30] Fassbinder had already filmed Fleisser's *Pioniere in Ingolstadt/ Pioneers in Ingolstadt* (1971) as well as his own play *Katzelmacher* (1969). Actors like Hans Brenner and Eva Mattes, in addition to Fassbinder's own stock company, performed as regulars in both the new *Volksstücke* and *Anti-Heimatfilme*.[31] Schlöndorff's TV-film *Baal* (1969) exemplifies, quite strikingly, the tie between the revaluation of the *Volksstück* and the Young German Film. It opens with a scene encountered in many subsequent *Anti-Heimatfilme*: a lone figure — Brecht's anarchistic poet as played by Fassbinder, garbed in his obligatory black-leather jacket — walks down an open road in long shot, sprawling fields surrounding him. The rebel in transit reminds one of a harried Heinrich Geiz *(Kombach)* as he trudges down a country lane at night followed by a relentless tracking shot. The scene similarly points ahead to Mathias Kneissl walking toward the viewer with gun in hand as a dutiful camera backs up to accompany his flight from the law. Schlöndorff's direct borrowing from *Woyzeck* (Heinrich Geiz speaks to Sophie about their illegitimate child: "Dear God in Heaven won't look at the little worm to check whether the amen was said before he was made") proves incontrovertibly just how consciously the new *Heimatfilm* appealed to the tradition of the critical *Volksstück*.

A second influence behind the transformation of the *Heimatfilm* is the Italo-Western. So-called "spaghetti Westerns" enjoyed enormous popularity during the mid- and late-sixties in West Germany, particularly among left-wing intellectuals. Sergio Corbucci's *Il Mercenario* (1968),[32] numerous movies with the gunslinger Django, and most definitively Sergio Leone's Clint Eastwood-trilogy (*A Fistful of Dollars* [1964], *For a Few Dollars More* [1965], and *The Good, the Bad, and the Ugly* [1966]), and the later *Once Upon a Time in the West* (1968) virtually deconstructed the cowboy epic.[33] Calling into question the heroic ideals of the American Western (while U.S. troops sought the national manifest destiny further west in Vietnam), the genre favored offbeat protagonists, outlaws who scorned traditional sources of authority. West German *Anti-Heimatfilme* would operate analogously, focussing on the disfranchised victims of German history, poachers and robbers rebelling against social structures that allowed them no other alternative. The most vivid example of the Italo-Western's impact on the critical *Heimatfilm* is Volker Vogeler's *Verflucht, dies Amerika/Damn This America* (1973), a work that depicts five Bavarian emigrants, convicts banished from their homeland who seek their fortunes (only to find perdition) in the Wild West of America. The discerning viewer easily recognizes the settings as the Spanish locales common to many "spaghetti Westerns."[34]

The third and often-obscured impulse behind the *Anti-Heimatfilm* remains Young German Film's reckoning with its national film tradition and its search for a wider audience. By the late sixties, filmmakers in the FRG had worked their way into an insular and self-indulgent phase, crafting alternative works in a country with, at best, a very marginal film (alternative or otherwise) culture, so out of touch with their audiences that fewer and fewer movies found distribution or exhibition. What good was it to have subsidy money if the finished products never received public screenings? Lacking its own distinctive voice, Young German Film, after its initial successes of 1966 and 1967, reverted to the *film noir,* and later the melodrama, confronting in these popular genres no small trace of the signs and codes of a German film praxis that had emigrated to America. Explorations and dalliances with Hollywood models would paradoxically bring much of Germany's expatriated film heritage home again. Fassbinder's reception of Sirk (who had left Nazi Germany for a prolific career in numerous Hollywood studios) and Wenders's regard for Hitchcock (who had learned his craft in Weimar Germany), as well as his evocation of Fritz Lang as a symbol for a shattered legacy, provide only the most conspicuous examples.[35] Herzog's admiration of F. W. Murnau and Lotte Eisner plus his continual borrowings from the "haunted screen" of the twenties[36] and the turn of the Berlin School to the *Arbeiterfilm* (worker film) of the Weimar Republic all represent further attempts on the part of Young German directors to link up with a legitimate national cinema. The Oberhausen signatories had announced their intention to create the new German feature film. To do so, they would have to do more than to proclaim their elders' cinema dead. They would have to come to grips with a problematic film tradition, to understand not only the past abuses of the medium under fascism and cold war politics, but to rediscover points in that past which would allow a possible cultural continuity.

The tradition summarized in the epithet *Papas Kino* represented an object of scorn for the brash beginners waging "a necessary revolution against the hegemony of the *Heimatfilm* and the 'weepy cartel' " (Hans-Jürgen Syberberg).[37] A showing of Gustav Ucicky's *Der Edelweisskönig/The Edelweiss King* (1957) at the 1971 Hof Film Festival (the traditional gathering place of the young directors), a screening meant as a ruse by the organizer Heinz Badewitz, caused a violent stir, a commotion that indicates just how virulently certain *Jungfilmer* hated *Papas Kino:*

> The film played on and suddenly a man stood in front of the screen, cursing and gesticulating. Vlado Kristl tried to cover the screen with his jacket, then he stormed onto the balcony and screamed to the audience: 'I refuse to have my film shown. I call on the others to do the same.'[38]

Kristl's colleagues, understanding Badewitz's prank, did not leave the festival. Some had started to realize a more effective means of confronting the once dominant praxis; they had begun to see that *Papas Kino* did not just mean the travesties of the Hitler and Adenauer eras. Certain elements of the national legacy could be reappropriated. Even a genre so often used in ideological campaigns as the *Heimatfilm* was in fact salvageable. Directors like Schlöndorff, Hauff, Vogeler, and Brandner sought a more dialectical relationship to the popular form, realizing its powerful potential for rewriting German history as well as its possible continuing appeal to the national audience they so decidedly lacked. They revived the genre with an eye to subverting its entire structure, reshaping it in line with a larger project: "We must try to learn and understand our history in a critical manner" (Schlöndorff).[39] Or in the words of Alf Brustellin:

> We have created only one film genre which could be called specifically German, the *'Heimatfilm,'* and we have let it go to seed. But when you think about it, it is precisely this genre, starring the common people, which is the ideal medium for telling the other version of history, for taking up the alternative tradition, that of the people of humble origin, the lower classes, the exploited, the forever defeated and the rebellious.[40]

The new *Heimatfilm* would amount to a critical confrontation with the legacy of *Papas Kino.*

The Subversion of a System

Critics stress how the new *Heimatfilm* "questioned the very bases of the genre: the assumption that life in the country is agreeable, desirable, and essentially unproblematic."[41] It dispelled the myth of the rural idyll and, in so doing, commented on the organizational structures of public life, past and present, in a way applying not only for the provinces. This design, though, needs more than the sketchy treatment it has thus far received. We need to re-examine the ideological foundations of the traditional *Heimatfilm* and contrast them with the constructions of subsequent rebuilders. Beyond this, closer attention must be directed to the formal terms of the renewal. Drawing on Willi Höfig's content analysis, *Der deutsche Heimatfilm 1947-1960*, I will summarize the main characteristics of the genre during its heyday in the Adenauer years, confronting each point with the contributions of Young German directors.[42] Since Höfig's generalizations do not transcend the thematic, I will reach beyond his categories to discuss the formal means by which creators of the *Anti-Heimatfilm* articulated their ambitious resolve.

One can portray the traditional *Heimatfilm* very accurately. In Höfig's words:

> It can be described as a clash between an 'open' and a 'closed' world, as the depiction of an ostensibly self-enclosed societal and value system and its confrontation with other systems lying outside its confines.[43]

Heimat (the homeland) takes on a positive value in contrast to the vagaries of the *Fremde* (the foreign). The polarity *Heimat-Fremde* amounts to opposing moral alternatives, a life bound in social and spiritual roots on the one hand, a world without firm customs and conventions, a realm of unsure possibilities and hazards on the other. The *Anti-Heimatfilm* turns this priority topsy-turvy. Both Mathias Kneissl and the Kombach peasants constantly hold up the *Fremde* as their great hope, for the *Heimat* offers them only misery and starvation. "Amerika is goned zu vergleicha mit Bajan," one character explains in *Mathias Kneissl*. "Ma hod ganz andore Schaasn." (The Bavarian text translates as: "America can't be compared to Bavaria. One has completely different opportunities.") In Schlöndorff's film, David Briel reads the letter of a recent emigrant to Milwaukee extolling the New World's endless resources; a later scene shows the Jew ready to leave for the United States.[44] One-tenth of the Hessian population emigrated in the 19th century, the voice-over narrator reports, quoting an apprentice's description of the penury and suffering which emptied entire villages.

Brandner expands upon the polarity *Heimat-Fremde* from another vantage point: the post-credits sequence opens with a stranger arriving from the city. The small town's luminaries—mayor, priest, druggist, hunter, police, as well as two prostitutes—greet the new teacher with a few perfunctory gestures and phrases. After the brief ceremony, one of the gendarmes says: "That's it," to which his partner tersely replies: "We'll see." The clipped response intimates the abiding distrust of anyone who might upset the precarious balance of the village. Brandner details the various measures a small town takes to maintain its sanctity: the civic government administers tranquilizers to everyone. So successful is the public pacification that the zealous police have next to no crime in their closely-controlled streets. *Heimat* becomes an elaborate system geared to ward off outside intruders or attacks from within.

Second, the *Heimatfilm* glorifies a sentimental attachment to a specific space, the idealized world of one's innocence with which one associates emotional well-being. People and milieu exist in a mystical oneness. The pantheistic harmony in this relationship is typically reinforced by cut-away shots from loving couples strolling through nature to landscape panoramas of flora and fauna. More poignantly, songs express the affective connotations of *Heimat:* "The homeland is my whole world," a character sings in Rudolf Schündler's *Wenn am Sonntagabend die Dorfmusik spielt/When They Play Music in the Village on Sunday Evening* (1953). "I'm going to stay where Fate holds me." These lyrics impart an emotional edge to all human activity, rendering everything—milieu, social relations, tradition, history—sentimental and beyond rational understanding.

The critical *Heimatfilm* subverts this whimsy. In Hauff's film all space outside the run-down mill occupied by the Kneissl family becomes dangerous ground. Forays into the outside world mean peril; one must deal with gendarmes, game wardens, and hostile villagers. Even the private sphere is not spared unannounced visitations by the police. No symbiotic relationship binds the Kneissl family to the Bavarian Forest; they seek in it the means of their material survival. The townspeople of Kombach likewise use the woods to their advantage in staging the robbery. Otherwise nothing indicates an emotional affinity to the space they inhabit. Instead one hears songs praising the rich soil of the New World:

> The time, the hour is here,
> We're leaving for America.
> The horses are already saddled;
> We're going to a foreign land.

> Coffee grows on every bush
> And is there for anyone who needs it....
> We're leaving for a land that's always green,
> Where even in winter roses bloom.

Brandner uncovers the violence lurking under a veneer of calm. At one point the sun goes down over a picturesque country home, an idyllic picture of a sprawling field. On the soundtrack, though, we hear a whip whistling through the air, one seen in the hand of the mayor in an earlier shot. The juxtaposition of sight and sound both deconstructs the tranquil facade and draws attention to the precarious price the villagers must pay for their pastoral innocence. They are not allowed to hunt in their own forest and on certain days may not even enter the woods. In the *Heimat* depicted by Brandner one treads very softly.

The third characteristic of the *Heimatfilm* is its closed system and all-encompassing immanence. Every conflict stems from attacks upon the *Heimatsystem,* be they from the outside world or within a single family. All problems find resolutions that reassert the validity of the homeland and tradition. The genre turns all human concerns into private affairs; the most serious dilemmas are overcome at the marriage altar. The new *Heimatfilm* demonstrates open narrative structures and conclusions which question, not reaffirm, the political systems in which the characters move. Voice-overs (spoken by Margarethe von Trotta) continually remind the viewer of the larger historical framework behind *Kombach,* juxtaposing the image of farmers huddled in a narrow kitchen over soup with the information: "Serfage was abolished only in 1820 in Hesse, but instead of bringing freedom, it just brought a heavier burden on the small farmers who couldn't live on their small piece of land." One cuts from the tired wives sitting at the table to a moving carriage with the royal treasure. As the camera tracks left to follow the wagon, we hear: "Kept ignorant throughout the centures, they were unable to see the cause of their miseries. Only emigration to the New World, poaching, or treasure hunting were seen as a way out of poverty." Another voice-over narrator provides the documented facts of Mathias Kneissl's life, quoting from court records and wanted posters. *Mathias Kneissl* and *Kombach* demonstrate how remnants of a feudal order undermine any hope for private solace. Kneissl never can get the money together he needs to wed his lover. Initially, Heinrich Geiz (in *Kombach*) cannot afford a humble wedding—at the same time a considerable tax is waged upon the populace so that the Princess of Hesse-Cassel might be married in luxury. Indeed, the wedding celebration Geiz affords himself with the money from the robbery draws attention to him and ultimately leads to the arrest and conviction of the peasants.

A further deviation from the closed system of the old *Heimatfilm* lies in endings that do not present spurious harmonies. Instead of providing affirmative conclusions, the filmmakers appeal directly to the spectator. At the end of *Kombach,* David Briel talks about cities that did not exist in the 1820s: Schlöndorff goes outside the film's diegesis to include subsequent experience extending to the viewer's present. Kneissl, sitting before his executioners and facing the audience, freezes into a static portrait: an image from the past engrains itself in the spectator's mind. *I Love You, I Kill You* closes with a dramatic act of rebellion: the hunter tracks down the teacher (who has been poaching in the village's prized forest) and brings him to the town square where the police shoot the lawbreaker. The hunter, who had earlier received an award for his "exemplary service," suddenly turns on the gendarmes and—in an act of grand refusal which breaks through the circle of meaningless ritual governing every activity in the burg—guns them down. As birds hoot loudly, we see a final close-up of gloved hands and smoking shell cartridges. The take lasts for some time and Brandner conspicuously does not punctuate the film with the word "Ende."

Fourth and finally, the *Heimatfilm* manifests a conservative and patriarchal structure; its plot logic aims to achieve—more often than not, restore—a normative order present at the narrative's beginning. Characters who question or attempt to alter the given become negative forces. The action typically ends with the original state once again intact. All three of the *Anti-Heimatfilme* under discussion do just the opposite; they analyze an oppressive patriarchy and show how it bears down upon those living under it. *Kombach* and *Mathias Kneissl* both have bipartite narrative structures that further an understanding of the truly malevolent social orders which the traditional *Heimatfilm* had taken for granted. One sympathizes with challenges to this sinister political machinery. Schlöndorff's film provides a double analysis: the first half of the movie traces the robbery in the Subach Valley back to its inception.[45] The narrative presents the act as one of dire necessity, as a labor that takes five attempts before succeeding. After the actual crime, another line of inquiry commences, an analysis of the official investigation led by the fastidious agent Danz. The government inspector has no illusions about the poor people's true condition; he uses it to solicit information from the villagers, promising rewards to informers. His interrogations break down the individual defendants, who in the end—prompted by Church and State—unconditionally reaffirm these authorities. (Heinrich Geiz is the sole exception: he remains rebellious to the end.) A final quotation follows the subdued reenactment of the public execution, one that passes judgment on the network of forces which violates the human spirit:

> What in you was a mountain
> They have levelled,
> And your valley
> Has been filled in.
> Over your stretches
> A comfortable road.

Hauff's film traces the decline of a family: authorities beat the father to death, imprison the mother, and incarcerate the children. At the start of the movie's second half, the lonely hero sits in a train, pondering his fate now that irate villagers have burned the family refuge. He has lost his job, has little chance of finding another one as an ex-convict, and lacks all hope of gaining the means to marry his lover. He sighs, gazes at the passing greenery, and faces the inevitable prospect of becoming a robber if he is to survive. Aligning itself with the desperate challenges to the public order, the new *Heimatfilm* (this applies equally to *Jaider—The Lonely Hunter*) delineates the oppressed people's motives and puts them into a larger context of victimization rarely written about in historical accounts. (One has mythologized Kneissl as something of a Robin Hood in Bavaria, but obscured the actual fact that the battle between poachers and feudal lords took on war-like dimensions in the 19th century.[46]) *I Love You, I Kill You* focusses on the patently patriarchal order of "Die Herren" ("The Masters"), overseers from afar who keep the township under total control. The rulers treasure the village's rich game preserve and enforce laws granting only themselves hunting rights. Brandner's film concentrates on the growing rage that begins with the teacher's idle poaching and culminates in the hunter's decisive revolt against the ritualistic cycle essentialized in the movie's curious title.

Kombach featured peasants "who survived the age of Martin Luther but did not live long enough to be energized by the age of Karl Marx."[47] The *Anti-Heimatfilm* in general centered around pre-revolutionaries who refuse to act as powerless objects in the hands of Fate or an inscrutable system. One emphasized exceptions to the rule, challenges to seemingly inexorable constellations. The failure of such ventures has less to do with a post-1968 leftist melancholy—as Wolfram Schütte insists[48]—than with the tragic course of German history and its "tendency for revolutions to fail and restorations to succeed" (Oskar Negt).[49] Schlöndorff, Hauff, and Vogeler meant to rediscover an obscured tradition of the oppressed, radical signs of life which manifested themselves in the form of "courage, humor, cunning, and fortitude." The point is not that the grand refusals went down in defeat, but in fact that they took place—and as Brandner's film suggests, can continue to do so. The scenes therefore take on a "retroactive force," calling into question "every victory, past and present, of the rulers."[50] In this manner the critical *Heimatfilm* found a new calling as a genre meant to shake the very foundations of German history.

Radical Picture Stories from the Homeland

The *Anti-Heimatfilm* took equally radical stylistic exception to its generic forebearer. Three major considerations suggest the formal terms of the new *Heimatfilm*'s reckoning with tradition. First, it problematizes the signifying process through constant references to the powerful potential exercised by images as recordings, stylizations, and distortions of reality. Unlike the "static, 'intentionally beautiful' representations"[51] of earlier *Heimatfilme,* tableaux bound in a straightforward picture-book aesthetics, Brandner's "Bildergeschichte aus der Heimat" ("Picture Story from the *Heimat*")—so runs the movie's subtitle—analyzes the stereotypical images produced by a regimented experience. School children paint uniformly bright-colored motifs consistent with the optimistic official line of the town's dignitaries. The eager pupils learn to equate single words with single associations: birds sing, flowers bloom, the State governs, and guns shoot. The natural and the human world all possess the same one-dimensionality for the town's inhabitants. And images, ones perceived by a populace already heavily sedated by drugs, supplant direct experience of reality. The new arrival to the burg walks past someone who takes a picture, counts to thirty, and remarks as he looks at the reproduction: "The new teacher." We then see the same person looking out of his camera, standing next to a friend who gazes into a kaleidoscope. Both, the film leads us to recognize, partake of the same monotone rosey-colored reality regardless of what instrument they use. Brandner from the beginning understates the story line and presents his narrative in a puzzle-like construction.[52] An early cut makes the director's distanciating design clear: he goes from a filmed representation of a hunter bending over his human quarry (presumably the old teacher who will be replaced) to a naive art rendering of the scene, contrasting brutal reality with its blithe stylization, in essence defining the relation of the new *Heimatfilm* to its predecessor.

Mathias Kneissl begins and ends with images that freeze into photographs, representations making clear the medium's inherent dialectic of the ephemeral and the permanent. Early in the film the camera duplicates the position of a still camera taking a picture of the family. The image captures a group of people in time, the same group we will see torn asunder in the course of the narrative. A photograph serves as historical memory: "Show everyone our photo and send them kindest regards" are the first words spoken in the film. A still of the incarcerated robber facing his executioners lingers at the movie's end; the camera records a plaintive appeal ignored by most historical accounts. Edgar Reitz speaks of how film can act as a sort of a magical power that brings the dead and the forgotten back to life, making otherwise lost images part of the present.[53] The new *Heimatfilm*, however, does not seek to preserve the myth of a timeless and transfigured reality. It functions in direct opposition to the conservative predilection of its generic tradition, undercutting the tendency to produce "a world that remained untouched by time or triumphantly resisted time's destructive effect, a world that itself is a souvenir of this past."[54] Schlöndorff's *Kombach* with its wood-cut tonalities historicizes moments out of a for-the-most-unwritten German history, providing alternative information not readily found in text books, history written from a point of view sympathetic to its victims, not its victors. The black-and-white starkness of Franz Rath's cinematography provides a further, most vivid contrast to the garish production values and soft-focus sentimentality of earlier *Heimatfilme*.

A second formal challenge of the new *Heimatfilm* lies in its unceasing textuality, its constant reference to texts within the larger filmic text. Unlike the artificial, closed, and non-reflexive likes of its predecessor, the *Anti-Heimatfilm* demonstrates much narrative self-consciousness. *Kombach* contains numerous quotations from German cultural history, from popular literature offering the peasants relief while simultaneously instilling in them the ideology of the ruling class. Schlöndorff shows how these seemingly quaint songs, poems, and stories fit into an insidious mechanism that preserves an oppressive hierarchy. We watch old women strain at the top of a hill as they pull a plow across a field, while at the bottom of the same hill their grandchildren learn a passage from the medieval epic *(Meier Helmbrecht)* recited by their teacher:

> Therefore remain content with plowing fields,
> For many a noble woman
> Will surely be made more beautiful by the peasant's labor.

Impressionable minds memorize Christian Fürchtegott Gellert's poem "Satisfaction with One's Condition" and a little boy reads the resigned words of Jeremias Gotthelf's *The Broommaker of Rychiswyl* while his parents listen approvingly. This literary tradition affirms the existing inequities, combining with the *Bible,* the teachings of Martin Luther, and fairy tales to keep simple people content with their wretched lot. Schlöndorff, in cataloguing this literature of affirmation, constantly juxtaposes it with the realities experienced by its unwitting consumers, thereby exploding the illusions created by the heritage and its surface *Gemütlichkeit* in showing the suffering it furthers. David Briel sees past the fairy tale harmonies in his speech at the wedding banquet:

> How marvelously is the world ordered! The people have furnished their house with chairs and benches and tables and a kitchen, and in it a fire burns, and they have coffee and milk and sugar and lovely dishes, and they do all of this for us. It's just like in the fairy tale 'Little Table Set Yourself.'

He pauses, then proceeds to destroy the idyll, claiming that all is not so simple. Fingering a gold coin, he concludes: "Without this we would have nothing."

Brandner, unlike Schlöndorff and to some degree Hauff, does not go outside the diegesis to quote official records and provide historical commentary. But he repeatedly introduces texts into his carefully designed narrative, ones that further disclose the violence behind a seemingly sedate context. Children sing "Die Gedanken sind frei" ("Thoughts Are Free") in a classroom as two gendarmes stand outside the school listening. One policeman repeats the lyrics with a sinister smirk, commenting on the distinct lack of autonomous thought or action in the systematically other-directed village. On several occasions Brandner cuts to a middle-aged man sitting in a bare room, looking out of the window, writing in his diary. "One day goes into the next unnoticeably," scribbles the inner emigrant. "Over our heads the seasons change. One can't do anything about it." These contemplations reiterate the fatalistic assumptions of the traditional *Heimatfilm,* assumptions that Brandner's narrative as a whole incisively calls into question.

Hauff, like Schlöndorff, plays off dispassionate official records with images that belie the historical documents. A voice-over narrator at one point reads a list of Kneissl's various crimes. On May 30, 1893, the Munich Criminal Court sentenced him to five years in prison for resisting and insulting the police as well as for attempting murder. The Kneissl house burns as the off-voice repeats the harsh verdict, a verdict we know from an earlier scene which in no way accords to reality: police invaded the Kneissl home without a search warrant, attempted to rape his sister, and made various other threats that finally provoked Mathias's brother to frighten the intruders with a gun. At another juncture, Hauff provides a related aural-visual contrast: we listen to the text of a wanted poster as we glimpse the clearly desperate Kneissl, lifelong victim of official intransigence, wearily trekking down a barren country lane.

A third formal consideration remains the dynamic array of visual—and aural—earmarks inherent to the *Anti-Heimatfilm,* usages that grew out of the rebellion against the functional postcard indulgences of the mass-produced movies from another era. A few examples can at least suggest the formal counterparts to the subversion of the genre's political content. Most apparent is the studied use of lateral tracking shots, tracing simple people driven by circumstance to lives of crime, following them in their flight from representatives of the State. Conspicuous, as well, is the careful use of depth-of-field to visualize social conflict, for instance the class differences stressed by the *mise en scène* of *Mathias Kneissl*'s opening shot: as the Kneissl family stands at the train station, a rich man's coach rolls into the scene, cutting across the frame and virtually covering them up so they can no longer be seen. Schlöndorff's placement of actors in the narrow Geiz family kitchen operates along similar lines to express a hierarchy even among the oppressed: the Jew David, although an accomplice, still must stand in the background as others sit down to eat.

Another common ploy is the conscious underlining of certain spaces and compositions by shots held for several seconds after a scene has played out (Schlöndorff lingers on the empty trail through the woods after yet another robbery attempt has failed and the dejected peasants trudge back to the fields) or by freezing action in a static tableau as we find in the off-center sepia image at the end of *Mathias Kneissl* and the numerous stationary holds at the conclusions of scenes in Brandner's film. Beyond this, one must note the creative use of sound in these works, especially the singular mixture of acoustic and natural noises in *I Love You, I Kill You*. Schlöndorff, as a further variation on his Brechtian penchant for using voice-overs to comment upon and counterpoint the staged fiction, also implements jazzy melodies and upbeat music out of keeping with the historical period he so painstakingly reconstructs.

The analytical *Heimatfilme* in sum attack the thematic and formal arsenal of previous exercises, replacing "images of a stereotypical, artificial world" (Peter Handke)[55] with powerful counter-representations meant to disclose the innermost workings of their respective settings and reflect on the German past—and present.

The Subsequent Path of the *Heimatfilm:* Coming Home

Contrary to popular misconceptions, the *Anti-Heimatfilm* did not disappear overnight as directors "moved from implicit to explicit criticism of the Federal Republic, to urban settings, and themes that were unambiguously contemporary."[56] German filmmakers carried on this tradition—in numerous directions. Not all subsequent *Heimatfilme* were as decidedly radical in their impetus, but seen together these films worked toward imparting a critical image of Germany. West German efforts in this vein include Niklaus Schilling's *Nachtschatten/Night Shadows* (1971) and *Rheingold* (1977), Fassbinder's adaptation of Kroetz's *Wildwechsel/Jail Bait* (1972), Vogeler's *Damn This America* (1973), Herzog's *Herz aus Glas/Heart of Glass* (1976), as well as Hans W. Geissendörfer's rendering of Anzengruber's *Sternsteinhof/Sternstein Manor* (1976), and Ulrich Edel's TV-version of Oskar Maria Graf's *Der harte Handel/The Brutal Barter* (1978). More recent variations on the *Heimatfilm* include Hans-Christof Stenzel's playfully irreverent *Sufferloh* (1979), Jörg Graser's *Der Mond ist nur a nackerte Kugel/The Moon Is Only a Naked Globe* (1980), and Klaus Emmerich's *Trokadero* (1980). *Heimatfilme* are not limited to the historical past, nor do they only take place in the country. Quite significantly, New German filmmakers have redefined and expanded accepted notions of the *Heimat*.

The most significant recent reformers of the Heimatfilm are Josef Rödl and Herbert Achternbusch. Rödl's films feature the same rural setting and its denizens. They are, in the director's words,

> designed to meet the need for honest films about people who live in an agricultural environment—who play themselves and thereby convey an authentic picture of their milieu, their way of life, their whole being.[57]

Albert-warum/Albert-Why? (1978) and *Franz-der leise Weg/Franz-The Gentle Path* (1980) take place in the small village of Darshöfen where Rödl grew up. His painstaking study of the town and its daily routines possesses anthropological rigor; the poignancy, though, of perceived and lived detail takes on a poetic lyricism that knows nothing of obtrusive symbolizing and literary contrivance. In one of his latest films, Herbert Achternbusch crawls out from under the Karl Valentin memorial on the Munich *Viktualienmarkt* (an open-air market in the city center). Continuing the zany folk tradition of the homespun comic, Achternbusch has made a private obsession with his *Heimat,* an enduring love-hatred of Bavaria, into the major theme of his films. In *Servus Bayern/Bye Bye, Bavaria* (1977), he verbalizes the brash program behind his contemporary *Heimatfilme:* "This place has made a wreck of me and I'm going to stick around until people start noticing it."

The earliest *Anti-Heimatfilme* of 1971 moved back in time to survey scenes from a past that official history had sought to repress. The creators sided with the vanquished, not the victors, realizing—as Walter Benjamin had—that "empathy with the victor invariably benefits the rulers."[58] Brandner flashed forward to a dystopian future that even more radically restated the underlying critique of a narrowness that knows only rules and no exceptions, of a reality that has become *gleichgeschaltet*. Taken together with more recent actualizations, these films re-explore the *Heimat,* finding in its midst an inexorable tendency over time to disdain the foreign, fear the unusual, and torment the weak. "Like strangers we live in our own house": Wolf Biermann's lyrics restate the sympathy present here for individuals disfranchised and pursued by the State. Over the years numerous West German filmmakers have attempted to reread German history in a critical manner and to look incisively at sectors of public experience—past and present—which cultural legitimators in the Federal Republic would rather ignore. Film in this way enhances a respect for the past and enriches a feeling for the present:

> Film has much in common with our ability to remember. It is not just the capacity to retain images and events, to salvage them from the march of time, but also the possibility to mix past and present in a way which causes them to merge.[59]

"We want to deal with the images of our own country." This resolve of the filmmaker collective that produced *Deutschland im Herbst/ Germany in Autumn* (1978), West German film's most thorough-going reflection on the *Heimat*,[60] this impetus guided the *Anti-Heimatfilm* from its inception in the early seventies. One reflected on the wrongs of the German past, hoping to bring about a less harrowing present, a German history in which one could take pride, a Germany in which one could feel at home. Numerous West German directors have, from the beginning, pursued the quest of Gabi Teichert, the leftist patriot who wants to understand past history in order to create a better future one. For, to quote the famous closing words of Ernst Bloch's *Das Prinzip Hoffnung/The Principle of Hope:*

> The basis of history... is the working, productive human being, who shapes and reshapes circumstances. When he finally realizes himself and his creations in an authentic democracy without self-denial or alienation, then something of which we have a faint glimmering as children will come about in the world, a place where no one has been before: *Heimat.*[61]

NOTES

An earlier, somewhat different version of this chapter appears as "Calamity Prevails over the Country: Young German Film Rediscovers the *Heimat*," in *Film und Literatur; Literarische Texte und der neue deutsche Film* (Bern/Munich: Francke, 1984).

[1] "Erfahrungen beim Erzählen von Geschichten aus der Geschichte," *Medium*, December 1979, p. 31.

[2] Werner Herzog, for instance, said in an interview with Jonathan Cott: "Filmmakers like myself started from zero—we didn't have the cultural continuity of France or the United States." "Signs of Life," *Rolling Stone*, 18 Nov. 1976, p. 53.

[3] Article entitled *"Heimatfilm"* in *rororo Filmlexikon*, ed. Liz-Anne Bawden and Wolfram Tichy (Hamburg: Rowohlt, 1977), I, 277.

[4] Willi Höfig, *Der deutsche Heimatfilm 1947-1960* (Stuttgart: Enke, 1973), p. 4. I acknowledge the crucial importance of Höfig's positivistic thoroughness for much background material. Nonetheless, I share the misgivings voiced by Ute Ganschow in a review of Höfig's book, most especially Ganschow's reservations about Höfig's uncritical appropriation of studies written during the Third Reich. See *Diskurs* (Cologne), Nos. 6/7 (1974), pp. 174-76.

[5] Ibid., p. 10.

[6] Höfig discusses the importance of the *Dorfgeschichte* on pp. 19-28. For a more differentiated view of 19th-century rural literature in Germany, see Hermann Kinder, *Poesie als Synthese: Ausbreitung eines deutschen Realismus in der Mitte des 19. Jahrhunderts* (Frankfurt: Athenäum, 1973). The role of the *Volksschauspiel* is discussed by Höfig on pp. 143-152.

[7] Quoted in Höfig, p. 21.

[8] Höfig draws particularly on Hans Moser and Raimund Zoder's *Deutsches Volkstum in Volksschauspiel und Volkstanz* (Berlin: de Gruyter, 1938).

[9] A sub-genre of the *Heimatfilm* evolved in which the effect of a play or film production on a village provided the central plot interest. See Höfig, pp. 151-52.

[10] Quoted in Höfig, pp. 149-50.

[11] Wilhelm Spickernagel, "Der Kinematograph im Dienste der Heimatkunst," *Hannoverland*, vol. 6, Sonderheft 3 (1912), p. 234. Quoted in Höfig, p. 153.

[12] Höfig, p. 143.

[13] *From Caligari to Hitler: A Psychological History of the German Film* (Princeton: Princeton U.P., 1947), p. 111.

[14] Oscar Kalbus, quoted in Höfig, p. 162.

[15] Quoted in Höfig, p. 164.

[16] Ibid., pp. 168-69.

[17] The title of the film *Ferien vom Ich/Vacation from Myself* (Hans Deppe, 1952) sums up the overriding tendency behind these movies every bit as much as a later title of an experimental effort presages a more critical direction: *nicht mehr fliehen/Stop Running* (Herbert Vesely, 1955).

[18] *nicht mehr fliehen: Das Kino der Ära Adenauer*, ed. Ulrich Kurowski, Michael

Brandlmeier, and André Gerely (Munich: Freunde des Münchner Filmmuseums, 1979), p. 5.

[19] Ibid., p. 6.

[20] Cf. Peter Brückner's general characterization of the sense of dislocation experienced during the epoch in *Versuch, uns und anderen die Bundesrepublik zu erklären* (Berlin: Wagenbach, 1978), esp. p. 18.

[21] See "Autorität und Revolte im deutschen Film: Nationale Leitbilder von Caligari bis Canaris," *Frankfurter Hefte,* January 1956, p. 22.

[22] See Wolf Donner, "Wenig Lärm um viel: Volker Schlöndorffs filmische Bauernchronik," *Die Zeit,* 2 Feb. 1971; and Alf Brustellin, "Die andere Tradition: Volker Schlöndorffs *Der plötzliche Reichtum der armen Leute von Kombach* im Münchner Theatiner," *Süddeutsche Zeitung,* 8 Feb. 1971.

[23] Hans Günther Pflaum and Hans Helmut Prinzler, *Film in der Bundesrepublik Deutschland* (Munich: Hanser, 1979), p. 26.

[24] See von Horváth's 1932 essay, "Zur Erneuerung des Volksstückes," in *Über Ödön von Horváth,* ed. Dieter Hildebrandt and Traugott Krischke (Frankfurt: Suhrkamp, 1972), esp. pp. 16-17.

[25] See " 'Ich schreibe Leben—aus Betroffenheit': Gespräch mit Marieluise Fleisser" (with Thomas Thieringer), *Süddeutsche Zeitung,* 9 Jan. 1974.

[26] *Über Ödön von Horváth,* pp. 91-95.

[27] *Materialien zum Leben und Schreiben der Marieluise Fleisser,* ed. Günther Rühle (Frankfurt: Suhrkamp, 1973), pp. 384-85. See also Hellmuth Karasek's discussion of "Die Erneuerung des Volksstücks," in *Die Literatur der Bundesrepublik,* ed. Dieter Lattmann, 2nd rev. ed. (Zürich/Munich: Kindler, 1973), pp. 660-88.

[28] Ibid., p. 403.

[29] Sperr also played the protagonist in the film version of *Hunting Scenes* and the shepherd Meier in *Mathias Kneissl.*

[30] See Thomas Thieringer, "Streit zwischen Autor und Regisseur," *Frankfurter Rundschau,* 14 March 1973. *Wildwechsel* is distributed in the US under the title *Jail Bait.*

[31] Fassbinder likewise played treacherous farmers in *Mathias Kneissl* and *Kombach.* Hauff provided an impressively effective Heinrich Geiz in *Kombach.* Schlöndorff made a cameo appearance as a station master in *Mathias Kneissl.*

[32] Cf. Wolf Lepenies, "Der Italo-Western—Ästhetik und Gewalt," in *Theorie des Kinos: Ideologiekritik der Traumfabrik,* ed. Karsten Witte (Frankfurt: Suhrkamp, 1972), pp. 15-38.

[33] See Christopher Frayling's comprehensive analysis, *Spaghetti Westerns: Cowboys and Europeans from Karl May to Sergio Leone* (London: Routledge & Kegan Paul, 1981).

[34] Another German Western filmed in Europe (in the Bavarian Forest) is Hark Bohm's *Tschetan, der Indianerjunge/Tschetan, the Indian Boy* (1972). For an appreciation of Vogeler's film, see Günter Herburger, "Arbeitslos im Wilden Westen," *Die Zeit,* 2 Nov. 1973.

[35] See Wim Wenders, "Sein Tod ist keine Lösung: Der deutsche Filmregisseur Fritz Lang," in *Jahrbuch Film 77/78,* ed. Hans Günther Pflaum (Munich: Hanser, 1977), pp. 161-65.

[36] See Werner Herzog, "Laudatio auf Lotte Eisner zur Verleihung des Helmut Käutner-Preises 1982," *Film-Korrespondenz,* 30 March 1982, pp. I-II.

[37] *Syberbergs Filmbuch* (Munich: Nymphenburger, 1976), p. 47.

[38] Heinz Badewitz, "Hof, ein Festival für die Provinz: Und ein Stück Geschichte des jungen deutschen Films," in *Jahrbuch Film 77/78,* pp. 128-39.

[39] Quoted in *Der plötzliche Reichtum der armen Leute von Kombach: Dokumentation mit Drehbuch* (Zürich: Kulturstelle der Eidgen. Technischen Hochschule, 1972), n.p.

[40] "Die andere Tradition," op. cit.

[41] John Sandford, *The New German Cinema* (Totowa, New Jersey: Barnes and Noble, 1980), p. 134.

[42] I draw from the summary on pp. 385-92 for the main points.

[43] Höfig, p. 266.

[44] In a rendering of Theodor Storm's *Ein Doppelgänger/A Double,* Ulf Miehe's *John Glückstadt* (1974), the director has his hero—contrary to the textual basis—take leave of rural Germany for America.

[45] One recalls the subtitle of Heinrich Böll's *The Lost Honor of Katharina Blum* (1974), a novel Schlöndorff and von Trotta adapted for the screen: "How Violence Develops and Where It Can Lead."

[46] See Joe Hembus, "Keine Schonzeit für Wilderer," *Zeit-Magazin,* 11 June 1971, p. 14.

[47] Peter Harcourt, *"The Sudden Wealth of the Poor People of Kombach," Film Quarterly,* Fall 1980, p. 63.

[48] "Linke Flucht in rechte Vergangenheit," *Frankfurter Rundschau,* 19 May 1971.

[49] "The Misery of Bourgeois Democracy in Germany," *Telos,* No. 34 (Winter 1977-78), p. 123.

[50] All three quotes from Walter Benjamin, "Theses on the Philosophy of History," in *Illuminations,* ed. Hannah Arendt (New York: Schocken, 1969), p. 255.

[51] Ulrich Gregor and Enno Patalas's general characterization of West German films of the fifties applies to the *Heimatfilm* in particular. *Geschichte des Films 1940-1960* (Hamburg: Rowohlt, 1976), II, 420.

[52] See "KINO-Interview: Uwe Brandner," *Kino* (West Berlin), June-July 1973, pp. 41-42.

[53] "Erfahrungen beim Erzählen," op. cit., p. 30.

[54] Hermann Bauschinger, quoted in Höfig, p. 81.

[55] "Vorläufige Bemerkungen zu Landkinos und Heimatfilmen," in *Ich bin ein Bewohner des Elfenbeinturms* (Frankfurt: Suhrkamp, 1972), p. 150.

[56] Sandford, p. 136. See also Pflaum/Prinzler, p. 29.

[57] From the program notes provided at the 1979 Berlin Film Festival.

[58] Benjamin, p. 256.

[59] Reitz, p. 30.

[60] *"Deutschland im Herbst:* Worin liegt die Parteilichkeit des Films?," *Ästhetik und Kommunikation,* June 1978, p. 124.

[61] *Das Prinzip Hoffnung* (Frankfurt: Suhrkamp, 1973), III, 1628. Werner Schroeter refers to this passage expressly in *Die Generalprobe/La Répétition générale/The Dress Rehearsal* (1980) while speaking of the German *misère.*

Chapter Five

Germany before Autumn: The Literature Adaptation Crisis

> *"Rather than ask, 'What is the attitude of a work to the relations of production of its time?' I should like to ask, 'What is its position in them?'"*
> —Walter Benjamin[1]

> Is It Possible to Make Films in German Today?
> —Title of a film project by Jean-Luc Godard turned down by German television

The Big Mess

During a few months in 1977, much controversy ensued in the FRG over an alleged *Literaturverfilmungskrise* (literature adaptation crisis). Perhaps no other single moment in the history of West German film has so dramatically exhibited the many problems inherent in a state-subsidized cinema in a country well-known for its strained relationship to the medium. It appeared for a few months as if the manifest destiny of West German filmmakers—for all their well-documented realistic ambitions and progressive persuasions—lay in illustrating literary classics from the 19th century or in recycling bestsellers. A few public statements from filmmakers and critics suggest the parameters of the dilemma:

—Germany and its historical aversion to sights and sounds which disclose its innermost workings: the country, claimed Wenders, "for this reason has for thirty years greedily soaked up foreign images, just as long as they have taken its mind off itself. I do not believe there is anywhere else where people have suffered such a loss of confidence in images of their own, their own stories and myths, as we have."[2]

—The primacy of the written word and the penchant for viewing film as an appendage to literature: "Once again we find among us a particularly fatal tendency not to trust the power of the filmic medium, but rather to construct films from the most classical literary sources possible in order to escape the danger of having to work with images and in that way tell our own stories" (Niklaus Schilling).[3]

—The tendency of public institutions to support only "safe" (i.e. uncontroversial and easily legitimated) projects during a time of political crisis: "The commissions support an asphixyating mediocrity; in three years at the latest they will have succeeded in providing perfectly boring illustrated versions of the entire bourgeois canon of the 19th century (preferably Fontane and Storm) for German classes in public high schools" (Hans C. Blumenberg).[4]

—The specter of censorship and an indirect but still undeniable official prohibition of critical realism: "When the economic, legal, or political powers that be have gone so far that film, theater, and literature can no longer deal with the central everyday social issues in a way that might produce works displeasing to those who govern, then one can no longer talk about the freedom of art, no matter how often and how loudly one makes claims to the contrary" (Gerhard Zwerenz).[5]

The literature adaptation crisis, paradoxically enough, coincided with a wave of excitement and fanfare directed toward New German Cinema on the other side of the ocean. In the midst of all the unbridled enthusiasm abroad, very little mention was made of the dire situation in the FRG. (As Fassbinder went through one of his most intense periods of depression while making *Eine Reise ins Licht/Despair,* he contemplated everything from emigration to suicide—right at the time his overseas adherents celebrated a retrospective of his work.) Few seem to have taken notice of the juncture in America. West German commentators later looked over the period of high-pitched emotions as one marked by over-reaction and hysterics, at best an ephemeral impasse that was quickly overcome. Over the years American critics and scholars have frequently made mention of dissatisfaction among the filmmakers toward their support systems, stressing that such criticism is inevitable given the iconoclastic views of the directors and their outspoken opposition to the FRG establishment in general.[6] One has tended, though, to avoid specifics when characterizing the terms of this opposition, resorting instead to such phrases as anti-bourgeois nonconformism, individualistic outrage, or humanistic protest.[7] West German filmmakers and many critics seemed to think literature was causing the downfall of New German Film in 1977. American accounts since the time blithely draw atention to New German Cinema's decidedly literary bias, viewing the dependence on *belles lettres* as a sign of an overrriding intellectualism, or alternately as "a strategy for attracting viewers to theatres."[8] An American observer as well-steeped in the specifics of West German film culture as the *Variety* correspondent in Berlin insisted once: "Literature is the backbone of German cinema. Remove that backbone from the history of New German Cinema, and it appears to be a jelly-fish."[9] The statement is correct—and worthy of further exploration.

The State of Things: An Inventory

American commentators by and large do not seem to know that the *Literaturverfilmungskrise* ever transpired. West German critics in retrospect seemed to stop talking about it overnight with the first signs of its passing early in 1978. Both responses have in essence obscured the more lasting significance of the literature adaptation crisis: the structures that caused it still very much abide today. Before I go on to an analysis of the phenomenon, I would like to list the films involved, not out of any positivistic fervor, but rather to show just how dominant the penchant for literature adaptation was during this time:

1976: Hans W. Geissendörfer, *Sternsteinhof/Sternstein Manor,* based on Ludwig Anzengruber's novel; *Die Wildente/The Wild Duck,* based on Henrik Ibsen's drama;

Heidi Genée, *Grete Minde,* based on Theodor Fontane's story;

Wolf Gremm, *Die Brüder/The Brothers,* which used motifs from Septimus Dale's short story;

Roland Klick, *Lieb Vaterland, magst ruhig sein/Rest Thou Tranquil, Beloved Country,* based on Johannes Mario Simmel's novel;

Thomas Körfer, *Der Gehülfe/The Assistant*, based on Robert Walser's autobiographical novel;

Theodor Kotulla, *Aus einem deutschen Leben/Death Is My Trade*, based on Robert Merle's novel;

Manfred Purzer, *Die Elixiere des Teufels/The Devil's Elixirs*, based on E.T.A. Hoffmann's novel;

Helma Sanders-Brahms, *Heinrich*, based on the life of the writer Heinrich von Kleist;

Volker Schlöndorff, *Der Fangschuss/Coup de Grâce*, based on Marguerite Yourcenar's novel;

Daniel Schmid, *Schatten der Engel/Shadows of the Angels*, based on Fassbinder's play, *Die Stadt, der Müll, und der Tod*;

Franz Seitz, *Unordnung und frühes Leid/Disorder and Early Sorrow*, based on Thomas Mann's short story;

Bernhard Wicki, *Die Eroberung der Zitadelle/The Conquest of the Citadel*, based on Günter Herburger's novella.

1977: Robert Van Ackeren, *Belcanto*, based on Heinrich Mann's novel, *Empfang bei der Welt*;

Alf Brustellin/Bernhard Sinkel, *Der Mädchenkrieg/The Three Sisters*, based on Manfred Bieler's novel;

Klaus Emmerich, *Heinrich Heine* based on the writer's life;

Ingemo Engström/Gerhard Theuring, *Fluchtweg nach Marseille/Escape Route to Marseilles*, based in part on Anna Segher's novel, *Transit*;

Rainer Werner Fassbinder, *Bolwieser/The Stationmaster's Wife*, based on Oskar Maria Graf's novel; *Frauen in New York/Women in New York*, based on Claire Booth's drama, *The Women*; *Eine Reise ins Licht/Despair*, based on Vladimir Nabokov's novel;

Eberhard Fechner, *Winterspelt*, based on Alfred Andersch's novel;

Hans W. Geissendörfer, *Die gläserne Zelle/The Glass Cell*, based on Patricia Highsmith's novel;

Wolf Gremm, *Tod oder Freiheit/Liberty or Death*, loosely based on Schiller's drama *Die Räuber*;

Horst Hächler, *Waldrausch/Forest Fever,* based on Ludwig Ganghofer's novel;

Peter Handke, *Die linkshändige Frau/The Left-Handed Woman,* based on his own story;

Fritz Matthies, *Paulines Geburtstag oder Die Bestie von Notre Dame/Pauline's Birthday or the Beast of Notre Dame,* which includes scenes from Harry Pauly's drama;

Wolfgang Petersen, *Die Konsequenz/The Consequence,* based on Alexander Ziegler's autobiographical novel;

Alexander Petrović, *Gruppenbild mit Dame/Group Portrait with Lady,* based on Heinrich Böll's novel;

Ottokar Runze, *Die Standarte/The Standard,* based on Alexander Lernet-Holenia's novel;

Daniel Schmid, *Violanta,* based on Conrad Ferdinand Meyer's story, *Die Richterin;*

Bernard Sinkel, *Taugenichts/Good-for-Nothing,* based on Joseph von Eichendorff's story, *Aus dem Leben eines Taugenichts;*

Herbert Vesely, *Der kurze Brief zum langen Abschied/The Short Letter to the Long Goodbye,* based on Peter Handke's novel;

Alfred Weidenmann, *Der Schimmelreiter/The Rider of the White Horse,* based on Theodor Storm's novella;

Wim Wenders's *Der amerikanische Freund/The American Friend,* based on Patricia Highsmith's *Ripley's Game* and motifs from *Ripley Underground.*

1978: Alf Brustellin, *Der Sturz/The Crash,* based on Martin Walser's novel;

Gustav Ehmck, *Neues vom Räuber Hotzenplotz/The New Adventures of the Robber Hotzenplotz,* based on a book by Otfried Preussler;

Klaus Emmerich, *Die erste Polka/The First Polka,* based on Horst Bienek's novel;

Wolf Gremm, *Die Schattengrenze/Frontiers of Darkness,* based on Dieter Wellershoff's novel;

Werner Herzog, *Nosferatu,* based on Bram Stoker's novel, *Dracula; Woyzeck,* based on Georg Büchner's drama;

Peter Patzak, *Das Einhorn/The Unicorn,* based on Martin Walser's novel;

Maximilian Schell, *Geschichten aus dem Wienerwald/Tales from the Vienna Forest,* based on Ödön von Horváth's play;

Peter Stein, *Trilogie des Wiedersehens/Trilogy of Farewell,* based on Botho Strauss's drama;

Christian Ziewer, *Aus der Ferne sehe ich dieses Land/From the Distance I See This Country,* based on Antonio Skármeta's short story, *Nix passiert.*

At first glance, such a catalogue suggests a rather disproportionate number of films based on literary sources. But one can hardly fault films as cinematically lively as *The American Friend, The Left-Handed Woman, Despair,* or *The Glass Cell* for their overdependence on literary sources. Wherein lay the crisis? Critics like Blumenberg proclaimed that the subsidy system was breeding an overabundance of films lacking either popular appeal or topical resonance.[10] Early in 1977, *Spiegel* reported that German film "prefers to move in a realm somewhere between Simmel and Fontane. Of the 28 films which the Project Commission of the FFA has thus far supported, 15 are literature adaptations."[11] As the *Tendenzwende* took a further turn for the worst and a full-going restoration transpired in the FRG, committee officials catered to the lowest common denominator for fear of stirring up controversy in an already turmoil-ridden and ideologically polarized climate.[12] Joe Hembus would reflect some years later on his experiences in the Project Commission and argue in favor of the generally good intentions of most officials, denying any overall conservative conspiracy. He would point out that the body expressly turned down prospective literature adaptations—among them, *The Devil's Elixirs, The Rider of the White Horse,* and *Group Portrait with Lady* —which failed to promise creative and independent renderings of their textual basis.[13] Be that as it may, in the wider view of things, something was decisively wrong.

Alfred Nemeczek, a journalist who also served on the Project Commission during the period, saw things differently. The main considerations guiding all deliberations—in keeping with the dictates of the FFG—were "quality" and "economic potential" *(Wirtschaftlichkeit)*. One could easily scuttle ambitious and potentially difficult projects by casting doubts on an application's box-office appeal—and one often did. (Fassbinder's controversial Frankfurt-film, which will be discussed below, received a negative disposition for that reason and others.) A table attached to Nemeczek's article roughly confirmed the *Spiegel* figures: of the 26 scripts based on classics and recent bestsellers, a full one-half of them had gained Project Commission monies. Scenarios with topical contents and contemporary issues did not fare very well at all: of 33 such proposals, only 10 found support.[14]

Hans W. Geissendörfer, asked in September 1977 why so few West German films addressed themselves to present concerns, answered that it was not due to the filmmakers' lack of interest in these matters. To his knowledge over 22 original scripts dealing with the problem of violence in the FRG (at a time when terrorism was a topic on everybody's mind) were in the Ministry of the Interior *(Bundesinnenministerium)* awaiting approval.[15] Few seemed to have received any, judging by the subsequent productions. Literature-oriented titles represented the FRG at the Cannes festival that year, *Heinrich* and *Group Portrait with Lady*, causing further outrage among filmmakers and critics.[16] These were perhaps representative films; they were not, however, the most important works made in the FRG during the time. Adding insult to injury, the government's choices for *Bundesfilmpreise* (State Film Prizes) that year provided final proof, if any more was needed, that *Literaturverfilmungen* enjoyed official favor: *Heinrich* received the award for the best feature film and five of the films decorated as the year's best were literature adaptations—not to forget Schlöndorff's mention as best director for *Coup de Grâce*.[17] Something was awry, but an explanation that only points to a handful of committee members, cultural politicians, and cautious TV editors as the culprits definitely stops too short.

Word and Image: Literature in German Film History

A series of contextual considerations helps to shed light on the *Literaturverfilmungskrise*. The escalating intolerance toward dissident points of view during the public uproar over terrorism in 1977 played a role. And, as we have seen in an earlier chapter, it was not mere coincidence that brought about the near collapse of West German film's more independent sectors. Avant-garde and documentary directors of crucial importance had stopped making films or moved abroad. Progressive framers of the *Arbeiterfilm* no longer found public television willing to support the genre. Even recognized talents with an international following (besides Fassbinder who suffered dearly in this period) like Herzog and Kluge had trouble in their search for subsidy money: both *Stroszek* and *Der starke Ferdinand/Strong Man Ferdinand* were rejected by the Project Commission. Some filmmakers, recognizing the strained situation, requited themselves to the tough *status quo,* and toned down their ambitions. Many would face charges of opportunism from critics and colleagues, although no one was willing to admit that his or her literature-based work had anything but compelling links to the present, an argument rarely borne out by final products.[18]

One can also look at the *Literaturverfilmungskrise* as the function of a subsidy system that demanded finished scripts for its deliberations, the logical extension of a culture's less than wholehearted embrace of the medium film. (Wenders's comments come to mind once again, as do Schilling's.) A pariah among the other arts, film received, in 1976, one-sixtieth of the public support granted to opera and theater. In other countries, filmmakers like Fellini and Resnais were viewed as cultural dignitaries; in West Germany, even the most visible directors enjoyed little public respect.[19] The national disdain for the visual medium was reflected in the way film projects gained public support: one submitted a *written* proposal, a script describing one's undertaking *in words*. Once approved, the scenario was to be closely followed. Those who did not faced the prospect of having to repay subsidy funds.[20] In no other nation does one encounter the script fetish and trust in words—as opposed to images—which one does in Germany. Filmmakers like Kluge would attack the approach as anathema to serious film praxis:

> 'Films are not written, they are made.' Numerous officials and committees nevertheless feel that an 100-page-long script is something with substance, they trust the words, instead of investing confidence in images.... Everything that is so crucial for the filmmaker like prior research, trips, background photographs, everything in essence which really prepares the film and enables a flexible production, is discriminated against by the subsidy guide lines.[21]

Obviously there is nothing inherently sinister or unusual about adaptations. From the very start of its film history (scenes from *Faust* served as shorts already at the turn of the century), Germany has known a particularly intimate relation between literature and film, a closeness marked equally by cooperation and tension. Virtually every writer of any significance has worked in the filmic medium, as supplier of story ideas and screenplays or, more recently, as writer-director. (And film has made an undeniable dent on German literature, both in thematic and formal terms.[22]) As the early makers of films sought to gain a respectability for a medium that most intellectuals associated with fairgrounds and the unscrubbed masses, they encouraged the collaboration of well-known authors and appropriated the bourgeois canon in the hopes of finding a middle-class following, especially after 1910. Few of the resulting *Autoren-Filme,* whose writers included Gerhart Hauptmann, Hugo von Hofmannsthal, and Johannes Schlaf, were successful in finding apposite formal means of transposing the literary contents into the new medium.[23] This would not be the case later in the Weimar Republic, where one can point to numerous examples of cinematically distinguished adaptations, such as F.W. Murnau's *Faust* (1926), G.W. Pabst's *Die Büchse der Pandora/Pandora's Box* (1928), and Joseph von Sternberg's *Der blaue Engel/The Blue Angel* (1930). But it was also a *Literaturverfilmung,* Pabst's rendering of Bertolt Brecht's *Die Dreigroschenoper/The Threepenny Opera* (1931), which would give rise to a fierce court debate over the degree to which a creator "owns" the artistic property he sells to the film industry, a controversy that would bring out numerous issues regarding the fate of intellectual workers in a capitalist economy, a "sociological experiment" recorded by Brecht in *Der Dreigroschenprozess/The Threepenny Trial* (1931). The cinema of the Third Reich included numerous adaptations of Kleist and various 19th-century realists; a biography of a famous dramatist (Herbert Maisch's *Friedrich Schiller,* 1940) served the same purpose as other life stories of great men did at the time: it presented the writer as a spiritual forebearer of the *Führer.*[24] *Literaturverfilmungen* played an integral part in film's subservient role under National Socialism as an unquestioning supporter of the state and official ideology.

Nowhere does the strained relationship between film and literature become more apparent in Germany than in the FRG during the years 1954–1958, a time when a plethora of illustrated literary classics appeared, movies based on the works of Ludwig Anzengruber, Wilhelm Busch, Gerhart Hauptmann, Erich Kästner, Thomas Mann, Theodor Storm, and Carl Zuckmayer, to name just the most prominent authors. *Literaturverfilmungen* in the fifties meant watered-down renderings of works hallowed by the now disfranchised bourgeoisie, picture book evocations of an idealized and less problematic past (primarily the era when the middle class enjoyed its prime), more often than not costume films peopled by popular stars and graced with high production values. In short, these films were the same sort of vacations from history observed in the *Heimatfilme* of the Adenauer years. Kurt Hoffmann, for instance, reduced Thomas Mann's complexly symbolic picaresque novel *Felix Krull* to a vehicle for the young Horst Buchholz (*Bekenntnisse des Hochstaplers Felix Krull/Confessions of the Confidence Man Felix Krull,* 1957); *Buddenbrooks,* in Alfred Weidenmann's 1959 version, was little more than an elaborate sitting-room drama. These films amounted to tours through the lost bourgeois past, pictures that found a receptive audience in a country seeking to reestablish ties with a shattered tradition. The *Literaturverfilmungen* of the fifties show no particular sense of any unique visual style (although Helmut Käutner, Rolf Thiele, and Kurt Hoffmann often strained to achieve distinctive signatures) or personal involvement on the part of directors engaged in the adapting process. This is one of the reasons why West Germany—among all other major European nations—was the last to develop its own *Autorenkino* after 1945.[25]

Adaptations and Transformations

In contrast to *Papas Kino*'s lackluster refurbishing of literary properties, Young German filmmakers used their sources mostly as creative springboards. Three of the four films crucial to the 1966 breakthrough had their basis in literature. Schlöndorff's *Der junge Törless/Young Törless* became not a painstaking reconstruction of Robert Musil's 1906 novel, but rather a study of pre-fascist mentality, a narrative that used a stark sense for imposing structures (columns, corridors, doorways) to capture the overbearing monotony and oppressive institutionality of the military academy. Peter Schamoni's *Schonzeit für Füchse/Closed Season on Fox Hunting* drew from Günter Seuren's book *Das Gatter;* many critics claimed Schamoni had managed to salvage an otherwise barren story in his filmic rendering.[26] Kluge reshaped his own short piece "Anita G." (from the collection *Lebensläufe*) in *Abschied von gestern/ Yesterday Girl,* merging the story basis with found elements from daily life and an abundance of different kinds of texts (e.g. ancient Egyptian incantations, the West German legal code, children's rhymes, popular tunes, and Brechtian intertitles) to form a collage-like matrix of fact, fantasy, and fiction.

Literature and film represented complementary forms for the *Jungfilmer*. Kluge, Edgar Reitz, and Wilfried Reinke published an essay in 1965 ("Wort und Film") which proved to be programmatic for Young German Film's subsequent dealings with literature through the mid-seventies.[27] Film, claimed the authors, can bring together verbal, acoustic, and visual expression, integrating them in elaborate patterns that allow the spectator to produce exciting and multifarious associations in his/her mind. One need not let words interact with images to further a naturalistic effect and a novelistic causality.[28] Dialogue, as one had learned from Godard and Louis Malle, could be edited every bit as creatively as images. Voice-over commentary and intertitles did not simply have to fill in what the visual track did not show; they could intensify the overall effect and at the same time distance the viewer from the narrative. Words need not always possess a distinct purpose in cinema (as plot information, character motivation, etc.). Why must everything have a fixed meaning? "Language in film may be blind."[29] One saw literature and its many discursive modalities as a potential ally, realizing

> that the arbitrary addition of interesting details, no matter what text one brings in, leads no doubt to an arbitrary result, but a result that can be successful, because 'he who offers a lot has something to offer for everyone.'[30]

Film has been seen as the art form most closely related to photography. This is not necessarily so, claimed Kluge and his cohorts. Looking at the way film, during its history, has constantly relied on the written medium, one might say its true soul mate is literature. The point remained to make more creative use of words and literary means than had previously been the case.

Prior to the *Literaturverfilmungskrise,* New German filmmakers, given their tendency both to script and direct their films as a consequence of the subsidy system and its institutionalization of *Autorenkino,* often turned to literature, rarely resorting to plodding or text-bound duplications of their sources, be they classical or popular, hallowed cultural icons or recent bestsellers. Schlöndorff, the most consistent *Verfilmer* over the years, has never been content merely to reproduce a text. He has invariably—on occasion less successfully—sought the reality behind the work. "It's always a case," he once reflected, "where literature discloses German history."[31] Directors in the main went beyond their textual starting points, adding a personal dimension to adaptations in a number of ways:

- Reshaping or shifting narrative tonalities: Ulf Miehe, wanting to escape the inexorable fatalism of Theodor Storm's *Ein Doppelgänger,* yet still not diminish the penetrating vision of the German *misère* inherent in the novella, had the hero of *John Glückstaadt* (1974) share the fettered existence of Storm's protagonist until the final scene: in Miehe's ending, Glückstadt boards a boat for America instead of shipwrecking in his homeland;

- Searching out one's personal thematic interest in a work: Fassbinder's *Fontane Effi Briest* (1974), for all its fidelity to the 19th-century novel, quite convincingly restates themes and interests present in the larger body of the director's corpus. The long subtitle to the film in fact applies in general for Fassbinder's unrelenting concern for the inextricable bonds between education and oppression. *Effi Briest* is every bit as much an adaptation of Fontane as it is a restatement of Fassbinder's overriding preoccupations. One might even call it a remake of *Martha* (1973) in an historical setting. This same principle informs Fassbinder's subsequent epic version of Alfred Döblin's *Berlin Alexanderplatz* (1980), another adaptation that summarizes and essentializes obsessions of a life's work;[32]

- Fashioning visual forms out of a source which accord to a personal world view: Werner Herzog's *Lebenszeichen/Signs of Life* (1967) contains an informing structure that one does not find in his source, Achim von Arnim's story, *Der tolle Invalide auf dem Fort Ratonneau.* The form is the circle, an objective correlative to Herzog's fatalistic belief in trapped human existence. The disturbed soldier's life on Kos involves futile labors, endless repetition which makes him feel a captive, subject to the whims of higher powers and mightier elements, ones that in the end overcome him in a valley of whirling windmills. Arnim's tale of how a lover's bravery prevents a disaster shares at best the venue of a fortress and certain character constellations with Herzog's film; the ultimate shape of *Signs of Life,* a film abounding in circles, stands as one of Herzog's making;

- Imparting a topical meaning to a work from another epoch: Schlöndorff's *Michael Kohlhaas — Der Rebell* (1969) proved to be an ambitious failure that sought to use the Kleistian protagonist's grand refusal in the face of authoritarian intransigence to depict the student rebellion of 1968 in a 16th-century setting. Other directors relocated classical texts in the present: Rudolf Thome couched

Goethe's *Die Wahlverwandtschaften* in a contemporary domestic arrangement (*Tagebuch/Diary,* 1975); Hans-Jürgen Syberberg updated Kleist's *Die Verlobung in St. Domingo* in his motorcycle gang version of 1970, *San Domingo*.

When one speaks of Young (and New) German Film's use of literature, though, one dare not only dwell on *adaptations*. Every bit as crucial and indeed more in keeping with a search for alternative discursive forms are the radical *transformations* of literature to be found for instance in the work of Jean-Marie Straub and Danièle Huillet. *Machorka-Muff* (1962) does not "tell" the story present in Böll's *Hauptstädtisches Journal/Bonn Diary*. Most adaptations presuppose no prior knowledge of the textual basis: they stand as independent narratives where story and history exist as functions of the filmic text.[33] Straub/Huillet at best quote passages out of Böll's satire, moving by leaps and bounds from one space to another, denying the spectator the assurances of spatial and temporal orientation. (An "establishing shot" of Bonn seen out of a hotel window does little to familiarize the viewer with the setting; the pan across the cityscape, if anything, adds to an irritating sense of dislocation.) *Nicht versöhnt/Not Reconciled* (1965) likewise only provides bits and pieces out of Böll's disjunctive family novel, *Billard um halbzehn/Billiards at Half Past Nine*. The directors make no attempt to sort out time and place for the spectator, to guide one through the complex chronology of three generations. Individual scenes in both films possess the character of primitive tableaux found in early cinema. Straub made a film about the specter of certain fatal patterns throughout modern German history in *Not Reconciled,* claims Martin Walsh, taking

> as his starting point the principle that film is 'a perceptual present' — that there is, in our experience of watching a film, no past tense. He then transfers this idea to the narrative organisation, eliding all the connectives that were present in Böll's novel, thereby formally underlining the historical principle that present and past are indivisible.[34]

Straub/Huillet found an apposite formal approach to the substance of Böll's novel while endeavoring to promote reflection on the way in which conventional narratives falsify history in their simple-minded causality and plodding linearity. (They would pursue the resolve even more radically in years to follow.) Another intriguing example of a narrative that simultaneously undermines and elucidates its textual basis will be dealt with in the next chapter, where I will turn to Wim Wenders's *Falsche Bewegung/Wrong Move* (1974), a commentary on Peter Handke's loose rendering of Goethe's *Wilhelm Meisters Lehrjahre/The Apprenticeship of Wilhelm Meister.*

Clearly the above survey limits itself to paradigms among the many possibilities at hand in West German output since Oberhausen. The short typology demonstrates at least some of the ways in which adaptations and tranformations of literary sources have brought about West German films with their own narrative, structural, thematic, and topical integrity, elements often missing when one looks at the works produced during the *Literaturverfilmungskrise.*

Pictures from an Exhibition: Phasing Discourse out of Story

It would be inaccurate to say that during the crisis period only undistinguished literature adaptations came out of the FRG. On the contrary, one can point to a number of impressive *Autorenfilme* made in these months, movies based on exciting original scripts (Schilling's *Die Vertreibung aus dem Paradies/The Expulsion from Paradise*), films set on the streets of present-day West Germany (Brandner's *halbe-halbe/Fifty-Fifty*), works grounded in the desire to expand the parameters of the cinematic medium (Nekes's *Lagado*). Realistic, reflexive, and experimental films *were* being made, for all the controversy over the lack of precisely this kind of filmmaking. These films were just not gaining the attention or notoriety found by the *Literaturverfilmungen.* When it came to festival representation and government prizes, the titles containing New German film's best ambitions went unnoticed. Exceptions to the rule like the above examples, Walter Bockmayer's *Jane bleibt Jane/Jane Is Jane Forever,* or Herbert Achternbusch's *Bierkampf/Beer Battle,* all reminded discerning observers of the alternative cinema's still uncompromised possibilities. There existed a potential overshadowed and often obscured by a series of factors: a recurring predilection for the stifling of critical voices in any public crisis, a political climate less than hospitable toward differing opinions, a stagnant film economy whose still dominant conservative fringe continued to call for commercially viable productions aimed at the lowest common denominator, a network of television and subsidy support systems which reacted to all of the pressures — not to mention filmmakers unsure about what to do in the tenuous situation, or ones eager to profit from it.

Thus arose a spate of *Verfilmungen,* works without any particular popular appeal (a fact substantiated by box-office figures) or allure for the more progressive film culture. The adaptations, above all, lacked authorial discursiveness and reflexivity, precisely the attributes that had marked previous successes of the *Autorenfilmer.* These narratives were couched in terms of "there" and "then"; their protagonists appeared as "he" and "she." Rarely—the only striking example is *Escape Route to Marseilles*[35]—did one encounter a meaningful connection between filmmaker and textual basis, a "here" and a "now" and an "I" and a "you."[36] In the few cases where directors expressly attempted such a merging of horizons, the final products bore little in common with the grand ambitions outlined in press booklets.

West German film critics voiced three main objections to the larger majority of the adaptations. First, one argued that the films showed more signs of technical expertise than personal involvement. Commentators had a hard time perceiving any indications of inspiration and enthusiasm in the perfectly crafted and elegantly photographed likes of *Grete Minde* and *Heinrich.* (Clearly, had either film appeared five years earlier, neither would have received the fierce opposition that came out of the strained constellations in 1977.) Cameramen like Thomas Mauch *(Heinrich),* Jürgen Jürges *(Grete Minde),* Dietrich Lohmann *(The Three Sisters),* and Jost Vacano *(Liberty or Death)* supplied sumptuous landscape images, overwhelming as single frames, but in the context of these films ultimately more illustrational than expressive in their effect.

Further, one attacked the *Verfilmungen* for their hopelessly literal penchant, a bland deference to the sources. (This complaint particularly confronted *Group Portrait with Lady.*[37]) These films were neither *Autorenkino* nor popular cinema, but rather—in the mind of Schütte—a timid *Nacherzählkino,* works that recounted stories without any narrative energy, stylistic urgency, or personal conviction. Finally, one seldom ran across anything here

> besides an unproductive—both politically and aesthetically—escape into ostensible cultural values, ones that stifle the imagination and which neither receive the scrutiny of a new interpretation nor have much to do with our vital interests, just as they do little toward furthering cinema's reclamation of reality.[38]

For all the brouhaha about certain films being relevant to current debates, one concluded that none of them really spoke to the present, even if Grete Minde appeared to be a 17th-century terrorist or the young outlaws of *Liberty or Death* looked like precursors of Baader and Meinhof. As so often before, critics asked pointblank: why all this indirectness? Why not forget the costumes and historical distance and simply make films about the West German present?[39] Things were not that simple and never had been.

Each of the three objections does hold up under closer examination, even if the critique as a whole unfairly singled out symptoms of a larger malady and treated them as the sickness itself. In general one attacked the *approach* of these films but paid less attention to the underlying implications of their subject matter—a curious deviation from the otherwide content-bound praxis of many West German film critics. The present context does not allow a lengthy explication of the films involved in the controversy. What follows is an overview of the films—made and unmade—generally associated with the *Literaturverfilmungskrise,* under three main headings.

(1) *Opas Kino rides again or the return of the same: the past that would not go away.* Both *Disorder and Early Sorrow* and *The Rider of the White Horse,* works made by older directors from the conservative branch,[40] refer back to earlier points in German film history. Each movie expresses a longing for private solace in the face of public confusion. Seitz quite explicitly demonstrates the continuity of his 1976 adaptation with another point in time where *Papas Kino* still held sway: *Disorder and Early Sorrow* begins with an extended quotation from a film Seitz produced in 1964, another Thomas Mann rendering, namely Rolf Thiele's *Tonio Kröger.* A series of newsreel images, scenes of socio-political unrest during the Weimar Republic, flash by to indicate the larger malaise in which the film's protagonist, the history professor Abel Cornelius, lives. Seitz identifies with the dutiful curator of the past who views the pressing present as a threat to his domestic tranquility.

Weidenmann, the director of *Rider of the White Horse,* had been decorated in the Third Reich for his blood and soil debut, *Hände hoch/ Hands Up* (1942). He had worked continuously and frequently through various regimes since the first effort. His rendering of Storm's novella bears much evidence of an aesthetics practiced in films of his made nearly twenty (e.g. *Buddenbrooks*) or thirty-some years earlier (*Junger Adler/Young Eagle,* 1944). Doing away with Storm's elaborate narrative frame and exercising utter fealty to the central story, Weidenmann is not a man for subtlety. He celebrates a strong and decisive hero, the dike-reeve Hauke Haien, a figure more powerful than his peers, an individual whose strength is a function of his isolation, a leader who defies the people he governs and even challenges the elements before — in a scene reminiscent of numerous deaths by water found in Nazi cinema — drowning in a storm. Haien is a man of destiny, a combination of the Hitler-surrogates abounding in films of the Third Reich with the tragic-individuals-overcome-by-forces-larger-than-themselves who appealed to the quietism of postwar audiences. Hauke Haien, clearly a much more defiant and vital personage than Professor Cornelius, nonetheless shares a common calling: both seek to erect bulwarks that will protect their private spheres from the incursion of outside forces, thematics very much redolent of films from the fifties. Purzer's *The Devil's Elixirs* and Horst Hächler's *Waldrausch* likewise unabashedly evinced the bankrupt aesthetics of *Papas Kino*.

(2) *Rebels with a cause or individualism and its discontents.* If the elders centered their emotional experience around the sanctity of their home life, then the younger generation sought to free itself from all constraints and ties in the name of an undefined autonomy. In the adaptations of New German directors during the period, one encounters troubled and absolute young people striking out against the stifling atmosphere which hinders their uncompromising quest for happiness. These thematics no doubt recall an earlier wave of knapsack films from the first days of Young German Film, titles like *Yesterday Girl, Es/It,* Gustav Ehmck's *Spur eines Mädchens/Trace of a Girl,* and Johannes Schaaf's *Tätowierung/Tatooing*.[41] Unlike the more tough-minded early works, the adaptations of the mid-seventies do not explore or problematize these rebellions; they show them happening. These presentations are often quite striking in their visuals, but rarely incisive in their rhetoric. Helma Sanders-Brahms begins *Heinrich* with the tormented artist's preparations for a suicide, then in a string of associative flashbacks (ones with little inherent continuity or overall rhythm) retraces the stations of his life-long martyrdom. What promises to be an analytical structure never takes shape. The words of his farewell letter could very well stand as a motto for many of the *Literaturverfilmungen* in this series: "The truth is that I was not to be helped on earth." *Heinrich* was, in the end, an overwhelming visualization of the "letters, documents of Heinrich von Kleist, his friends, relatives, and contemporaries." It aes-

theticized a life of pain and glossed over the writer's many character quirks, viewing him mainly as an isolated monad—Kleist did have important contacts with contemporaries!—with no chance of ever realizing his design for happiness.

Grete Minde likewise featured a stranger in a world of rules which has little understanding for exceptions. The daughter of a Spanish Catholic mother raised in a stern North German Protestant environment (the Saxon town of Tangermünde in the 17th century), Grete becomes an outcast, someone who nonetheless refuses to let herself be victimized. Heidi Genée's identification with Fontane's heroine was total; similarly, the first-time director did little more than demonstrate how imposing the constraints were in which the young girl existed, justifying her final act of arson against the unforgiving town. The approach at best bastardized the *Anti-Heimatfilm* by equating history with a never-ceasing inhumanity and intolerance. Unlike the films from the 1971 renaissance, Genée's debut lacked discursive rigor and differentiating vigor.[42]

Insisting on the authenticity of the lived moment, the protagonists of the *Literaturverfilmungen* try to run away from history. Both *Heinrich* and *Grete Minde* have idyllic interludes where their heroes enjoy solace in venues far away from the world of strictures and responsibility: Kleist finds momentary bliss as a farmer, Grete comes into her own briefly in a puppet theater.

Brustellin/Sinkel used a World War II setting (Prague between 1936-1946) as a backdrop for their attractive heroines' private lives and loves in *The Three Sisters*. "We wanted," the directors claimed, "to show how uninhibited self-realization starts off freely and sensuously, but then, slowly but surely, is destroyed and rendered impossible by the men who make history."[43] Typically, no attempt ensued to distance the adaptation from the apolitical quest for self-actualization described— but rarely problematized—in Manfred Bieler's novel.

Sinkel's *Good-for-Nothing,* a project conceived in the early seventies, meant to shape the Eichendorff short story to depict the post-1968 generation's rebellion against the reality principle and the work ethic. In keeping with Sinkel's other zany nonconformists, the young hero leaves home and duty behind him to set out for Italy, the traditional goal of German *Wanderlust*. The director wanted to draw a parallel between Eichendorff's stultifying Berlin and the equally uninhabitable present-day FRG. Likewise, his hero—similar to Peter Schneider's Lenz who had escaped the empty theorizing and antiseptic intellectualizing of

Berlin after the student movement to find hope, vigor, and solidarity down south[44] — was to glimpse an alternative life style in Italy. Critics were for the most unconvinced by the updating of the late Romantic work and the few spectators who managed to see it before it disappeared from cinemas were not overwhelmed either.[45]

Geissendörfer's *The Wild Duck,* unrelenting in its fealty to Ibsen's play despite the deconstructive resolve with which the filmmaker had initially approached the work,[46] was yet another example of a penchant for dramatizing individual flights into worlds of illusion and private whimsy. Geissendörfer, West German film's most ardent advocate of identification cinema and the ploys of conventional narrative,[47] stuck very closely to his source, letting Robbie Müller's otherwise so expressive camera defer to sets and performances. The filmed drama showed the many challenges posed by the reality principle, one which only obliquely corresponded to the West German reality from which the *Literaturverfilmungen* derived.

(3) *Fassbinder and his friends: how hard it is to make difficult films.* Just what happened to proposed *Literaturverfilmungen* whose bearing on the West German present was more direct? The experience Fassbinder had on two occasions during the crisis period provided striking examples of the fate of critical realists during the time. His renderings of Gerhard Zwerenz's novel, *Die Erde ist unbewohnbar wie der Mond/ The Earth Is as Uninhabitable as the Moon,* caused a violent debate in the spring of 1976. The script submitted to the FFA was denied subsidy money; the committee members feared the project might well confirm already existing anti-Semitic sentiments and perhaps engender new ones. A play Fassbinder derived as well from Zwerenz's book — *Der Müll, die Stadt und der Tod/Garbage, the City, and Death* — received sharp words and wide commentary, even though it remained unperformed and undistributed by its publisher. The work dealt with urban speculation in Frankfurt and featured a Jewish business magnate as its hero, a ruthless wheeler-dealer who appeared as the product of an inhuman system, not the mere incarnation of cultural stereotyping. To the chagrin of many, however, the figure possessed a number of decidedly negative character traits indistinguishable from the most vile anti-Jewish abuse. And beyond this, Fassbinder couched the work in a Genet-like symbolism, writing dialogue marked by expressionistic staccato and creating an atmosphere bound in an end-of-the-world desperation.

The controversy began with Joachim Fest's attack on the unreleased printed version of the play. He scorned it as pornography, a collection of crude clichés, the work of a "left-wing fascist," paradigmatic for a fashionable anti-Semitism among certain progressive circles.[48] Suhrkamp, Fassbinder's publishing house, immediately shelved the book in which the play was to appear out of fear for the misunderstanding it might cause. The FFA had earlier justified its negative disposition to the script of the novel adaptation (a work different from the more surrealistic play only loosely based on Zwerenz's book) by referring to the Film Subsidy Law and the clause denying support to films that "injure moral or religious feelings." As the scandal continued, few people agreed with Fest's charges of anti-Semitism and left-wing fascism. Still, Fassbinder found little support and few defenders. Many cast doubts on the play's aesthetic and political worth. Wilfried Wiegand's response expressed matters in frighteningly clear terms: the actions taken against the play could not be seen as censorship, but rather as legitimate control measures necessary to ensure the viability of a democracy. The real fault of the drama lay in its approaching a still sensitive topic with insufficient artistic means. After Auschwitz one dare not write a bad drama about Jews.[49] Three years later, with the public screening of the American film *Holocaust* on West German television, the overwhelming majority of critics would hail the commercial production for undertaking a task people claimed had been neglected by filmmakers in the FRG.

Fassbinder replied that his entire work supplied copious evidence for his sympathy with minority groups and the oppressed. He had merely sought to bring a matter heretofore unbroached into public discussion. Guilt-ridden deference to Jews in postwar West Germany masked an underlying problem. In an interview he quoted Robert Neumann's phrase, "Philosemities are anti-Semites who love Jews."[50] In all of the fierce jeremiads written *post Festum,* one noticed much attention directed at a single play (whose novel basis had been on the market for several years without causing any comparable outbursts) and an individual artist but only halting discussion on the part of faultfinders about the social constellations and historical situation from which *Garbage, the City, and Death* issued.[51]

A year later WDR announced its plans to produce a 10-part adaptation of Gustav Freytag's controversial novel of 1855, *Soll und Haben/ Deficit and Balance.* Even before a single script was completed, the *Frankfurt Allgemeine Zeitung* voiced serious misgivings about the project, doubting how one could make a film out of a book full of anti-Semitic and anti-Slavic sentiments — especially by a filmmaker "against whom the reproach of aggressive anti-Semitism has been raised."[52] Several weeks later, in what appeared to be a direct response to the article, the WDR proclaimed it would not pass the assignment onto the Bavaria studio as planned. The undertaking could too easily lend itself to public misunderstanding. Nowhere, except in the *FAZ* notice, had it been insinuated that Fassbinder had a faithful reproduction of the Freytag-epic in mind.

The director's own essay describing the shelved project spoke of an ambitious resolve to turn the novel on its head, to read it against the grain. *Soll und Haben* was for Fassbinder an important document depicting the way in which the German middle class developed by demarcating itself in a number of directions: it stood aside from the proletariat, took internal refuge from the nobility, and above all isolated itself from foreigners and Jews. The rise of the bourgeoisie in Germany is inextricably bound with the increasing accumulation of capital — and was it not precisely this drive that one projected onto the Jewish minority as being its governing motivation?

> The bourgeoisie therefore needed the Jews so that it would not despise its own motivations, so that it could feel proud and large and strong. The final consequence of such subconscious self-despising was the mass extermination of Jews in the Third Reich: in reality one wanted to eliminate that which one did not want to acknowledge in one's own person.[53]

Once again the fear of possible misunderstanding and public disapproval caused an examination of the contradictions and historical tensions inherent in the German past and still operative in the FRG present to be stifled.

The sociologist Oskar Negt, speaking at the 1977 Römerberg-conference, wondered why West German films contained so little German history. Zwerenz likewise queried why so few films were being made about current developments in the Federal Republic. Fassbinder's experiences made it clear what sort of treatment such undertakings could expect:

> The critical realists are being turned into Western dissidents by virtue of the documented and undeniable facts which they depict because our authorities equate critical literature with political opposition.[54]

And these experiences were by no means isolated examples—just the most conspicuous ones among many less-publicized others. Eberhard Fechner similarly sought to confront the social mechanisms and modes of behavior which allowed fascism to flourish. Working from Alfred Andersch's novel *Winterspelt* (1974), the director presented his script to the Project Commission. The application was rejected with the curious explanation that the film had "too much story." Puzzled by the response, Fechner turned to a member of the FFA who told the director in confidence: "Change the communist in your script into an antifascist and everything will be fine." Fechner made the revision, and late in 1977 he completed *Winterspelt*.[55] Others were not lucky enough to get a second chance.

Last Words: After the Fall

By the end of 1977 the crisis reached a climax, taking on even more grotesque proportions. On the day industrialist Hanns-Martin Schleyer's body was found in the trunk of a car, Bavarian TV changed its program from the slated Jerry Lewis film to *La Règle du jeu*. The network interrupted the screening, though, well into the movie, ceasing the broadcast without explanation. It appears that nervous officials suddenly had become unsettled by the prospect of two attempted murders in the film's final reels. In the aftermath of the autumn confusion, filmmakers found public television ill at ease, unwilling to support any undertaking bearing the slightest resemblance to the recent occurrences. The more political violence dominated people's thoughts, the less West German institutions seemed inclined to allow open discussion of the problem. This did not only mean the squelching of any thorough-going or radical investigations of the topic. It applied as well, in the words of Florian Hopf, "for simple detective stories in which for instance a criminal attempts blackmail by kidnapping someone; it applies even for works in which a socially humiliated man constantly under pressure from above suddenly starts running amok."[56]

Two films reflected on the crisis from very different perspectives, providing West Germany's most subversive *Gremienfilme* (an epithet usually reserved for bland films that issue from an institutionalized cinema of subsidies and TV cooperations), critical works probing the mechanisms controlling independent image-making in the FRG. Hellmuth Costard's *Der kleine Godard an das Kuratorium junger deutscher Film/The Little Godard* continued a project initiated years before by

Vlado Kristl,[57] an attempt to make a film without a script—for how can one summarize a work based on images before these images have come into existence? Costard aimed

> to shoot feature films without imagination; to use the undisturbed course of events as the perfect *mise-en-scène;* to create, through montage and the use of several cameras, an impression of direction; to give the spectator the transparent illusion he's caught up in a story.[58]

But the project could not gain subsidy support without a script, even though the very point of Costard's experiment was to avoid the prevailing literary bias and to rebel against the primacy of the screenplay. "Only perverse fantasy can save us," the director (quoting Goethe) had declared in the motto to his infamous and outrageous short, *Besonders wertvoll/Particularly Noteworthy* (1968), an irreverent provocation that scorned the Film Subsidy Law. But imagination, much less perverse fantasy, could not develop in an environment ruled by committee guidelines and cultural bureaucrats. "In other words," Jan Dawson summarized the dilemma, "the life, shape and future of that elusive dream, 'the alternative cinema,' lie in the hands of a non-alternative Establishment, and even radical self-expression needs conservative endorsement and commercially produced technology."[59] Bearing out the validity of insights voiced decades ago in Brecht's *Threepenny Trial, The Little Godard* both through its impetus and in its final form showed the "inseparable relationship between politics, economics and aesthetics; because it shows how, even in a free society, we can be censored even in our dreams."[60]

Deutschland im Herbst/Germany in Autumn was to be the most significant cinematic enactment of the hysteria-ridden climate that had fostered the *Literaturverfilmungskrise*. One scene from the independent production has particular bearing on the present discussion, namely Schlöndorff/Böll's *Antigone*-sequence. Members of a public television commission meet to preview a rendering of Sophocles's *Antigone* made for the series "Youth Discovers the Classics." An argument takes place not about the production proper but over a "distancing text" meant to deny any identification on the part of those involved in the film with the potentially subversive contents of the play. Various versions of the *Distanzierungstext* come under discussion. The first is not clear enough, claims one member; it could be misconstrued. The second attempt likewise lends itself to possible misinterpretation. A final disclaimer text shows the entire cast dressed in street clothing, declaring:

> It is unavoidable, even inevitable, that in many plays, even classical ones, violence is depicted. We distance ourselves from every form of violence and we do this in the names of the filmmakers, the direction, the entire ensemble, the stage workers, the ticket sellers, in the name of all those directly or indirectly involved with the production.

This text too causes raised eyebrows. It degrades the Sophocles-play, says one discussant. Worse than that, says another panelist, it sounds artificial, indeed ironic. "And irony is what we need least of all." A TV editor, by now at wit's end, suggests simply screening *Antigone* without any preface. Have things come so far that one can no longer stage classical dramas? A perturbed member of the committee, a government spokesman, responds harshly:

> The next word will be censorship and the one after that fascism. Try to understand our situation: we're fighting with our backs up against the wall. I ask myself if it's really necessary, exactly at this point in time, to stage *Antigone:* denied burial, rebellious females, and this ominous visionary, this Teresias, a precursor of the prophets—a sort of forerunner of the intellectuals. Young people will misunderstand this as a call to subversion.

In the end the film is put on ice while one waits for quieter times.

Films like *Germany in Autumn,* Margarethe von Trotta's *Das zweite Erwachen der Christa Klages/The Second Awakening of Christa Klages,* and Helke Sander's *Die allseitig reduzierte Persönlichkeit-REDUPERS/The All Round Reduced Personality-REDUPERS,* all shown early in 1978 at the Berlin festival, gave rise to renewed hope regarding alternative image-making in the FRG. As the highly emotional storm of 1977 finally passed, so too did West German cultural life take on a semblance of normalcy. Schütte, pointing to the large number of films screened in late 1977 and 1978 grounded in more tangible current settings, announced: "It looks as if our film finally, at long last, has found and taken up contact with the real-life world around us."[61] Correct as his analysis might have been at the moment, there still was cause for a less sanguine assessment. The underlying dilemma had not gone away. The *Literaturverfilmungskrise* was over; the structures that had produced it remained intact. Filmmakers still had to bear the scrutiny of committee members, many of whom knew little about film and cared even less for the medium. (Others did fortunately.) They still—in most instances— had to submit finished scripts if they were to find support for their images, alternative or otherwise. (There were of course exceptions like the liberal ZDF which often granted certain filmmakers more leeway.) TV stations continued to stand under the dictates of *Ausgewogenheit,* meaning that attempts to deal with pressing topics in an unpopular or controversial manner more often than not could hardly expect encouragement—or backing. Finished films continued to be withdrawn, postponed, or rescheduled at less opportune hours whenever the prospect of public disfavor posed itself.

The successes of New German Cinema demonstrate in the mind of American critics how "a lot of government money is paying for new films by new directors, with excellent results."[62] The *Literaturverfilmungskrise* demonstrates how successfully government-sponsored institutions can stifle creative and critical filmmaking during a period of political turmoil, periods of which German history doubtlessly has not seen its last.

NOTES

Some of the thoughts expressed in this chapter appeared in *"Deutschland im Vorherbst:* Literature Adaptation in West Germany," in *Kino: German Film,* No. 3 (Summer 1980), pp. 11-19.

[1] "The Author as Producer," in *Reflections,* ed. Peter Demetz (New York: Harcourt Brace Jovanovich, 1978), p. 222.

[2] "That's Entertainment: Eine Polemik gegen Joachim C. Fests Film *Hitler—eine Karriere,"* *Die Zeit,* 5 Aug. 1977. Wenders was addressing himself to Fest's problematic documentary. His conclusions, nonetheless, apply in the present context and came from the period in question.

[3] Quoted in Hans C. Blumenberg, "Das Jahr des Teufels," *Die Zeit,* 8 July 1977.

[4] "Im Würgegriff des Fernsehens: Das Kino auf der Suche nach dem intelligenten Kommerzfilm," *Die Zeit,* 2 Sept. 1977.

[5] Speech delivered at the 1977 Römerberg-conference in Frankfurt, published as "Die falschen Stoffe: Anmerkungen zu den Themen deutscher Filmemacher," *Jahrbuch Film 77/78,* ed. Hans Günther Pflaum (Munich: Hanser, 1977), p. 46.

[6] See Charles Eidsvik, "The State as Movie Mogul," *Film Comment,* March-April 1979, p. 63; and Rob Baker, " 'New German Cinema': A Fistful of Myths," *Soho Weekly News,* 23 March 1978, p. 22.

[7] See Baker, " 'New German Cinema' "; and Vincent Canby, "The German Renaissance—No Room for Laughter or Love," *New York Times,* 11 Dec. 1977.

[8] Charles Eidsvik, "Behind the Crest of the Wave: An Overview of the New German Cinema," *Literature/Film Quarterly,* Vol. 7, No. 3 (1979), p. 176.

[9] Ronald Holloway, "The Backbone of German Cinema," *Kino: German Film,* No. 3 (Summer 1980), p. 25.

[10] "Im Würgegriff des Fernsehens," op. cit. See also Peter Buchka, " 'Wir leben in einem toten Land': Haben die deutschen Filmemacher nur noch die Wahl zwischen äusserer und innerer Emigration?,*" Süddeutsche Zeitung,* 20 Aug. 1977.

[11] " 'Ab morgen reich und ehrlich': *Spiegel-*Report über die deutsche Filmindustrie (I),*" Spiegel,* 10 Jan. 1977, p. 110.

[12] See Blumenberg, Buchka, and also Wolfram Schütte, "Herrscht Ruhe im Land? Warum? Emigrationsabsichten, Kritik-Schelte und flaue Filme: die Situation," *Frankfurter Rundschau,* 6 Aug. 1977.

[13] *Der deutsche Film kann gar nicht besser sein: Ein Pamphlet von gestern. Eine Abrechnung von heute* (Munich: Rogner & Bernhard, 1981), p. 366. Hembus's panegyric to the subsidy system appears earlier in the book on pp. 304-08 under the heading, "Ich liebe das Gremienkino."

[14] "Ganz schön heruntergekommen: Erfahrungen in der Projektkommission," in *Jahrbuch Film 78/79,* ed. Hans Günther Pflaum (Munich: Hanser, 1978), p. 169.

[15] Klaus Kirschner and Christian Stelzer, *Die Filme von H.W. Geissendörfer—Gespräche, Materialien* (Erlangen: Selbstverlag der Videogruppe Erlangen, 1979), p. 12.

[16] See e.g. Peter Buchka, "Fatale Politik mit schmutzigen Bildern: Die Bundesrepublik präsentiert sich in Cannes mit *Heinrich* und *Gruppenbild unter Wert*," *Süddeutsche Zeitung,* 26 May 1977.

[17] Other *Verfilmungen* receiving awards were *The Conquest of the Citadel, Grete Minde, Group Portrait with Lady,* and *The Three Sisters.*

[18] See Hans Günther Pflaum and Hans Helmut Prinzler, *Film in der Bundesrepublik Deutschland* (Munich: Hanser, 1979), p. 44.

[19] Buchka, " 'Wir leben in einem toten Land.' "

[20] Kluge, as noted in chapter three, ran into precisely this problem with *Gelegenheitsarbeit einer Sklavin/Part-Time Work of a Domestic Slave* (1973).

[21] "1980: Auf Lorbeeren kann man schlecht sitzen: Anmerkungen zur Filmförderung und zur kreativen Praxis der Filmemacher," in *Deutscher Filmpreis 1951-1980,* ed. Manfred Hohnstock and Alfons Betterman (Cologne: Bachem, 1980), p. 78.

[22] See *Kino-Debatte: Texte zum Verhältnis von Literatur und Film 1909-1929,* ed. Anton Kaes (Tübingen: Niemeyer, 1978); also, *Hätte ich das Kino! Die Schriftsteller und der Stummfilm,* ed. Bernhard Zeller (Stuttgart: Klett, 1976).

[23] Alfred Estermann, *Die Verfilmung literarischer Werke* (Bonn: Bouvier, 1965), pp. 192ff.

[24] For an overview of literature adaptations during the Nazi period, see Francis Courtade/Pierre Cadars, *Geschichte des Films im Dritten Reich,* trans. Florian Hopf (Munich: Hanser, 1975), pp. 248-52.

[25] See the analysis in Hembus, pp. 3-168.

[26] Robert Fischer and Joe Hembus, *Der neue deutsche Film 1960-1980* (Munich: Goldmann, 1981), p. 247.

[27] The article first appeared in the journal *Sprache im technischen Zeitalter,* No. 13 (1965). It was reprinted in Klaus Eder and Alexander Kluge, *Ulmer Dramaturgien. Reibungsverluste* (Munich: Hanser, 1980), pp. 9-27. All citations are taken from the latter source.

[28] "Wort und Bild," pp. 12-16. Cf. Noël Burch's observation in "An Interview with Noël Burch," *Women and Film,* Vol. 1, Nos. 5-6 (1974), p. 30: "The idea that there are two tracks—an image-track and a sound-track—is something that people are not even remotely aware of in any sense, and therefore are not aware of the fact that essentially these are two different productions happening.... The dominant concept is that the image produces the sound."

[29] "Wort und Bild," p. 21.

[30] Ibid., p. 24.

[31] *Die Blechtrommel: Tagebuch einer Verfilmung* (Darmstadt/Neuwied: Luchterhand, 1979), p. 48. See Schlöndorff's contributions in the discussion "Film als Requisit der Literatur?," *Film Forum,* March 1979, pp. 86-103.

[32] See Fassbinder's article, "Die Städte des Menschen und seine Seele: Einige ungeordnete Gedanken zu Alfred Döblins Roman *Berlin Alexanderplatz,*" *Die Zeit,* 14 March 1980.

[33] Noël Burch, "Porter, or ambivalence," *Screen,* Winter 1978/9, p. 97.

[34] *The Brechtian Aspect of Radical Cinema* (London: British Film Institute, 1981), p. 54.

[35] The film does not have an American distributor nor is it included in the

FRG's large Embassy library. Cf. Ingemo Engström and Gerhard Theuring, "Dossier: *Escape Route to Marseilles*," trans. Barry Ellis-Jones with intro. by Steve Neale and Paul Willen, *Framework*, No. 18 (1982), pp. 22-29.
[36] Cf. Geoffrey Nowell-Smith, "A Note on History/Discourse," *Edinburgh '76 Magazine*, p. 27.
[37] See Buchka, "Fatale Politik mit schmutzigen Bildern": "And really one can hardly speak about images here; at best one can talk of illustrated sentences."
[38] Schütte, "Herrscht Ruhe im Land?"
[39] See, for example, the last paragraph of Hans C. Blumenberg's review of *Good-for-Nothing* and *Liberty or Death*, "Kostümfest ohne Ende: Literaturverfilmungen nach Eichendorff und Schiller," *Die Zeit*, 27 Jan. 1978.
[40] Seitz has been and still remains best known as a producer (and occasional director) of literature adaptations. Although his film politics bear more in common with the established sector, he nonetheless has produced several significant Young German Films, among others works by Straub/Huillet *(Die Chronik der Anna Magdalena Bach/ The Chronicle of Anna Magdalena Bach)* and Schlöndorff *(Törless, Die Blechtrommel/ The Tin Drum)*.
[41] The *Aussteigerfilme* ("drop out films") of the late seventies and early eighties contain a similar impulse. Cf. Adolf Winkelmann's *Die Abfahrer/On the Move*, Uwe Friessner's *Das Ende des Regenbogens/ The End of the Rainbow*, and Norbert Kückelmann's *Die letzten Jahre der Kindheit/ The Last Years of Childhood*.
[42] Cf. Wilfried Wiegand, "*Grete Minde*—eine fragwürdige Materialschlacht," *Frankfurter Allgemeine Zeitung*, 30 June 1977.
[43] Quoted in the press booklet provided for the film by the *Filmverlag der Autoren*.
[44] Peter Schneider, *Lenz* (Berlin: Rotbuch, 1973).
[45] During the summer of 1981, Alexander Kluge was reputed to be recutting the film.
[46] See Kirschner/Stelzer, op. cit., p. 9.
[47] Ibid., p. 26: "There are certain rules that one should not change for the spectator, because one will otherwise frustrate him."
[48] "Reicher Jude von links: Zu Fassbinders Stück *Der Müll, die Stadt und der Tod*," *Frankfurter Allgemeine Zeitung*, 19 March 1976.
[49] "Gefährliche Klischees: Zur Diskussion um Fassbinder," *Frankfurter Allgemeine Zeitung*, 2 April 1976. Cf. Jean Améry, "Shylock, der Kitsch und die Gefahr," *Die Zeit*, 9 April 1976: "Fassbinder is obviously no anti-Semite. He is only (as the author of *this* play) a poor dramatist and—what is decisive in the given context—an unpsychological and unphilosophical thinker and an unhistorical person."
[50] "Philosemiten sind Antisemiten" (Interview with Benjamin Heinrichs), *Die Zeit*, 9 April 1976.
[51] Shortly before the controversy began, Daniel Schmid completed a film version of Fassbinder's play (featuring the author) entitled *Schatten der Engel/ Shadows of the Angels*. It was shown in the "Quinzaine des Realisateurs" at the 1976 Cannes festival. The script to the film as well as a documentation of the entire public debate are published in *Schatten der Engel: Ein Film von Daniel*

Schmid nach dem Theaterstück "Der Müll, die Stadt und der Tod" von Rainer Werner Fassbinder (Frankfurt: Zweitausendeins, 1976).

[52] Editorial preface to Hans Mayer's "Ist Gustav Freytag neu zu entdecken? *Soll und Haben*/Aus Anlass eines Fernsehprojekts," *Frankfurter Allgemeine Zeitung*, 26 Feb. 1977.

[53] Rainer Werner Fassbinder, "Gehabtes Sollen—gesolltes Haben: Der Streit um die geplante Gustav-Freytag-Verfilmung," *Die Zeit*, 11 March 1977.

[54] Gerhard Zwerenz, "Linker Antisemitismus ist unmöglich," *Die Zeit*, 9 April 1976.

[55] See Brigitte Jeremias, "Wer schlägt uns denn das Kino tot? Römerberg-Gespräch in Frankfurt," *Frankfurter Allgemeine Zeitung*, 2 May 1977. Cf. also Hans-Jürgen Weber, "Alles andere als ein Schlachtenspektakel: Eberhard Fechner verfilmt den Roman *Winterspelt* von Alfred Andersch," *Tagesspiegel* (Berlin), 18 Dec. 1977.

[56] "Deutschland im Herbst '77: Schwierigkeiten von Filmemachern/Manche Stoffe angeblich nun unmöglich," *Frankfurter Rundschau*, 31 Dec. 1977.

[57] Kristl had made subversive *Gremienfilme* at various points in his career, most notably *Film oder Macht/Film or Power* (1970). See the collection of his scripts and miscellaneous commentaries on film in *Sekundenfilme* ed. Wolf Wondratschek (Frankfurt: Suhrkamp, 1971).

[58] This is quoted from the introductory narration to *The Little Godard*. For the complete opening text, see *The Films of Hellmuth Costard*, ed. Jan Dawson (London: Riverside Studios, 1979), p. 19.

[59] Dawson, p. 6.

[60] Ibid., p. 8.

[61] "Endlich bei uns angekommen: Bundesdeutsche Film 1977/78," in *Jahrbuch Film 78/79*, ed. Hans Günther Pflaum (Munich: Hanser, 1978), p. 45.

[62] Baker, op. cit., p. 22. The passage goes on: "The German Establishment is paying well—and presumably quite happily—to promote a 'radical' new German cinema which may present them as cranky old fogies to the rest of the world, but at least it is presenting them well. Germany has risen again and the world has to sit up and take notice."

Chapter Six

The New Sensitivity and the New Filmmakers: Subjective Factors

> *"How and under what conditions can the subjective factor inscribe itself as an objective factor in the historical process?"*
> —Rudi Dutschke[1]

> *"It is hardly fortuitous circumstance that has caused a stirring of feelings directed toward Germany and its history."*
> —Alexander Kluge and Oskar Negt[2]

Autorenkino: Dead or Alive?

West German filmmakers have followed many courses in time since Oberhausen. Their most crucial project has been an ongoing dialogue with German history, a confrontation with the continuities of past and present. The dialogue, as previous chapters have indicated, has known its many side-tracks, numerous interruptions, and recurring threat of breakdown over the last two decades. The exchange has taken very provocative shape especially when filmmakers have posed themselves directly as partners in the larger discussion—as subjects. (The

Literaturverfilmungskrise for a time silenced or stunted many voices.) One can describe this participation as a forwarding of discourse in the face of ready-made history, as a recognition of the need for memory in order to regain otherwise forgotten experience, as an ongoing struggle against the mechanisms that stifle authentic human response and hinder the open flow of information and ideas. Rather than feign finality or omniscience, many filmmakers — often ones not known so well outside of West Germany — have forefronted their enunciations as a function of limit, leaving questions half-answered, conclusions tentative, and making it clear that little distance exists between the fictional subject and the enunciating one. Fassbinder's sequence in *Deutschland im Herbst/ Germany in Autumn* (the topic of a special epilogue to follow), Jutta Brückner's *Hungerjahre/Hunger Years,* and Herbert Achternbusch's cinema of disenchantment: these are only several examples among many of a tendency present since Oberhausen, but particularly conspicuous since the mid-seventies, films governed by the subjective factor. Before I take on this many-faceted phenomenon, I need to talk about how previous critics have addressed the matter of subjectivity.

The large majority of American commentators approach the question in a roundabout manner, claiming simply that the young filmmakers work as individuals, linked only by loose connections to the past or their peers. Subjectivity is de-historicized and equated with artistic eccentricity. The images the directors produce are "fresh," "new," "different." Enjoying creative freedom, the willfully independent creators combine "remarkable levels of craftsmanship with stunningly original visions." Werner Herzog, perhaps the most significant example of the "important cinematic pioneers," amounts to something of a "magician." Watching one of his films represents "the nearest thing to transcendence one is likely to encounter in a movie theater."[3] New German Cinema means a collection of independents, "a most unmovement-like movement." The directors "have not advanced a common aesthetic or thematic 'politique'; their interests are disparate; they are not close friends."[4] The rhetoric here celebrates the self-reliant and defiantly idiosyncratic *auteur.* Though not unknown in West German discussions and no stranger to French accounts, "the myth of the romantic visionary" as the basis of the FRG's so consumingly personal cinema has taken on the status of accepted opinion in the United States.[5]

A related argument finds critics speaking of West German filmmakers' cultivation of the self at the expense of history. The *Jungfilmer* "are Germans for whom the Third Reich and the war are cloudy memories at best, and more likely only overheard reminiscences."⁶ This line of reasoning has found its most hyperbolic extension in Raymond Durgnat's jeremiad, "From Caligari to *Hitler*." More abundantly than anywhere in the western world, more strikingly than in any of the other "new waves," claims Durgnat, one finds in New German Cinema the tendency to wallow "in a pit of historical amnesia."⁷ Americans reveling in their own "Me-Generation" love to follow the ego trips of these Romantic wayfarers, transcendental travelers who are grand when it comes to shaping frames, composing images, and deconstructing narratives, but decidedly maladroit when they take on history:

> If the Sixties tried to live in a yellow submarine, the Seventies experience was a decade in bondage to NeubabelScyberneticsburg—with no dreams, no tribe, no family, strong ethical or historical roots to mediate between a forlornly narcissistic Me and a system which Herzog's original title for *Kaspar Hauser* neatly sums up: *Every Man for Himself and God Against All*. Herzog, Syberberg, and Godard are all Grand Masters of the one-liner, as well as anti-dramatic lyricists, because they're sharpshooters with one-shot minds—logical rather than dialectical dramatic. Maybe it's therapeutic to dream of being an impervious ego, making history Homerically and failing Wagnerianly. And since Young Germany has the worst case of historical amnesia, combined with heavy subsidies for film, we shouldn't be surprised that it provides the poets laureate for an international intelligentsia hard hit by culture- and future-shock.⁸

Durgnat, one must add, does his fair share of off-target shooting in an attack full of precious and ponderous puns—not to mention considerable indications of the author's own lapses of memory.⁹ He attempts to absolutize Herzog's and Syberberg's sort of filmmaking as the dominant praxis in West Germany today:

> The cult of the 'egotistical sublime' arises from, and in turn perpetuates, two artistic disadvantages: a historical wipe-out, and a substitution of 'magic' personality ascendancies for the warp and woof of social with individual factors.¹⁰

These charges come as no news to those familiar with West German film critics' continuing claim that the young filmmakers have never achieved a productive working relationship to their own times.¹¹ What is (perversely) fascinating about Durgnat's prose in "From Caligari to

Hitler" —whose style might be likened to a high-brow version of *Bild-Zeitung* invective, the rodomontade of someone ever ready to sacrifice the truth for a turned phrase—is the way in which it blends a sometimes valid critique of American appropriations with the rhetoric of West German film's most rabid domestic assailants.

A third direction in considerations of subjectivity and West German filmmaking is a tact often pursued in the FRG: *Autorenkino* is dead. The *Literaturverfilmungskrise* assumes the proportions of a near final act in a long and drawn-out struggle. Many West German filmmakers have divested themselves of personal commitment and individual flair as a result of the never-ending pressure of public institutions. Their films have ceased to be as intimate as those of the mid-sixties, both in their direction and subject matter. As certain other *auteurs*, in the wake of festival accolades and foreign acclaim, have gained access to larger budgets, star casts, and wider distribution and exhibition outlets, the romantic anti-capitalism of Young German Film has given way to the industrial aestheticism and impersonal glossiness of New German Cinema. The history of West German film becomes in this light one of devolution, a movement from *Törless* to *Tin Drum*, from *Katzelmacher* to *Lili Marleen*, from *Autorenkino* to *Produzenten-* and *Kommerzkino* —in sum, a betrayal of the ideals voiced in the Oberhausen Manifesto in favor of a continuing approximation of the dominant cinema:

> The history of West German film of the last ten years, or let us be more exact, the seventies, is...the history of an increasing estrangement. The authors disappeared more and more from their films; what remained was only a more or less talented technical aplomb.[12]

For all their individual differences and varying approaches, one can point to a commonality of concern in a number of West German filmmakers. Since Oberhausen they have travelled a very rocky road, but one can—contrary to American chroniclers—discern a continuous course in time. Despite apparent—and in some cases, like those of Herzog and Syberberg, often real—signs of solipsism, West German film has a decided regard for history and many dialectical talents, especially among directors (e.g. Kluge, a host of feminists, and an array of documentary filmmakers) Durgnat conveniently overlooks. To reduce a rich and many-sided national cinema down to the work of five figures, as the British critic does without justifying his choices or seeking to be representative, makes matters all too simple. Even if West German film does have a rapidly developing host of commercial artisans, efficient technicians like Wolfgang Petersen, Ulrich Edel, Hans W. Geissendörfer, and as of late, Volker Schlöndorff: for all the big budgets and box-office appeal enjoyed by an increasing number of films from the FRG, there remains a much larger body of *"dreckige kleine Filme,"* dirty little films produced on small budgets by artists willing to make up in personal energy what they might lack in technical expertise or production values.

The works we will be dealing with below are variations on the theme of the problematic and problematized subject, a continuing and crucial motif in West German filmmaking. Some comments regarding the context shaping this preoccupation are in order prior to any closer evaluation of paradigmatic examples.

The Melancholic Left in the Wake of the *Tendenzwende*

Three interrelated dilemmas confronted West Germany's progressive artists during the seventies: the haunting memory of the student movement's glaring failure, the attendant demise of collective pursuit, and the presentiment of terrorism. For all the apparent signs of stability people abroad generally associated with West Germany (economic prosperity, low unemployment and inflation rates, a decisive and firmly entrenched leadership), the basic tenor of the FRG seen from within took on more discordant notes at times: massive security checks, a radical decree, blacklisting, an atmosphere of suspicion towards dissident groups, and state-sponsored denunciation campaigns against radicals. One no longer spoke of infiltrating the establishment and altering public experience by gradually marching through the institutions. The hopes harbored by the SDS faded into disillusionment couched in less political terms. Tabloid tastemakers rejoiced as writers retreated from predominantly engaged and oppositional literature to much more personal and subjective modes of expression, stories of sickness and private turmoil, intimate depictions of growth and change. One seemed to have fled from participation in the *Aussenwelt* to an exploration of the *Innenwelt* — in the official version at any rate. The bourgeois press attempted to enlist what it referred to as the "New Subjectivity" in a larger cause: to register "a cultural reversal from the political-emancipatory 1960s to an envisioned neo-romantic interiority for the

1970s."[13] One influential conservative critic heralded the trend as "a return to a necessary perspective, one that—as a consequence of a one-sided politicization of literature—had all too often been neglected in recent years."[14]

Leftist commentators attacked this discourse of authenticity for its resignation and *l'art pour l'art* elitism.[15] Belittling such navel-picking, intellectuals like Michael Schneider saw in this dominant current of the seventies a chronic melancholy, utter narcissism, and an abiding inability to think dialectically. Solipsism merged with self-pity, misanthropy blended with disenchantment: "Everywhere these authors look, all they see are defective people, defective relationships, a defective environment..."[16] The prevailing cultural metaphors centered around ice, winter, and the apocalypse, expressions of what Schneider labelled a "negative romanticism":

> If the 19th-century Romantics—in the wake of the failed bourgeois revolution—had fled backwards in time to a world of dreams and fairy tales, their contemporary negative counterparts—after the collapse of their own former political and existential utopias—have taken flight into the shadowy perplexing images of a world that only appears to them as a nightmare, as a never-ending horror film, one that they have been documenting with almost masochistic thoroughness for some ten years now.[17]

The Collapse of Collectivity

The student movement had aroused hopes regarding the value of shared dreams and collective endeavor. "Our most important experience," Schneider wrote in retrospect, "was realizing that we could achieve something through cooperative action and solidarity."[18] As the APO *(Ausserparlamentarische Opposition* or Extra-Parliamentary Opposition), riddled by dogmatism and factionalism, crumbled into splinter groups and government marginalization of radicals further undermined political activists on the left, the euphoria of street demonstrations and mass meetings gave way to cynicism regarding common pursuit and a marked hostility toward any ideology couched in the language of rationality. To use Michael Rutschky's terminology, one shifted from the desire to actualize theoretical contructs ("eine Sehnsucht, Allgemeinbegriffe zu leben"[19]) to the utopian notion of remaining undefined by social mechanisms ("die Utopie der Unbestimmbarkeit"[20]). Primal homogeneity became the new ideal for many, as one rejected all organizational frameworks.[21] One embraced an experience central to T. W. Adorno's philosophy: the social process which shapes individuals just as decisively works at deforming them. So much West German literature of the seventies reaffirms the insight, stressing how the seminal human experience in our times is fear, a fear grounded in the belief, as Rutschky points out, that

> The outside world is cold and mean; whoever steps into it becomes subject to its laws and perforce also becomes cold and mean and must forget the good and warm interior world.[22]

No matter how widespread the sensibility was during the epoch, there was little commonality among exponents of the *Utopie der Unbestimmbarkeit*. One effect of the persuasion remained the tendency to see others as functions of the hostile *Aussenwelt*.[23]

For West German filmmakers, at least the male vanguard of the "New German Cinema," this everyone-for-himself approach threatened to become the prevalent *modus vivendi*. (Feminist filmmakers, for the most ghettoized and ignored by the mainstream of German film culture well into the mid-1970s, did not accord to the general trend while attempting to create their own organizational substructures.) The initial pronouncements of the Oberhausen signatories had been long obscured. The old dreams of a national cinema bound in personal visions, alternative images, and critical realism, all of which would take shape as parts of a continuing dialogue with West German audiences: these were pushed aside for the moment as directors competed for subsidy monies, television funding, and media exposure. Just how could one realize collective aims within a support system of government institutions and public commissions whose guidelines reduced directors to supplicants and monads?

The Presentiment of Terrorism

Unsettled by the student movement's resolve to infiltrate the establishment, troubled by increasing signs of dissatisfaction among workers who felt their interests betrayed by the collusion of union leaders and SPD heads, irritated by the rise of political groups whose appeal transcended traditional party allegiances (e.g. ecological activists like "the Greens" and citizen initiatives), and finally called to arms and given an ostensible excuse for repressive counter-measures by a small circle of extremists, the West German government struck back with awesomely systematic precision.[24] The surveillance and security checks which became a part of the everyday sought to ferret out not only the miniscule number of actual terrorists; the campaign focussed as strongly on potential dissidents, so-called "sympathizers," who in thought or deed supported the acts of the RAF. Many members of the left understood the despair and vehemence behind the acts of the Baader-Meinhof group. Few concurred with the criminal acts themselves.

Terrorism, nonetheless, as a discursive practice, shared much in common with strategies utilized by numerous cultural producers. In a certain sense one could speak of terrorism as a misunderstood version of Critical Theory, as critique running wild. Adorno—as Rutschky argues a bit too schematically—insisted that the calling of philosophy was to develop a sense of authentic existence:

> And again and again he [Adorno] demonstrated that one cannot live *like this* or *like that* or *in such a manner*, that all of this is not really living. This was the central motif of his philosophy: critique—one that can allow individual identity to develop as an exact negation of every aspect of the societal process.[25]

The terrorists in this light had left the realm of intellectual discourse and sought to live out their critique, using their bodies instead of words as modes of expression, ultimately signing their actions with their corpses. They posited themselves as a living critique, forgetting though that their bodies were only signs, and in so doing obviating any mediation between the specific and the general. (Adorno, one suspects, would have viewed their acts for this reason as ones of false negation.) The official treatment of the incarcerated RAF-members (strict isolation in the specially-designed maximum security prison in Stammheim, severe limitations on their interactions with people from the outside) as well as the intense controversy over where one would bury the dead bodies of the trio Baader, Ensslin, and Raspe: do not such counter-measures attest to a government awareness of the persuasive power of this *Körperpolitik?* Indeed even commentaries seeking to understand the logic behind the explosive terrorists acts invariably caused their authors difficulties with authorities, another indication of how the West German state readily linked theorizing about and practicing of terrorism. The Frankfurt School, so declared various politicians, must take the blame for providing the intellectual backdrop for the RAF violence.

Many of the most painful autobiographies and chronicles of sickness abounding in West German literature of the seventies gain poignance from their authenticity. Authors like Ernst Herhaus *(Die Kapitulation)*, Bernward Vesper *(Die Reise)*, and Günther Steffens *(Annäherung an das Glück)*, among many others, recount traumatic and excruciating experiences from their own lives. The documents both evoke great personal suffering as well as summoning forth considerable discomfort in the reader. The texts, reflections of the torments of inner worlds, assume the function in the outside world as attacks, as physical assaults, ones marked by a consuming directness. The work of Herbert Achternbusch provides the most striking enactment of this tendency, especially his film *Bierkampf/Beer Battle,* in which the director/protagonist actually becomes physically violent with strangers.

We turn now to some examples of the "New Sensitivity," films possessing a similar deformation of protagonist and environment, works portraying characters who combat the terms of the outer world and seek to privilege the rights of the inner self. Each example, we shall see, contains a subversive potential beyond the seeming glorification of the radical subject. Likewise, these films communicate a profound social experience, a more encompassing historical context, factors all too readily obscured by previous celebrators and critics of the "New Sensitivity."

Peter Handke's *The Left-Handed Woman:* Specularity and Hunger for Experience

Die linkshändige Frau/The Left-Handed Woman (1977) readily lends itself to a discussion of the so-called "New Subjectivity" and its ostensible static duality between individual and society, its strained relationship between subject and object. An advocate of a pure and autonomous literature, Handke poses a paradigm and a problem: a paradigm insofar as he represents *the* central example of this dominant trend in West German cultural output of the seventies,[26] a problem because he offers little help in any attempt to rescue the "New Subjectivity" from conservative appropriators (who laud its putatively unideological directness and revel in its neo-romantic interiority) much less from leftist critics (who attack its supposedly undialectical tendencies, its deformation of self and environment, its ahistorical fatalism).

Handke, well known for his ardent disdain of politics, his ivory-tower reclusiveness,[27] and his outspoken sympathy for an aestheticism characteristic of earlier epochs, insists one must approach him and his work on the author's own terms: "What biology maintains, what psychoanalysis maintains, how Marxism defines me, all of this leaves me totally cold."[28] One can only criticize him, so he has often said, in terms of his own self-image.[29] *The Left-Handed Woman* was Handke's attempt to create a film with the intensity of myth,[30] a work whose pristine images speak so directly that they do not require interpretation: they are adequate in and of themselves. This image-making, though, did not take place outside of history. For some time now I have suspected there lies a more subversive potential, indeed a crucial historical experience behind Handke's defiantly under-narrated film[31] — despite its author's incessant claims to the contrary.

The Left-Handed Woman is a film marked by an extreme impenetrability, an inexorable elusiveness, and a seeming obliviousness to topical concerns. At the center of the film—as in Handke's prose—stands the specular subject. Seeing is being for Handke's protagonists. Their mode of vision has much in common with the moviegoer who sits in the dark and partakes of filmic spectacles. Bloch, the ex-welder in *Die Angst des Tormanns beim Elfmeter/The Goalie's Anxiety at the Penalty Kick*, cannot blend bits and pieces of haptic reality into a meaningful whole. He constantly escapes to cinemas where he breathes more easily. The hero of *Der kurze Brief zum langen Abschied/The Short Letter to the Long Goodbye* wends his way through the United States rediscovering images well known to him from John Ford films. The manifest destiny of the journey is an interview with the director of *Young Mr. Lincoln* and *She Wore a Yellow Ribbon*. Keuschnig, the main character in *Die Stunde der wahren Empfindung/The Moment of True Feeling*, stands on the street in the novel's closing scene and regards passers-by: "The people coming toward Keuschnig looked like people who had been filmed a long time ago; in reality they had ceased to exist—what he saw was only the latest film with them in it."[32]

The author of the entries in *Das Gewicht der Welt/The Weight of the World*, Handke's journal, is a compulsive film buff and the otherwise anchoritic dweller of a Paris suburb residence, the lover of solitary pleasures who seeks experience unbesmirched by the everyday, who shies away from the company of most people. Handke appears in the collection of fleeting moments and fragmentary observations as an updated version of the *flâneur*, the man of leisure who goes botanizing on the asphalt, a solitary promenader who reduces the outside world to a film. " 'By chance he looked out of the window and saw...' (one could as a rule say the same of me)," Handke notes in the journal.[33] At another point he reflects upon a movie about himself, "a film made or even just imagined by me with the title *Mein Leben:* a long sequence of black film on which only occasionally something would flash by," the "something" being not other humans or himself, but leaves gliding over an empty street.[34] A world of unpeopled images gazed upon by a camera eye: this is *Mein Leben* as envisioned by the writer—as well as *The Left-Handed Woman* as realized by the director.

The Left-Handed Woman, like the journal entries, amounts to a succession of images unreeling in what seems to be a self-contained sphere, what one critic has described as a "black hole."[35] Its protagonist—who is, by the way, right-handed—constantly stands at windows, peering out, watching the world pass by, the same world from which she retreats, cutting herself off from husband and friends, and even at times her son. A curious and sudden revelation, much like Keuschnig's "moment of true feeling," prompts her reaction, one that might be taken for a feminist awakening were it not for the way in which the narrative repeatedly undercuts Marianne's friend Franziska, the promoter of women's groups and spokesperson for raised consciousness. Franziska becomes just one more link in a chain of signifiers which attempts to provide "explanations" for Marianne's odd behavior.[36] In her husband's mind Marianne is a "mystic." Others fear for her welfare, claiming that all this being alone will have frightful consequences. But the Woman refuses to listen to what others have to say about her, insisting on the integrity of her self-imposed isolation. "Say what you will," Marianne declares while looking into a mirror. "The more you think you can say something about me, the more I'll free myself from you."

A character who stands beyond the interpretations of her peers (and by extension the audience), a writer who only allows himself to be approached in terms of his self-image: the Woman is a thinly clad surrogate for the director, one could say, a vehicle to demonstrate Handke's theses about being alone and the power of isolation, thoughts uttered often in the Paris journal and in various interviews.[37] The Woman's staring at street life and her treks through the city bear much in common with the behavior of Handke's camera, its impressionistic attentions, its way of concentrating on found objects, and focussing with unblinking intensity on transient phenomena.

The opening frames of *The Left-Handed woman* contain still-lifes for the most lacking human presence, shots in which the objects glimpsed serve no narrative purpose or—as we will come to realize—diegetic function. Blades of grass next to railroad tracks rustle as a train passes; newspapers fly into the air as other locomotives whiz by an empty platform; out of a train window the camera peers onto the urban scape. As in similar shots throughout the film, we cannot identify the perspective with any character: the images have an independent existence. One is reminded of Yasujiro Ozu, a filmmaker highly regarded by Handke and other New German directors. We see a poster of the Japanese master in Marianne's house and watch the Woman take in a screening of Ozu's 1931-comedy, *Tokyo Chorus,* signs of just how influential the director's vision has been for Handke's film.³⁸ Ozu, as Noël Burch has pointed out, often employed "pillow shots," cut-away still-lifes of landscapes and everyday objects devoid of human presence. Much more than simple metaphors or mere aesthetic exercises, such shots of rooftops, laundry drying on the line, smoke stacks or tea kettles, impart a sense that humans are not the sole center of the inhabited world. Pillow shots, according to Burch, subvert the anthropocentrism normally found in dominant narrative cinema:

> Unmoving, often lasting a long time (seldom less than five seconds, which we at least experience as long for an 'unpeopled' shot), fully articulated from the graphic point of view, they demand to be *scanned* like paintings, not like *inhabited* shots, which, even in Ozu are relatively more centred around characters.³⁹

Pillow shots suggest a concrete world existing outside our everyday consciousness, a world waiting to be discovered, a living world beyond the compositional center of the film's narrative.

Handke's corresponding images—petals falling off a tulip in a restaurant, the shaking leaves of a yellow flower as a train speeds by—bring the inanimate to the fore and make it a point of focus. Handke's pillow shots echo Marianne's image-making, her relentless staring at street life and constant gazing out of windows. Enunciating and fictional subject, Handke and Marianne, share a similar perspective: the world as image and imagination. The glasses the Woman wears while translating are framed by rims very much like ones we recall from pictures of Handke, a detail perhaps, but a telling one.

One is tempted to pass off the film, as many West German critics indeed have, as hermetic and solipsistic, a precious work fashioned by a writer-director obsessed by movies and ridden with an acute case of cinematic consciousness. (He would later translate Walker Percy's *The Moviegoer.*) *The Left-Handed Woman,* one might very well say, is the product of an artist who increasingly has sought to escape the sullied confines of the present, to discover a sovereign distance from social categories and topical concerns. However easy it might be to invoke the epithets so commonly found in leftist diatribes against Handke— narcissistic isolationism, objectless subjectivism, negative romanticism[40]—one remains struck by the virulent nature of Handke's image-making, aware of an atmosphere of refusal and a shock character beneath the surface placidity of *The Left-Handed Woman,* for all its slow pacing, long static takes, visual austerity, and dramatic minimalism.[41] The problem remains, though: how does one gain access to the social content of a film that has been so systematically sealed off; how does one broach historical considerations given the fierce subjectivity and radical aestheticism framing *The Left-Handed Woman?*

Insights found in T.W. Adorno's *Kierkegaard: Construction of the Aesthetic* (1933) allow a start in the direction of a more dialectical appropriation of Handke's film and his work in general. Adorno's difficult essay is crucial in our context precisely because the critical philosopher sought in it to demystify Kierkegaard's mystifications, to solve the apparent riddles of bourgeois idealism, and to demonstrate how "Kierkegaard's gloomy motives have good critical sense as soon as they are interpreted in terms of social critique."[42] The Woman, a fictional extension of the filmmaker, embodies what Adorno's essay terms the *bourgeois intérieur,* an enclosed monad that seeks to expel external history from its experience. Reality is not allowed to extend into its living sphere, "but only to appear in optical illusion, just as in a peephole."[43] The intrusion of the outside world is constantly combatted, in the Woman's case by reducing the real to a specular representation, the same tendency present in the detached camera's penchant for eliminating temporal and spatial continuity in its decentered still-lifes. This image-making does not, however, take place outside of history, no matter how emphatically the image-maker might insist on the unfettered nature of his vision, just as his fictional surrogate declares her autonomy from the views of others.

The tendency to shape the world into a bundle of sense impressions lacking narrative dimensions, the stress on haptic randomness and the eschewal of politics and history: these prevail in West German autobiographical literature of the seventies. Social criticism in such writing takes on an autistic quality, submits Rutschky, where "inner processes appear as fluttering movements of the outside world, one from which the individual, driven by an unbearable fear and displeasure, tries to free itself."[44] For adherents of the New Subjectivity, the outside world becomes identical with the limits it imposes on individual freedom. One embraces what Rutschky calls an "Utopie der Unbestimmbarket," i.e. a desire to remain undefined by social mechanisms and organizational frameworks, paradoxically enough in a society which on the one hand promotes a public ideology of individual fulfillment and yet on the other hand increasingly creates conditions that stifle real self-actualization.[45] Marianne, one can say, dramatizes this predicament, showing how interiority and the hope for some undefined alternative state are the results of a situation in which an individual feels less and less able to impress itself upon the world it inhabits. Her insistence on the primacy of her experience comes as a reaction to the lack of control she has over the objective processes that determine her.

"The manner in which human sense perception is organized, the medium in which it is accomplished," Walter Benjamin once wrote, "is determined not only by nature but by historical circumstance as well."[46] Behind Handke's world of seemingly impenetrable images meant to stylize and thus tame an otherwise oppressive reality, a dangerous *Aussenwelt,* lies a radical idealism that manifests itself as a precariously grounded self-sufficiency. Moving through disenchanted spaces and crowded streets, Benjamin describes elsewhere, "involves the individual in a series of shocks and collisions."[47] It is appropriate that the Woman's gaze is similar to that of the camera, for film was the medium that arose as a response to the shock character of modern urban life. Walking through intersections and plunging through crowds, the individual must look in all directions in order to begin to cope with present-day society's over-production of signs. The nervously gazing pedestrian becomes "a *kaleidoscope* equipped with consciousness," the result of modernity's public experience, one that "has subjected the human sensorium to a complex kind of training."[48]

Marianne—and Handke—bear out such training in their attempts to find a means of preserving subjective life against the onslaughts of ideology and technology, to maintain a semblance of individuality in the face of the challenges of modern life under advanced capitalism.

There are numerous examples one might cite from *The Left-Handed Woman* which bear out this insight. I will limit myself to an extended quote from the prose text:

> It was almost night. The woman and the child were in the center of the city, at a snack bar between two big office buildings, and the child was eating a pretzel. The roar of the traffic was so loud that a long-lasting catastrophe seemed to be in progress. A man came into the snack bar; he was bent almost double and had his hand on his heart. He asked for a glass of water and gulped it down with a pill. Then he sat down, stooped and wretched. The evening bells rang, a fire truck passed, followed by a number of ambulances with blue lights and sirens. The light flashed over the woman's face; her forehead was beaded with perspiration, her lips cracked and parched.[49]

Marianne may find occasional solace and fleeting well-being in her isolation or communings with her son. She still remains an inhabitant of this larger world with its frightening dissonance. "Even the objectless subject," Adorno notes, "with its inner history is tied to historical objectivity."[50] *The Left-Handed Woman,* meant as a celebration of the independent subject, actually reflects the same subject's intense vulnerability, its precarious status within modern constellations—as well as something else: its intense hunger for a richer experience, a voracious *Erfahrungshunger.*

Why are there compelling links between New Subjectivity and New German Film, the continuity between Handke's desire for an unencumbered existence and his cinemorphic seeing? Why is it that many young people in the Federal Republic have in recent years rediscovered the cinema as a place where they can still an otherwise unsated hunger for experience, where they partake of images without feeling a need to interpret them? These hours in the dark somehow allow one for a moment to regain one's bearings in a world one normally thinks of as chimeric. Herbert Achternbusch insists:

> I don't want to think at the cinema. I want to see. I scoff at the kind of cinema which won't let me rediscover my own feelings. I demand a sense of justice back from cinema. To keep going cinema was always important to me. Too much has been lost in my dreams.[51]

Rutschky describes the orientation found by the post-1968 generation in movie houses as being bound in the dreamlike fascination with the intensity of isolated images: the corporeal world comes alive, freed from the conditioning forces that structure the everyday, liberated from the discursive framework that limits certain signs to particular meanings, that imposes *Sinn* (meaning) on *Sinnlichkeit* (sense experience).[52]

Insights found in Kracauer's *Theory of Film,* the source of Rutschky's notion of *Erfahrungshunger,*[53] shed a more benign light on Handke's recourse to cinemorphic seeing and his characters' reduction of reality to pillow-shot representations. Marianne's hunger for experience manifests itself as a fascination with transient images caught on the wing, as Kracauer would put it, material life at its most ephemeral: weather vanes, street signs, store-front shutters, the empty chairs in a church. For her—and Handke—the world at times becomes "a flow of random events involving both humans and inanimate objects," a world sought out by the specular subject who for the most feels out of touch with things and looks for a way to enjoy "the illusion of vicariously partaking of life in its fullness."[54] Perhaps the most traumatic experience after the student movement was the sense of how little control the individual has over the forces, mechanisms, and processes that shape how it lives. This world of technology, other-directedness, commodity fetishism, has only grown more complex for the exponents of the New Subjectivity. A widespread feeling of impotence provided the background for many West German writers and filmmakers working in the seventies. Numerous disillusioned intellectuals sought compensation in a world not abounding in amenities. For many of them filmgoing and filmmaking afforded a sanctuary. In Kracauer's words: "In the cinema 'one grasps all of it,' as the woman teacher put it. There the frustrated may turn into the kings of creation."[55]

No matter what Handke or critics of various persuasions would have us believe: Handke's work bears the marks of a virulent social experience and is hardly devoid of reality. Even the militantly hermetic likes of *The Left-Handed Woman* opens itself up to a larger historical discussion and provides a critique of modernity. The film in this sense portrays a private rebellion at whose center lies a defiant attempt to assert one's own gaze, to pose personal discourse in the face of more uniform modes of experience. Handke remains so continually exciting precisely because, while pursuing this resolve to assert the primacy of his vision, he makes us aware of how limited this perspective is—as well as suggesting the forces that have imposed these limits on him and other subjects who hunger for experience.

Wim Wenders's Rerouting of Handke's *Wrong Move*

In 1969 Wim Wenders and Handke collaborated for the first time in what would become a long-standing and still-continuing working relationship.[56] The product was a twelve-minute short entitled *3 Amerikanische LPs,* a film about rock and roll consisting of music, shots from a moving car, and conversations between the two artists about the predominance of "emotions and images" in American pop tunes.[57] An overriding attention to sense experience very much informed a persuasion that flourished in Munich during the late sixties—an antithesis to the strident program of the student movement—commonly referred to as *Sensibilismus.* To a great degree the predilection influenced productions coming out of the *Hochschule für Fernsehen und Film* from which Wenders graduated in 1970. The *Sensibilisten* eschewed logical systems and political categories, insisting on the integrity of the subjective experience in all its immediacy and directness. One relied on the momentary uniqueness of lived encounters. There existed an unspoken taboo against intellectualizing what one perceived: direct experience of the world was enough in and of itself.[58] Munich's *Sensibilisten* made films with extended travelling shots and long takes. They pointed their cameras out of apartment and car windows onto the streets. The works had a contemplative tenor and little if any story line; they consisted of series of images meant to capture the ineffable feel of things.[59]

Sensibilismus represents an early form of the tendency journalists would later designate as the "New Subjectivity." Wenders, very much a friend and colleague of Handke, would seem to be a prominent adherent of the trend. Even American commentators have seen *Falsche Bewegung/Wrong Move* (1974), a film scripted by Handke and directed by Wenders, in these terms. J. Hoberman spoke of it as "the most introspectively German example of the New German Cinema" yet screened in New York.[60] Vincent Canby was put off by its chilly contours: "The movie...deals in heightened experience through vivid colors and in the amplification of small sounds, while...it pays no attention to the feelings and emotions of others."[61] The Handke-scenario that Wenders adapted—as we will see: rewrote—is loosely based on Goethe's classical *Bildungsroman, Wilhelm Meisters Lehrjahre/ Wilhelm Meister's Apprenticeship. Wrong Move,* in its final version, reflects a profound variance between Handke and Wenders for all their apparent similarities. *Wrong Move* is a seminal text in that it touches upon so many crucial facts of German tradition. The film draws a line of influence from the 18th-century "novel of education" to present-day concretizations of the problematic notion of *Bildung* found in the book. Wenders comments both on Goethe *and* Handke, posing the central question of the artist in Germany and his intellectual dilemma, reflecting on the ideal of self-cultivation German intellectuals have embraced throughout the centuries: the assumption that inwardness is "the source of human distinction."[62] Wenders did not write the screenplay for *Wrong Move;* he did, though, produce the final draft.[63] What follows is a catalogue of the major changes the director effected in rerouting Handke's *Wrong Move* while translating the script (which exists in print[64]) into its ultimate form.

Wenders confines the narrative point of view to his protagonist. We do not—as in Handke's script—read Wilhelm's journal entries or follow his superimposed handwriting on the screen.[65] Instead we hear him speak in voice-over and we perceive events from his vantage point. The spoken words become the mutterings and speculations of someone unable to carry on a meaningful dialogue with those around him. Handke's third-person narrative (his preferred form) gives way to a first-person one. Wenders shows us an individual very eager to see his life as an ongoing story and yet unable to transcend his own person, incapable of placing himself in a context of experience which includes other people and things.[66] Wenders intimates how thoughts simmer in Wilhelm's head, a mind steaming with unfinished notions. Wilhelm looks for things to express, not really knowing why he wants to write or quite able to find the gumption to do so. His reflections, productions of an interior monologue, often appear as ones the writer still has not put to paper. *Wrong Move* takes the shape of a first-person narrative whose overall author questions the limitations of the narrator's tunnel vision.

Wenders changes the itinerary of Wilhelm's trip. Instead of an excursion to the romantic and rural likes of Soest,[67] a picturesque corner of the German landscape, Wilhelm's train ride takes him to Bonn, the capital of the FRG. The first signs of public insanity and collective fear he encounters during a morning stroll do not transpire in an obscure corner of North Rhine-Westphalia; they take place in the capital of West Germany. Even more emphatically than Handke, Wenders shows how Wilhelm's disquiet stems from a specific environment, one which "induces those choices that taken together become his character."[68] In general Wenders does not linger over the isolated details, the random sights and sounds which take up much of Handke's screenplay. There are two reasons: first, the first-person narrator is so self-involved that he—as Therese points out—overlooks many things around him. Second, Wenders less and less shared Handke's radical fascination with found objects and isolated images as he developed. In his evolution as a filmmaker, Wenders has increasingly ceased making films "in which the people are not the most interesting element" and instead centered his narratives around character.[69]

Wilhelm does not accept things and people as independent entities, but rather sees the external world as a mirror. Other persons become projections of possibilities unexamined, latent, or only vaguely recognized by the aspiring writer. In company Wilhelm feels alone because he cannot grasp people's otherness. Each character takes on a role in his life script; actualities exist only insofar as they find counterparts within Wilhelm. The silent and dreaming Mignon is a creature of unspoken gestures and intimations. She represents an intensified version of Wilhelm who has trouble finding words and whose stormy silences weigh heavily on those around him. The old man embodies the past Wilhelm cares little for, one he only seems to know from newsreels. Contrary to Handke's script, Laertes does not sing Goethe texts, but instead plays a harmonica in an eerie way evocative of the nemesis figure portrayed by Charles Bronson in Sergio Leone's *Once Upon a Time in the West*. He stands as a specter from the past, a past Wilhelm sees as an encumbrance, one he (futilely) tries to elude by chasing the musician out of his life.[70] Wilhelm's relationship with Therese becomes a vehicle for him to gather experience so that he might write. In a voice-over shortly before he phones the actress (a scene we do not find in the scenario), Wilhelm relates how glimpsing her in the train had seemed to promise an adventure, one he must pursue even if he worries about what kind of commonplaces he will have to utter. Only after the telephone conversation does he produce the maudlin and unconvincing love poem he reads at the breakfast table the next morning. The rotund poet the group meets during its morning walk recites lyrics that express a disconnectedness Wilhelm knows well. "Why," Bernhard whines, "must there be such an inexorable distance between me and the world?" Wenders emphasizes the linkage between the two by framing them when they first appear together in a deep-focus composition, a shot that makes it look as if the poet's head stretches out of Wilhelm's. The world as image and imagination: Wenders's film both depicts and comments upon a narcissist who perceives others as an extension of himself.

The Industrialist's lengthy perorations on loneliness as a factor in German intellectual history and as a reality in the FRG do not unfold as a commentary we accept without reservation. This runs counter to Handke's script, for the emphatic self-sufficiency contained in the ode to solitude only restates what the author has said in public and written in his journals.[71] Wenders adds an edge to these musings by having an actor with a heavy French accent (Ivan Desny) deliver them. Without this distancing from the scripted speech, Wenders once explained, "You'd stop listening to that character after a while, because all he does is complain. It's hard to listen to someone immersed in self-pity."[72] Wilhelm becomes the interlocutor in this discussion which is really a monologue; he listens attentively. Later he will use the blood from a wound on the Industrialist's hand to pen his day's diary entry, recycling another's suffering for his own purposes. Once again, Wenders takes two discrete scenes (the Industrialist's speech and Wilhelm's midnight ramblings) and fuses them in a way that both transcends and changes the meaning of Handke's conception.

At one juncture in the script, Therese suggests to Wilhelm that they form a theater group, quite in keeping with the quest for a German national theater in Goethe's novel.[73] Wenders presents a significant variation on the theme in that Wilhelm's peregrinations index the situation of film in West Germany. The personal journey reflects another course in time, one that will undergo more thorough exploration in *Im Lauf der Zeit/Kings of the Road,* whose title Wilhelm utters in a dream. He rides a bicycle past a cinema in his hometown which is playing *Die Rückkehr der reitenden Leichen/The Return of the Mounted Corpses,* the German-dubbed version of a third-rate Spanish horror movie from 1973.[74] Later he stands in front of the *Stern-Kino* in the Bonn town square where Francis Ford Coppola's *The Conversation (Der Dialog)* runs. During the stay in Frankfurt, Mignon and Laertes watch Straub/Huillet's *Die Chronik der Anna Magdalena Bach/The Chronicle of Anna Magdalena Bach* on television[75]; later Wilhelm, Mignon, and Therese take in Peter Lilienthal's *La Victoria* at a drive-in. The four films provide a reflection on the film art in West Germany along two axes. First, they comment on the dynamics governing film distribution and exhibition: foreign-made genre fare gluts the dying provincial houses; American films occupy the more profitable first-run *Kinos* in the big cities[76]; a German film made by two foreigners with a mélange of subsidy money, television funding, and private backing plays on TV and reflects the tenuous existence of another subsidized artist; a political film made by a formerly exiled German Jew about a distant country's social climate unreels in an *Autokino*. Second, the four films show the possibilities inherent in the cinematic medium, ranging from throwaway escapism to reflections like Coppola's on public intrusions into the private sphere, from Straub/Huillet's self-conscious scrutiny of the narrative process to the straightforward commitment of *La Victoria*. The order in which these references appear provides a commentary as well on Wilhelm's growing awareness of the limits of his self-indulgent and apolitical behavior.

The script and film end in very different ways, the logical outcomes of two very different journeys. In the script, Wilhelm takes refuge in the snow on top of the *Zugspitze*. As a storm rages, we hear the superimposed sound of a typewriter getting louder and louder. Wilhelm in his solitude, the trip's manifest destiny, will now be able to write.[77] In the film's conclusion the youth enjoys no *Magic Mountain*-like sense of mystical enlightenment in the snow. He does not feel the ecstatic heights, the Olympian reserve of Caspar David Friedrich's "Wanderer above the Mists," a painting which the final shot ironically evokes. He is stuck, plain and simple, in a cul-de-sac, forced to draw the painful consequences: "It seemed to me as if I had missed out on something, and as if I were missing out on something with each new movement." No clacking typewriter provides a sign of hope. Wilhelm remains as unable as he was at the start to produce books. A weary soul faces the prospect of living out his fugitive life alone. Wenders, much more radically than Handke, questions the German tradition of self-cultivation in showing Wilhelm's passage through the FRG to be a series of false moves, for the would-be *Literat* fails to consider anything but his personal well-being and intellectual improvement. *Bildung,* as Hegel defined it, is "the apprenticeship, the education of the individual at the hands of the given reality."[78] Wenders's *Wrong Move* demonstrates the liabilities of a cultural tradition, one still at work today as a shaping force in artistic life, which fetishizes the Self at the expense of the Other, which ignores the object in the name of the subject, and which constantly combats challenges from the outside world only to find that there is no escaping from history.

Why Herbert Achternbusch Runs Amok

Fade into the beginning of *Der junge Mönch/The Young Monk* (1978): "A freshly destroyed landscape, a landscape that steams." A voice-over narrator (the director) comments:

> Like children
> The men in power ruled
> Like criminals
> They destroyed the world.[79]

"I've given up wanting to understand, comprehend, and analyze everything," Heinrich Böll once confessed. "The explosions of Achternbusch seems to me less private in nature than exemplary for an experience of life and the world which we older generations cannot fathom."[80] Herbert Achternbusch indeed bears much in common with contemporary emanations of anarchistic behavior, with the Frankfurt *Spontis,* the street activists in Zürich, the house-occupiers in West Berlin. Like these discontented youths, Achternbusch reacts out of fear and loathing, reeling from a sense that the world he lives in has a malign purpose. His films reflect this troubled experience: as a director (and writer) he seeks meaning but only finds confusion. He rides on the wings of fantasy but invariably crashes. Similar to the Swiss urban Indians or the Flörsheim hut-dwellers, Achternbusch likens himself to a Comanche, a renegade on the rampage, well aware of how hazardous it is to remain passive when on dangerous ground. The new generation of protestor does not appeal to the utopian ideals and theoretical rhetoric of the student movement. That is not to say, though, that this new activism lacks expression or direction. The aesthetics of the "no-future" protestors, maintains Adolf Muschg, "reveals itself in the totality of the means of expression, which are conceived as references to a full and intact existence. One 'occupies' the walls in which one dwells with images of one's own fears and desires."[81]

Achternbusch, a latter-day *Stürmer und Dränger,* fashioning works charged with hyperbole and verbal dynamism, a successor of the classical avant-garde who militates for the power of unbridled creativity and actively attacks the culture establishment, Achternbusch speaks for the angst and outrage experienced by unemployed and disfranchised *Teens und Twens.* House occupiers frequently wave placards bearing the writer's famous outcry: "You don't have a chance, but go ahead and try anyway!"[82] Greenland is the alternative, claims Achternbush,[83] a precursor of the Swiss youths who have renamed Zürich *Republik Grönland* and made the city the operating base for their continuing "battle against the pack ice."[84] Herbert Achternbusch, a paradigm for a new sensibility older generations have trouble understanding. Achternbusch, as Heiner Müller put it, "the classical representative of the anti-colonial resistance war in the occupied territory of the FRG."[85]

As a filmmaker, Achternbusch assumes an extreme position in his native cinema, at once a pessimist more virulent than the fatalistic Werner Herzog, and yet, still an indefatigable activist, a zany rebel running wild. He does not get sidetracked in the metaphysical dead-ends, in the inexorable circles that enclose and fetter Herzog's suffering heroes. Achternbusch's despair stems from the tangible facts of empirical existence, not from the whims of a cosmos where whirl is king. "This place has made a wreck of me," he rages, "and I'm going to stick around until people start noticing it."[86] His films overwhelm the viewer at times, but in these tantrums, provocations, and laments speak much more than simple self-indulgence, misanthropy, or the shrillness of unmediated subjectivity. A cinema of disenchantment fashioned by someone enchanted with the cinema, at once earnest about the oppressive quality of the everyday and yet resilient enough not to succumb to its numbing lack of humor, Achterbusch's films celebrate the power of creation despite all odds—which, for someone in the FRG making willfully independent films, can be considerable. These films await their rightful due in the United States, a country which for all its receptiveness to New German Cinema still remains quite unaware of some rougher—and more subversively lively—edges.

Achternbusch sees no split in his identity as filmmaker and writer. He envisions his entire output in all its variety as one single book, a larger work in progress. A complex set of cross-references, recurring situations, and persistent locales and personages lend the credibility of a microcosm to these efforts, at whose center the mythos-maker Herbert Achternbusch stands. Writing like filmmaking is for him self-stylization, personal hagiography, and yet more than mere egomania. Achternbusch does not only enact heroic postures; he also dramatizes the insecurity that lies behind the need for such self-glorification.[87] Literature and film issue from the author's unique experience. They reflect impotence at the hands of authority and visions of possibility as well, both harrowing nightmare and liberating dream. Realism for

Achternbusch means thinking with one's own head; not just *creating* but *asserting* one's vision.[88]

Reading Herbert Achternbusch, as one critic has noted, is like watching a mind at work, not in the process of sober reflection, but in the throes of vital necessities, of sweating and dreaming.[89] The author's experience flows before us, not in a continuous manner, but in leaps and bounds, jumps from present to past, switches from one perspective to another, shifts from diegesis to exegesis. A cinematic consciousness governs Achternbusch's writing and links it on the surface to that of Handke. The differences, though, demonstrate telling shifts of focus in otherwise cinemorphic worlds. The novel *The Left-Handed Woman* contains numerous discrete and careful descriptions. The narrative moves from one neatly-framed moment to another, sometimes via slight jerks, more typically though through continuity transitions. One finds little of Handke's still-life imagery in Achterbusch, however. Achternbusch's protagonists often stare into the distance, but quite unlike the window-gazing and street-strolling we find in Handke's Marianne. Image after image drifts by Handke's specular subjects, but they remain for the most unmoved, outside of the reality for which they paradoxically hunger. Achternbusch's personages never escape the concrete existents that circumscribe how they live; the locales they inhabit and the landscapes they tread persist throughout their most bizarre visions. One may dream in Achternbusch's films, but one always wakes up—and never very pleasantly. Handke's characters seek self-sufficiency. Achternbusch's characters cannot afford such detachment. They rarely are allowed to forget how dependent they are, no matter where they go. Society must be convoluted, maintains the author, because it constantly forces you to make up in thought what it fails to grant you in reality.[90]

Garish book jackets announce a world of desperate dreams and frantic hopes, ones echoed in high-strung titles. Achternbusch's stories betray the same jerkiness one finds in the films: one scene leaps to the next without any preparation or with only the vaguest binding links. Wisecracks interrupt the pathos of long monologues, nonsensical turns-of-phrase irreverently detract from story lines. Visuals coexist with printed pages; grainy black-and-white fotos with pithy captions accompany the prose accounts. Achternbusch's style: a blend of disparate textures, moods, and tonalities which intermingle and impart to his work a convincing integrity. "I always start with a simple story," he relates, "but I tell it so fantastically and wildly and tenderly and abusively and passionately and urgently that one finds a slice of life in front of them."[91] This variety of possibilities obtains equally in the filmic extensions of this prose.

Beer Battle (1977), more deliberately than any other Achternbusch-film to date, interweaves private obsession and public expression. The director's films entail both self-aggrandizement and self-destruction; visions of grandeur invariably end in suicide or murder. They dramatize the creator's inner life, but they never cease to stress the imposing reality that has shaped his anxieties, insecurities, and shortcomings. An inexorable social context frames each and every act: narrow Bavarian inns, order-giving institutions that stifle authentic existence (police, TV, church, schools), organizational structures that define how people interact in public and in private.

Beer Battle poignantly enacts Achternbusch's vendetta toward his homeland. With the raucous Munich *Oktoberfest* as a backdrop, Achternbusch invaded the beer tents and side-shows with a camera team on what he later described as "a kamikaze mission."[92] He did not reduce onlookers to local color, though, mere trappings for his own cinematic spectacle. He made those present an integral part of the event. Virtually every shot of the film contains an openness, a fluid sense that reality surrounds all sides of the frame and—in a number of ways—determines the goings-on within the image. At more than one point the director loses control of his film and takes flight from angry celebrants. For all the seeming *Gemütlichkeit* in the crowded beer halls, beneath that jolly facade lurks an undeniable amount of hostility and aggression, especially towards behavior that interrupts the drunken oblivion. *Beer Battle* blends a documentary account of the 1976 *Oktoberfest* with Achternbusch's self-stylized passion play. *Cinéma vérité*, happening, and psychodrama all at once, the film merges fiction and reality, demonstrating forcefully Achternbusch's obsessive cinema of disenchantment and its singular confrontation of the real and the reel.

A would-be policeman (played by Achternbusch, who often assumes the roles of his oppressors and fixations) wanders through the *Oktoberfest*, causing confusion and fomenting anger wherever he goes. In a series of three flashbacks we learn that the imposter—chagrined by a life that commands no respect, not even from his wife—has stolen the uniform he proudly flaunts. Two policemen onto the ruse disguise themselves in black-face and chase the culprit through the beer tents. Meanwhile, the unconvincing peace officer runs from one woman to another, seeking the succor denied him at home, while his wife dogs his steps. Finally seeing that his life has no meaning (even with a uniform), the distraught character swears he must take leave. He retreats off-frame and several moments later lies dead on the beer garden sawdust with friends, lovers, and pursuers standing over him.

Structurally, *Beer Battle* seems at first glance to be a series of loosely-connected tableaux, shot for the most from the front, highly gesticulatory in nature, scenes that abound in long takes, or when there is cutting, in abrupt changes of angle. The double pursuit by police and spouse imparts the semblance of story logic to otherwise coincidentally-ordered confrontations. Quite often the camera will linger on a person for a long while as he or she tells stories of woe or cracks a joke. For all these signs of arbitrariness, the film contains some distinct tightening devices, above all its narrative frame and rhythmically-spaced series of three flashbacks. It begins and ends with low-angle shots of the towering Bavaria-statue on the *Theresienwiese*. We open with signs of hope, partaking of the light of day and blue sky in the background. Not so the conclusion, though, where we look into the distance and see balloons drifting alongside the matriarch into the night sky. A title reinforces the narrative *cul-de-sac:* "And so it ends."

This dialectic between the discovered and the staged, between the arbitrary and the intentional, the discursive and the precise, likewise obtains on a formal level. Nearly every shot has an authentic background, yet for all its found qualities, the film remains highly composed. Even though we have moments where people are absent from the image (as one finds in Handke's cutaway still-lifes), such shots never suspend Achternbusch's narrative. We always sense that this is an inhabited world and that these objects and structures represent extensions of its denizens. Unavoidable signifiers of the Bavarian environment (brass bands, *Lederhosen,* pretzels, wind-up toys, liter mugs, *Hackerbräu,* dirndls) coexist with aspects of the cultural heritage underlined by the director (quotes from *Lohengrin,* hymns of praise to the Virgin Mary, folk songs, and naive paintings). Amateur actors from Achternbusch's stock company intermingle with a cast of thousands. *Beer Battle* is a film about how an environment shapes an individual, a person who in turn tries to shape his own image of it. We see Achternbusch at one point framed in front of a map of Lake Starnberg.

Later on, we glimpse him attempting to sketch the same body of water in a table top beer puddle.

Making reality into one's own film, i.e. shaping empirical existence into one's own representation, is not as simple as the dreamer first imagined. No world as image and imagination as with Handke—for the world has its own will; to represent it, one must accept its challenges. An extended hand-held take provides the high point, a *tour de force* through the beer-drinking crowd. In his script Achternbusch talks of the eight-minute shot, "this daring leap into the thick of things, into the mass, the attempts to deal with it from one table to the next, its anger and my ability as a policeman." Never, he claims, was he so alive, so physically present.[93] The director quickly found that his Groucho- and Harpo-like ploys (skulking down the lanes insulting people and jumping onto their laps, drinking from unoffered glasses of beer, absconding with food or bits of clothing) may bring laughter in the cinema, but in a humorless reality such shenanigans provoke ire, indeed move spectators to acts of violence. Fists fly, the punches are real. Angry bystanders jump into the film and run after Achternbusch, but this is no staged fiction. Chased out of a hall, the frightened figure cowers behind a door and then hides under a bench fearing further attacks. Like Werner Herzog, who once filmed an angry volcano, Achternbusch journeyed into an inferno. Unlike his colleague, though, he *did* experience an eruption, one he did not have to leave the city of his birth to find.

"We have to scream out loud, otherwise we'll find ourselves dead and buried."[94] Achternbusch's films demonstrate *Autorenkino* in its purest and most radical sense, for they present a world with its own distinctively disquieting character, one fashioned and experienced by an individual who writes scripts, plays the lead role, uses his friends and familiar landscapes as actors and locations, as well as directs, produces, and (in some cases) distributes the films. Unlike many of his more flexible and compliant colleagues, Achternbusch does not make arrangements. He has never enjoyed (even after some considerable public successes) a particularly comfortable relation with film subsidy boards and television networks. He refuses to accept circulating notions of realism or conform to what committees consider viable. The most difficult thing about the everyday, he argues, is coming out of it unravaged.

At a time when numerous West German directors plan their next international coproduction or another multi-million mark project, Achternbush represents an anachronism. Twenty years after the Oberhausen Manifesto, he still makes gritty, low-budget films, ones marked by a willful outrageousness and anarchistic idiosyncracy. His work harkens back to early Young German productions like Franz Josef Spieker's *Wilder Reiter GmbH./Wild Rider, Inc.* (1966), or more to the point, to Vlado Kristl's *Der Brief/The Letter* (1966) and *Film oder Macht/ Film or Power* (1970). Among all the directors working in the FRG today, Achternbush most emphatically aligns himself with Sohrab Shahid Saless, an Iranian exile living in West Berlin, an outsider who makes sensitive films about what it is like to be a stranger in a hostile foreign country.[95] Kluge, one of the few directors who has not forsaken the ideals of Oberhausen, evokes Achternbusch's deepest admiration. A film like *Die Patriotin/The Patriot* shows that "dreams need not be an ersatz for an unfinished reality. Reuniting these realms is a task for the individual."[96] Clearly this notion is central to Achternbusch's cinema. Refusing to take seriously the thought garbage *(Denkschütt)* that clutters the air he breathes, fighting against images that sand off reality's rough edges, denigrate minds, tell lies, and ruin lives, Achternbusch does not allow himself to become coopted as yet another eccentric who sings striking tales of woe and alienation.

Consciously outlandish, Achternbusch will not settle down. Despite contemporary culture's relentlessly assimilative ploys, its way of making pleasing entertainments out of the most avant-garde challenges, Achternbusch stands firm.[97] Resisting easy veneration and facile cubby-holing, Achternbush remains West Germany's most direct filmmaker, an anarchist whose art knows no distinction between public and private, an activist who better than anyone else has articulated the new aesthetics of the grand refusal, and has dramatized a malaise felt by a large number of frightened and angry people living in West Germany today.

Fade out to a title taken from Achternbusch's *Die Stunde des Todes/The Hour of Death:*

> A human being is stronger than a dying river.
> A human being overcomes the concrete infernos.
> A human being observes the remains of the industrial insect.
> A human being has left gluttony behind him.
> A human being has found the mountain of his confidence.
> A human being has accepted his chances for survival.[98]

NOTES

Portions of the section on Herbert Achternbusch appear in a longer career appreciation in *New German Filmmakers: From Oberhausen through the 1970s,* ed. Klaus Phillips (New York: Ungar, 1984).

[1] Rudi Dutschke and others, *Rebellion der Studenten oder Die neue Opposition* (Hamburg: Rowohlt, 1968), p. 69.

[2] Alexander Kluge, *Die Patriotin* (Frankfurt: Zweitausendeins, 1979), p. 28.

[3] Peter Gambaccini, "The New German Film Makers," *Horizon,* June 1980, p. 22.

[4] Diane Jacobs, "Hitler's Ungrateful Grandchildren: Today's German Filmmakers," *American Film,* May 1980, p. 34.

[5] Cf. Sheila Johnston's discussion, "The Author as Public Institution: The 'New' Cinema in the Federal Republic of Germany," *Screen Education,* Nos. 32/33 (Autumn/Winter 1979/80), esp. p. 67.

[6] Rob Baker, " 'New German Cinema': A Fistful of Myths," *Soho Weekly News,* 23 March 1978, p. 22.

[7] "From Caligari to *Hitler,*" *Film Comment,* July–August 1980, p. 60.

[8] Ibid., p. 70.

[9] A few examples among many others: "In *Not Reconciled,* Straub [sic] touches on a prodigious theme: the machinations of German architects since 1945" (p. 60). In fact much of the film's action takes place prior to 1945; it depicts three generations of architects. Straub/Huillet's *Othon* was made in 1969, not 1979 (p. 61). The elevated railway one sees in Wenders's *Alice in the Cities* is in Wuppertal, not Amsterdam (p. 62). *Alice* was not "Wenders' exam film" (p. 62); *Summer in the City* was. Durgnat claims that "the Seventies saw a synchronization of the Germanic ego (reliberating itself as Adenauerean, cold-war pressures relaxed) with American individualism" (p. 63), but at best leaves it at such cultural clichés without delving into the specifics of the epoch. The specter, he argues, "that stalks Adenauer's Germany is not just Hitler's but Bismarck's" (p. 63). The point could be debated—but Durgnat is discussing films made much later during *Brandt's* and *Schmidt's* chancellorships!

[10] Durgnat, p. 65.

[11] See, for instance, Hans Günther Pflaum and Hans Helmut Prinzler's summary appraisal in *Film in der Bundesrepublik Deutschland* (Munich: Hanser, 1979), p. 68.

[12] Klaus Eder, "Der Glaube ans grosse Geld: Über einen industriellen Ästhetizismus," *Jahrbuch Film 79/80,* ed. Hans Günther Pflaum (Munich: Hanser, 1979), p. 103. See also Hans C. Blumenberg, "Im Tal der toten Augen: Eine Passage durch neue Filme aus Deutschland," *Die Zeit,* 24 April 1981.

[13] Russell Berman, "Opposition to Rearmament and West German Culture," *Telos,* Spring 1982, p. 144.

[14] Marcel Reich-Ranicki of the *Frankfurter Allgemeine Zeitung,* quoted in Hans-Gerhard Winter, "Von der Dokumentarliteratur zur 'neuen Subjektivität': Anmerkungen zur westdeutschen Literatur der siebziger Jahre," *Seminar,* May 1981, p. 95.

[15] See Delf Schmidt, "Gegen die Placebo-Literatur: Eine Vorbemerkung," in *Literaturmagazin 11: Schreiben oder Literatur,* ed. Nicolas Born, Jürgen Manthey, and Delf Schmidt (Hamburg: Rowohlt, 1979), p. 15.

[16] *Den Kopf verkehrt aufgesetzt oder Die melancholische Linke: Aspekte des Kulturzerfalls in den siebziger Jahren* (Darmstadt/Neuwied: Luchterhand, 1981), p. 256.

[17] Ibid., p. 257.

[18] Ibid., p. 144.

[19] *Erfahrungshunger: Ein Essay über die siebziger Jahre* (Frankfurt: Fischer, 1982), p. 25.

[20] Ibid., p. 43.

[21] Berman, p. 143.

[22] Rutschky, p. 41.

[23] Ibid., p. 57.

[24] Cf. Heinz-B. Heller, "Literatur in der Bundesrepublik: Literatur im Zeichen der Rezession, Neuen Linken und 'Tendenzwende,'" in *Sozialgeschichte der deutschen Literatur von 1918 bis zur Gegenwart* (Frankfurt: Fischer, 1981), pp. 646-48.

[25] Rutschky, p. 64.

[26] Handke, although an Austrian citizen and not without his ties to the national literature of his homeland, accords as well to developments generally associated with literary life in the FRG.

[27] Cf. the programmatic title of the collection of his early essays: *Ich bin ein Bewohner des Elfenbeinturms/I Am an Inhabitant of the Ivory Tower.*

[28] "Die Tyrannei der Systeme," *Die Zeit,* 9 Jan. 1976.

[29] See, for instance, Handke's violent response to an attempt to cubbyhole him, in "'Und plötzlich wird das Paar wieder denkbar': *Spiegel*-Interview mit dem Schriftsteller Peter Handke über Gefahren und Chancen des Alleinlebens," *Spiegel,* 10 July 1978, p. 140.

[30] "'Es soll mythisch sein, mythisch!': *Spiegel*-Redakteur Siegfried Schober über Peter Handke bei der Verfilmung seiner *Linkshändigen Frau*," *Spiegel,* 2 May 1977, p. 177ff.

[31] The term comes from Stephen Dwoskin, who used it to describe his films. See "Dwoskin Speaks," *On Film,* Winter 1978-9, p. 8. Ruth Perlmutter applies the term to *The Left-Handed Woman* in "Visible Narrative, Visible Woman," *Millennium Film Journal,* No. 6 (1980), p. 19.

[32] *Two Novels by Peter Handke,* trans. Ralph Manheim (New York: Avon, 1979), p. 102.

[33] *Das Gewicht der Welt* (Frankfurt: Suhrkamp, 1979), p. 232. See also Handke's recent collection of essays, *Das Ende des Flanierens* (Frankfurt: Suhrkamp, 1980), esp. pp. 93-97.

[34] *Das Gewicht der Welt,* p. 31.

[35] Perlmutter, p. 19.

[36] In this light a feminist spectator of the film might justifiably restate a question Handke poses in *Das Gewicht der Welt* (p. 18): "She sees a film made by a man about a woman and wonders: 'What does he think he's doing anyway?'"

[37] See the comments in the *Spiegel*-interview cited in note 29.

³⁸ Wenders reputedly introduced Handke to the films of Ozu.
³⁹ *To the Distant Observer: Form and Meaning in the Japanese Cinema,* rev. and ed. Annette Michelsen (Berkeley/Los Angeles: Univ. of Calif. Press, 1979), p. 162.
⁴⁰ See Roman Ritter, "Die 'Neue Innerlichkeit' —von innen und aussen betrachtet, *Kontext 1* (1976), pp. 245ff. See also Uwe Timm, "Über den Dogmatismus in der Literatur" in the same volume, pp. 25ff.
⁴¹ See Perlmutter, p. 19.
⁴² Adorno, "On Kierkegaard's Doctrine of Love," *Studies in Philosophy and Social Science,* Vol. 8, No. 3 (1939-40), p. 423.
⁴³ *Kierkegaard: Konstruktion des Aesthetischen,* 3rd rev. ed. (Frankfurt: Suhrkamp, 1966), p. 82. For a cogent summary and analysis of the difficult text, see Susan Buck-Morss, *The Origin of Negative Dialectics: Theodor W. Adorno, Walter Benjamin, and the Frankfurt Institute* (New York: Free Press, 1977), pp. 114-21.
⁴⁴ Rutschky, p. 77.
⁴⁵ Ibid., p. 70.
⁴⁶ "The Work of Art in the Age of Mechanical Reproduction," in *Illuminations,* ed. Hannah Arendt (New York: Schocken, 1969), p. 222.
⁴⁷ "On Some Motifs in Baudelaire," *Illuminations,* p. 175.
⁴⁸ Ibid.
⁴⁹ *Two Novels by Peter Handke,* p. 130.
⁵⁰ *Kierkegaard,* p. 63.
⁵¹ *Die Atlantikschwimmer* (Frankfurt: Suhrkamp, 1978), p. 119.
⁵² See Rutschky, pp. 150ff.
⁵³ See the section "Hunger for Life" in *Theory of Film: The Redemption of Physical Reality* (London/Oxford/New York: Oxford Univ. Press, 1960), pp. 167ff. Cf. Rutschky's lengthy discussion of Kracauer and the applicability of his theory of film to the seventies, pp. 187ff.
⁵⁴ Kracauer, p. x and p. 169.
⁵⁵ Ibid., p. 171.
⁵⁶ Their joint efforts have resulted in *Die Angst des Tormanns beim Elfmeter/The Goalie's Anxiety at the Penalty Kick* (1971) and *Falsche Bewegung/Wrong Move* (1974). *Alice in den Städten/Alice in the Cities* (1973) has many points in common with Handke's roughly contemporaneous novel *Der kurze Brief zum langen Abschied/The Short Letter to the Long Goodbye* (1972). (The book was adapted for TV by Herbert Vesely in 1977.) During the summer of 1982, Wenders directed a production of Handke's *Über die Dörfer/Over the Villages* in Salzburg. Although Wenders finished a script based on Handke's novel, *Langsame Heimkehr/The Slow Return Home* (1979), he was denied subsidy and television funding for the project and was forced to drop it.
⁵⁷ See Jan Dawson, *Wim Wenders* (Toronto: Festival of Festivals, 1976), p. 19.
⁵⁸ See Wolfram Schütte, *"Falsche Bewegung:* Wim Wenders neuer Film nach Peter Handkes Drehbuch," *Neue Zürcher Zeitung,* 18 April 1975. I am grateful to Wolfgang Längsfeld for numerous insights about *Sensibilismus.*
⁵⁹ Cf. Dawson, p. 23, where Wenders says: "There's a quotation I have

pinned on my wall: it's one of the few theoretical things about film-making that I can accept completely: 'Die Möglichkeit und der Sinn der Filmkunst liegen darin, dass jedwedes Wesen so aussieht, wie es ist' ('The possibility and the meaning of the film art lie in the fact that every being is just the way that it appears to be')."

[60] "Wenders in Wanderland," *Village Voice,* 13 Nov. 1978, p. 78.

[61] "Screen: Wenders's *The Wrong Move* [sic]," *New York Times,* 25 Jan. 1980.

[62] Martin Swales, *The German Bildungsroman from Wieland to Hesse* (Princeton: Princeton Univ. Press, 1978), p. 151.

[63] Dawson, p. 4. Handke as a rule has desisted from trying to influence the final visual shape Wenders has given to his scripts. As Wenders said at the 1978 Athens Film Festival in Athens, Ohio, his successful collaborations with Handke derive to a great extent from Handke's ability to leave the director alone during the actual filmmaking process.

[64] *Falsche Bewegung* (Frankfurt: Suhrkamp, 1975).

[65] Cf. *Falsche Bewegung,* pp. 8-9.

[66] Cf. Swales, pp. 32-33: *Bildungsromane* "suggest that there is an inalienable need in man to have a story, to know himself as part of that linear flow of experience which cannot be halted at will. For it is the story which binds together contingencies into the weighty sequence of a human destiny."

[67] *Falsche Bewegung,* p. 15. Wilhelm says: "Soest in Westphalia, right away I smell fresh bread and hear bells ringing between panelled houses."

[68] The phrase is used by Donald Richie in a discussion of Ozu's films, ones much respected by Wenders. *Ozu* (Berkeley/Los Angeles/London: Univ. of Calif. Press, 1974), p. 165.

[69] Dawson, p. 22.

[70] See *Falsche Bewegung,* p. 28, where Wilhelm says to the old man: "...I don't want to know about anything from before. I have no feeling for the past." Cf. Christopher Lasch, *The Culture of Narcissism* (New York: Norton, 1979), p. 26: "A denial of the past, superficially progressive and optimistic, proves on closer analysis to embody the despair of a society that cannot face the future."

[71] See the *Spiegel*-interview cited in note 29.

[72] Dawson, p. 24.

[73] *Falsche Bewegung,* p. 37.

[74] The Spanish title is *El ataque de los muertos sin ojos.* The film was directed by Amando Ossori.

[75] The Handke script calls for them at that point to watch Carl Dreyer's *La Passion de Jeanne d'Arc* (p. 70).

[76] The *Stern* is a cinema that has been partitioned into two screens, a tendency particularly typical of urban exhibitors not only in the FRG during the last decade.

[77] *Falsche Bewegung,* p. 81.

[78] Quoted in Swales, p. 20.

[79] *Die Atlantikschwimmer,* p. 359.

[80] "Alltag einer zerfetzten Welt: Über *Der Tag wird kommen,*" in *Herbert Achternbusch,* ed. Jörg Drews (Frankfurt: Suhrkamp, 1982), p. 75.

[81] "Kampf gegen das Packeis," *Spiegel*, 31 Aug. 1981, p. 183.
[82] *Die Atlantikschwimmer*, p. 199.
[83] Ibid., p. 303: "In Greenland there is a lot more ice," he tells a German TV journalist in *Servus Bayern/Bye Bye, Bavaria* (1977), "but not as much as we have."
[84] See Reto Hänny, *Zürich, Anfang September* (Frankfurt: Suhrkamp, 1981).
[85] Quoted in Achternbusch's essay, "Die Autobahn in den Gehirnen," *Die Zeit*, 28 Feb. 1981.
[86] *Die Atlantikschwimmer*, p. 304.
[87] Benjamin Heinrichs, "Herbert Achternbusch: *Die Stunde des Todes*-Beschreibung eines unbeschreiblichen Buches," *Die Zeit*, 21 March 1975.
[88] *Es ist ein leichtes beim Gehen den Boden zu berühren* (Frankfurt: Suhrkamp, 1980), p. 151.
[89] Benjamin Heinrichs, "Der Kopf ist ein Abgrund. *Der Tag wird kommen:* Herbert Achternbuschs sechstes Buch," *Die Zeit*, 12 Oct. 1973.
[90] *Die Atlantikschwimmer*, p. 260.
[91] Ibid., p. 265.
[92] Ibid., p. 8.
[93] Ibid., p. 293.
[94] Ibid., p. 246.
[95] *Es ist ein leichtes*, p. 146.
[96] Ibid., p. 152.
[97] Cf. Irving Howe, *Literary Modernism* (Greenwich, Conn: Fawcett, 1967), p. 24.
[98] *Die Atlantikschwimmer*, p. 173.

Epilogue

Life with Fassbinder: The Politics of Fear and Pain

> *"When RWF described to me his plans for a novel, I encouraged him. Fassbinder's working title was* Journey into the Interior of the Soul *or* Journey into the Interior of Fear. . . . *The novel, by the way, was never written.*
> *It was supposed to have been written in Paris. Then in New York. . . . The journey into the interior of soul-fear was not to be embarked upon in words."*
> —Gerhard Zwerenz[1]

Private Psychodrama or Public Passion Play?

Shameless exhibitionism that goes so far as to make bodily and emotional disfunctions into objects of spectacle[2]; narcissism raised to and transformed into "a higher form of political commitment"[3]; or, the recording of private fears evoked by a public crisis as a historical document[4]; or, still another possibility, a carefully-staged fiction, scripted, composed, and choreographed, meant less as a self-portrait of its director/lead role than as an enactment of the predicament experienced by many West German intellectuals in the late seventies.[5] These are some of the ways previous commentators have understood the Fassbinder-sequence in *Deutschland im Herbst/Germany in Autumn*

(1978). For all the dissonance in this international chorus, a common refrain can be heard: the scene is crucial to the entire omnibus film. The 26-minute passage functions as the pivotal center upon which the success or failure of the collective enterprise rests. In light of Fassbinder's recent death, I think one can go even a step further. The Fassbinder-sequence, in its singular merger of documentary confession and fictional self-stylization, represents West German film's most provocative variation on the theme of the problematic *and* problematized subject, a preoccupation that in hindsight more and more looks like *the* central obsession of intellectuals living in the FRG during the seventies.

Of all the various contributions to *Germany in Autumn,* Fassbinder's stands out by dint of its length, its position at the start of the film after a short prologue, but most importantly by virtue of its apparent ambiguity. It is at once extremely accessible and yet highly irritating in its rawness; it is apparently forthright, but in a way somehow elusive. "Is Fassbinder still Fassbinder," one critic wondered, "when he plays the lead role in a film about himself?"[6] On the one hand a documentary account of several excruciating days spent during October 1977 in the claustrophobic and sparse confines of the director's Munich apartment: *cinéma vérité* replete with grainy textures, long takes, and original sound. On the other, a film whose careful framing, subtle high-contrast lighting, and deep-focus compositions leave the viewer dubious as to how much—if anything—was left to coincidence, an intimation confirmed by the discovery that Michael Ballhaus, Fassbinder's cinematographer in many of his most stylized efforts, provided the camera work. (Likewise, the mother's smirk after her call for "an authoritarian ruler who is very good and very nice and orderly" suggests these lines came from a script and not the heat of a spontaneous conversation.)

Forefronting the subject in an environment hostile to public expressions of subjectivity, Fassbinder joined a group of similarly daunted filmmakers to react collectively. Troubled by the state of emergency, shellshocked from the colliding stimuli bursting forth dramatically out of the arsenal of a long repressed and still burdensome past,[7] Fassbinder and his cohorts realized that they, as participants in the German autumn, could not assume a perspective outside of the goings-on. "We are not," they emphatically declared, "the Supreme Court of History."[8] Viewing themselves as a multitude of voices which for the most had been denied a public forum during the fall's media blackouts, the gathering of filmmakers framed their project as instant history, a seizing hold of memories as they flashed by in a catastrophic moment in time.⁹ Placed strategically at the film's beginning, the Fassbinder-sequence assumes a crucial function: it dramatizes the paralysis of the human subject in a film that only came about because a collection of equally stunned subjects joined forces and responded collectively.

Despite the passage's apparent narrative integrity and self-enclosure, the sequence entertains a vital relation to the film's other parts, a nexus noted by many commentators in West Germany, but one for the most oversimplified or underdeveloped. The passage serves a contrapuntal function; it enacts the collective's worst fears, showing a subject so overwhelmed that he cannot actively respond, a reaction shared neither by the director Fassbinder who *did* produce the film, not by his colleagues, nor by *Germany in Autumn* as a whole. We return to the interrelated complex of crises discussed in chapter six, the dilemmas that confronted progressive cultural producers in the FRG during the turbulent decade, i.e. tne melancholic left, the collapse of collectivity, and the presentiment of terrorism. The seeming impasses posed by the Fassbinder scene—even more radically than in previously mentioned examples of what others have cast off as the "New Subjectivity"—are resolved, indeed sublated in the wider framework of *Germany in Autumn*.

Melancholy Becomes Mourning

Seen in isolation, the Fassbinder-sequence could be said to dramatize the deformation of self and environment, to portray the melancholic left so often lamented about in the seventies. Plugged into the world by only a phone, staggering through a grimly furnished and eternally dark apartment, Fassbinder appears inert, distraught, and afflicted. West German film's most conspicuous and controversy-loving public presence has retreated to an anchoritic existence. Like Walter Benjamin's "urban individual," he insulates himself by sealing his life off from reality. In the manner of Peter Handke he takes flight into the *Innenwelt*. (The film's first shot quite poignantly witnesses the concerned figure trying to take back statements made in an interview.) Only once does the camera focus on the world outside of the flat as Fassbinder gazes fearfully onto the nocturnal streets of Munich. The *Aussenwelt* only poses a threat. Public events overwhelm the bystander, official explanations of the Stammheim suicides stagger the imagination, police footsteps on the stairs cause panic, and the entire situation impresses on the individual his ultimate impotence. "What I think or don't think," Fassbinder says to Ingrid Caven on the phone, "doesn't make a bit of difference." Shutters remain closed and Fassbinder will not leave the refuge: "I'm afraid. I feel I can't get away."

The director, whose major project would become a psychological history of the Federal Republic, a constant commentator on the dent made by public institutions on private hopes, assumes a much more constrained view, that of a narcissist, someone who reduces the world to a private microcosm and who forces its inhabitants to heed his dictates. Arnim—who appears in the film's initial shot as an extension jutting out of the director's back—takes on the role of a servant subject to Fassbinder's every whim and frequent fits of pique.[10] At one point Arnim's hand enters the frame and clears off a glass: the lover is reduced visually to a function, a convenience. ("He only bosses me around," protests Arnim, whose pet name for RWF is appropriately "Bully.") Just as he uses the public forum to disclose tawdry aspects of his private interactions,[11] something a good number of critics deemed as problematic, so does Fassbinder allow us less than attractive glances at his face. The camera lingers at two junctures on reflections of the director, once after he has vomited and stares at his disheveled self, and later, while he lays out lines of cocaine and gazes down onto a pocket mirror. Fassbinder, frenzied and caught up in his own misery, demonstrates to a tee all the symptoms Freud associated with the melancholy individual:

> ...A profoundly painful dejection, abrogation of interest in the outside world, loss of the capacity to love, inhibition of all activity, and a lowering of the self-regarding feelings to a degree that finds utterance in self-reproaches and self-revilings, and culminates in a delusional expectation of punishment.[12]

Viewed within the larger context of *Germany in Autumn*, Fassbinder's inability to respond to the events transpiring outside his flat with anything but violent and self-destructive behavior represents the first reaction within a patterned series of other alternatives, including

—Gabi Teichert's active inquiries: she treks outdoors in search of the essence of German history. She wants to see things in their perspective, to discover a *Zusammenhang;*

—Franziska Busch's eager work for a politically-engaged media group, even if she in private "belongs to" (a less than felicitous turn of phrase in the sequence) a TV editor. She partakes of an interview with Horst Mahler, seeking an explanation for the collapse of the German left; and

—Mahler's own theoretical articulation of the crisis points in the development of a progressive opposition in the FRG. The space from which he speaks is—like Fassbinder's—a confined one. But light permeates the room, books line the shelves, and Mahler speaks with quiet and confident gestures. The camera will rise at the end of the sequence to an open window and the light of day, one framed though by prison bars.

As an explicit antithesis to Fassbinder's torpor, the film concludes with a scene in the Dornhalden cemetary which dramatizes not melancholy, but rather the difficulty of mourning. Masked faces replace Fassbinder's naked body, balled fists in the funeral crowd provide a defiance the director's idly masturbating hand does not, and the omnipresent police surveillance forces take over for a self-indulging camera. Public manifestations of sadness under these impossible conditions supersede the filmmaker's private bathos. The final scene incorporates the vulnerable, consternated, and yet still contrary reactions of the mourners not simply as emotional responses, but as the initial expressions of a not-yet operative public sphere in search of appropriate and effective ways to channel its feelings, as one West German critic put it, "Powerlessness as the reaction of a still-silent counter-public sphere trying to articulate itself while it continues to gather experience."[13] *Germany in Autumn* recorded and simultaneously provided the first larger attempt to gain a forum for the disfranchised group of young West Germans, leftist patriots without a *Heimat*.

Autorenkino and Cooperative Cinema: Same Difference

Cooperative cinema *(Kooperationskino)*, one of Kluge's pet notions, was an often-hoped-for and rarely realized ideal of the Young German filmmakers. In 1969, Volker Schlöndorff, Werner Herzog, and Peter Fleischmann, among others, spoke of a long-range project bearing the title *Über Deutschland/About Germany*. Over a number of years, the directors planned to make roughly 100 short and medium-length documentaries.

Monographs of individual events, groups, or persons which would allow us to draw conclusions about the circumstances in which we live.... These films should be undertaken with the clear intention to develop a readily identifiable national style of documentary filmmaking.[14]

Despite such initiatives and Kluge's persistent attempts, *Kooperationskino* remained by and large an undeveloped aspiration.

Fassbinder, the most self-sufficient and resilient of the West German *auteurs*, brought distinct associations with him to *Germany in Autumn*. Most of the audience knew well of his infamous stint with the Frankfurt *Theater am Turm* during the mid-seventies, the way in which his ensemble structured along lines of co-determination had crumbled under his authoritarian leadership. Much media attention had focussed on Fassbinder's falling-outs with former collaborators, on the way his putative socialist ideals were belied by patriarchal working methods.[15] We see the director renowned for his exploitation of actors on the set demonstrating the same ruthlessness in private with his mother and lover. The few shots of the director at work index a creator hardly wont to collective pursuit: we watch him spotlighted in the dark, dictating the script of *Berlin Alexanderplatz* into a cassette recorder. Repeatedly during the sequence we cut to a discussion between Fassbinder and his mother about the possibilities of democratic behavior within the FRG. Shrieking when his interlocutor fails to answer questions directly, gesticulating wildly, and frequently interrupting, Fassbinder replicates the closedness of the dominant forms of public discourse at the time; his intolerance and brutal dismissal of other viewpoints manifest the same intransigence which moved the state to invoke a *Gleichschaltung* in the media coverage of the events surrounding the abduction of Hanns-Martin Schleyer. Fassbinder's denial of dialogue (one argument with Arnim ends in fact with the director slamming his lover to the ground and throwing him out of their apartment), if anything, shows how even silenced leftist subjects had internalized the public inability to promote a free-flowing discourse in the everyday.

Germany in Autumn as a whole, though, provided more than a momentary alternative to the institutionalized self-serving directors like Fassbinder knew well. Clear connections to subsequent joint ventures like *Der Kandidat/The Candidate* (1980) and *Krieg und Frieden/War and Peace* (1983) indicate the continuing appeal of the collective production model, as does the recent film of a Berlin feminist collective, *Aus heiterem Himmel/Out of the Blue*.[16] Likewise, the solidarity manifested in the 1978 constellation, for all the divergent viewpoints,[17] has led to the formation of more effective group strategies. An alliance of short *Autorenfilme* (after all, the form with which the Oberhausen activists had started), *Germany in Autumn* merged single contributions within a larger framework, a framework conferred about and voted upon by the participants. The lesson: *Autorenkino* and *Kooperationskino* need not represent contradictory conceptions.

Taken by itself, Fassbinder's contribution, the product of a recognized *auteur,* readily invites confusion. Given its three-fold inscription (Fassbinder simultaneously functioning as filmmaker, actor, and character), the scene befuddles the viewer trying to pin down the ultimate enunciating subject, the overall point of view. (Is Fassbinder simply portraying himself, giving us an intentionally critical look at his life, or just playing a role?) But placed within the context of *Germany in Autumn,* the short film provokes the spectator to try and understand the sequence in inter-textual terms—as Gabi Teichert would say: in its *Zusammenhang*—not simply as the vision of an *auteur* who has made a large number of films with their stylistic and thematic continuity, but as one part of a larger vision, as one voice in a more encompassing discussion. Could this undercutting of auteurist appropriation be the reason why this film has enjoyed such a relatively lukewarm reception in the United States, why it does not entertain the cult status of many other Fassbinder titles, why American enthusiasts so rarely mention the film in their discussions of the director's canon?

The cooperative framework moves one to identify the Fassbinder-sequence as a particular enunciation (however complex and many-faceted) within a meta-discourse, one whose breaks, sequential leaps, associative montage, and contrapuntal tonalities invite the viewer *not* to perceive it as "history" in the Metzian sense, i.e. as a chronicle of completed events resting "upon a denial that anything is absent or that anything has to be searched for."[18] The viewer is forced to consider the scene as an integral but hardly definitive part of a larger text, one whose indeterminacy encourages—demands—audience participation. What Kluge once said about another cooperative undertaking applies here: "Instead of statements the film generates relationships.... Only the bogus public sphere [*Scheinöffentlichkeit*] forms an order or unity..."[19] Fighting the closed character of the inauthentic (but very powerful) existing public sphere, *Germany in Autumn* includes the audience as an interlocutor in a larger discussion of how one can deal with an unordered reality and the heterogeneity of experience, remonstrating the spectator—as Benjamin once wrote—to "wrest tradition away from a conformism" that threatens to suppress and conceal the present moment's connection to and dependence on the past,[20] a past not simply given, but one we know only through the mediation of human subjects.

Body Politics and the Discourse of Terrorism

In a number of ways, the Fassbinder-sequence replicates the body politics *(Körperpolitik)* of fear and pain.[21] Hiding out in his apartment as if he were a fugitive, fearing the police have bugged his phone ("Go ahead and listen," he says at one point to an imagined microphone) or will invade his flat, the battered victim of two years of public vilification, the director who was called a "left-wing fascist" in the *Frankfurter Allgemeine Zeitung* and repeatedly denounced as an anti-Semite, Fassbinder shows considerable indications of battle fatigue. He constantly rubs his aching head, breathes deeply, bursts into tears, and consumes drugs and alcohol to numb his anguish.

In a long take we watch Fassbinder talking on the phone with his ex-wife, framed in a medium close-up. He has just risen from bed and is still undressed. "They're dead," he mutters, "Baader, Ensslin, and Raspe." He describes the "suicides," chugging a brandy Arnim brings him. As the camera zooms back to a medium shot, we see Fassbinder still talking, gently masturbating while he queries whether the trio really killed themselves. The body shrouded in dark and shadow (with only a suggestion of light from open windows through the kitchen doorway in the background) lingers before the camera in all its corpulence, replacing *Sinn* with *Sinnlichkeit,* i.e. meaning with sensuality,[22] the sensuality of fear and pain, reactions etched into the unbearably long take. In a subsequent scene Fassbinder emerges from the toilet where we have watched him bent over retching; he turns to Arnim (and the spectator) and asks "What're you looking at?" In self-consciously offering himself as an object of spectacle, Fassbinder, in the manner of the exponents of *Körperpolitik,* overdetermines his body as a form of inscription, presenting it as a

—*commodity:* audiences are allowed a voyeuristic look at the private life of a recognized public figure;

—*weapon:* the body becomes an instrument of dominance and submission;

—*narcissistic surface:* the body as site of self-stylization[23] and object of mirror images;

—*potential corpse:* the kaput and lonely figure on the apartment floor serves as a haunting foreshadowing of the individual found dead early in the morning of June 10, 1982 in another Munich flat, a body that would become every bit as much the scene of public necrophilia and media ravaging as the remains of terrorists which one sees in a later sequence of *Germany in Autumn*.

Fassbinder's appearance in the omnibus-film stands in marked contrast to the less conspicuous presence of other representative leftist figures in the film: the decidedly unsensual and highly cerebral Horst Mahler, the relatively subdued performance of Wolf Biermann in a TV studio, and the almost lacking physical presence of Alexander Kluge, a filmmaker whose voice continually provides off-screen commentaries, whose editing very much determined the ultimate shape of the entire project,[24] but a person whom we only fleetingly glimpse amidst a group walking in long-shot. "Words are also good, Gottlieb, and what is said," Fassbinder at one point reads out of *Berlin Alexanderplatz*, a novel for whose words the director seeks to find adequate images. The impact of the sequence in the apartment, though, remains primarily one imparted by pictures of the filmmaker's body, images that—judging by the attention focussed on the scene in the West German press[25]—seem to have made a more lastingly tangible impression than the different rhetorical strategies pursued in other portions of the film: Mahler's lengthy monologue, Biermann's song and poem, Kluge's quotations and associative montage, Schlöndorff/Böll's insights into violence and public broadcasters, among others. "The truth of mortal beings," Fassbinder once said, "can only be captured in reflections."[26] Looking at the 50-some shots that constitute his contribution to *Germany in Autumn* in the wake of his recent death, one cannot help but see in these reflections West German film's definitive variation on the theme of the problematic (within the short scene) and problematized (in the context of the larger film) subject. It is a portrayal bound in the private turmoil of the FRG's most well-known advocate of the subjective factor, a performance inscribed by body politics speaking the language of fear and pain, a discursive practice quite prevalent in that country during the 1970s.

The Subjective Factor in the Course of Time

Within West German film history, the increasing recourse of certain directors—quite often ones not recognized outside of the FRG—to a discourse that presents the hopes of the subject while dwelling on its limits, this discourse issues as a response to the continuing awareness of the dangers posed by an impersonal cinema that serves larger causes, be it a cinema that actively supported a fascist regime as was the case during the Third Reich, or be it a cinema that legitimated a conservative *status quo,* helping to reaffirm the condition of comatose passivity found during the Adenauer era. Within the postwar context, this subjective strain of cinema stems from a double awareness of just how limited the possibilities are for changing the fatal socio-political constellations vested in modern German history—and, nonetheless, the awareness of how necessary such efforts are if one is to prevent future disasters. Tradition, and this applies some 40 years after Benjamin wrote his "Theses on the Philosophy of History," still continues to impress upon the subject the lesson "that the 'state of emergency' in which we live is not the exception but the rule."[27]

Much of West German film is predicated upon this insight, the feeling that in the speeding express train of time, one must pull the emergency brake. The particular urgency expressed by works like *Germany in Autumn,* Kluge's *Die Patriotin,* Herbert Achternbusch's *Das letzte Loch/The Last Hole,* Helke Sander's *Der subjektive Faktor/The Subjective Factor,* and parts of Werner Schroeter's *Die Generalprobe/The Dress Rehearsal,* among many other decidedly personal films that have come out of the FRG in the last half-decade, lies precisely in their desire on the one hand to mediate subjective experience within a historical framework and the relentless awareness on the other hand of the hindrances the human subject has encountered in its attempts to constitute itself as such during the course of recent German history. "It's somehow striking," the directors of *Germany in Autumn* wrote in a variation on Adorno,

> tools of torture are industrial products of modern society; but the protest against these tools of torture—in the form of imagination, memory, 'revenge'—still remains human products. In this way an apparent imbalance holds sway: the overwhelming presence of the world of facts, the impotence of humans in the face of it. But the point is not to let this apparent state of affairs fool us.[28]

NOTES

A slightly different version of this essay appears as "Life with Fassbinder: The Politics of Fear and Pain," in *Discourse*, No. 6 (Fall 1983), pp. 75-90.

[1] *Der langsame Tod des Rainer Werner Fassbinder: Ein Bericht* (Munich: Schneekluth, 1982), p. 104.

[2] See Gail Williams, "Germany in Autumn," *Hollywood Reporter*, 27 March 1979: "When Fassbinder takes the helm... the film's structure deteriorates into a stream-of-consciousness shapelessness.... Emotions are effectively laid bare (as are bodies), but Fassbinder's self-indulgence dominates this portion of the film."

[3] Vincent Canby, "Film: 13 Directors Make *Germany in Autumn*," *New York Times*, 5 April 1979.

[4] Wilhelm Roth, in *Fassbinder*, trans. Ruth McCormick (New York: Tanam, 1981), p. 191.

[5] Knut Boeser, "Ohnmächtig ohne zu resignieren," *Ästhetik und Kommunikation*, June 1978, p. 125. Also, Jan Dawson, "*Germany in Autumn & Eine Kleine Godard* [sic]," *Take One*, November 1978, p. 44.

[6] Boeser, p. 125.

[7] Cf. Alexander Kluge, *Die Patriotin* (Frankfurt: Zweitausendeins, 1979), pp. 28ff.

[8] "*Deutschland im Herbst:* Worin liegt die Parteilichkeit des Films?," *Ästhetik und Kommunikation*, June 1978, p. 124.

[9] Cf. Walter Benjamin, "Theses on the Philosophy of History," in *Illuminations*, ed. Hannah Arendt (New York: Schocken, 1969), p. 255: "To articulate the past historically does not mean to recognize it 'the way it really was' (Ranke). It means to seize hold of a memory as it flashes up at a moment of danger."

[10] Arnim Meier, who shared the Munich Reichenbachstrasse apartment with Fassbinder, took an overdose of pills a few months later. The suicide provided the impetus for Fassbinder's act of mourning for his lover, the film *In einem Jahr mit 13 Monden/In a Year of 13 Moons* (1978).

[11] In so doing, Fassbinder takes recourse to another favorite topos of West German artists during the seventies: *Beziehungsprobleme*, i.e. the obsessive preoccupation with one's relationships with friends and lovers. See Michael Rutschky, *Erfahrungshunger: Ein Essay über die siebziger Jahre* (Frankfurt: Fischer, 1982), pp. 51ff.

[12] "Mourning and Melancholia," in *A General Selection from the Works of Sigmund Freud*, ed. John Rickman (Garden City, NY: Doubleday, 1957), p. 125.

[13] Lothar Schwab, "Friedhofslandschaft mit Polizei," *Ästhetik und Kommunikation*, June 1978, p. 128.

[14] Robert Fischer and Joe Hembus, *Der neue deutsche Film 1960-1980* (Munich: Goldmann, 1981), p. 277.

[15] A cartoon by Chlodwig Poth (West Germany's counterpart to G.B. Trudeau) essentialized this disparity. Bearing the title "Keiner wäscht Rainer" (which can either mean "No one washes cleaner" or "No one takes Rainer to the

cleaners"), the caricature dramatized the gap between collective pretensions and actual authoritarian praxis. In one strip the director says: "Of course I allow co-determination. *I* take care of it." ("Natürlich gibt es bei mir Mitbestimmung. Hier bestimme *ich* mit.")

[16] *The Candidate* (1980) was an omnibus-film addressed to the candidacy of Franz Josef Strauss in that year's Chancellor election. Kluge, Schlöndorff, Stefan Aust, and Alexander von Eschwege were the contributors to that film as well as *War and Peace*. The latter centers on the growing anti-war movement in West Germany; Fassbinder had planned to provide an episode before his death. *Out of the Blue,* a collection of nine short films centering around the fear of nuclear warfare, was introduced on West German TV during the summer of 1982.

[17] For a discussion of the various strategies considered, see *Die Patriotin*, pp. 20-23.

[18] Christian Metz, "History/Discourse: Note on Two Voyeurisms," trans. Susan Bennett, *Edinburgh '76 Magazine*, p. 21.

[19] "Selected Writings of Alexander Kluge: Theory and Literary-Cinematic Practice of the *Auteur* Film," trans. Skip Acuff and Hans-Bernhard Moeller, *Wide Angle,* Vol. 3, No. 4 (1979), p. 29.

[20] "Theses on the Philosophy of History," p. 255.

[21] Cf. Rutschky, pp. 83ff.

[22] Ibid., p. 150.

[23] Even while presenting what looks to be a realistic scene of himself at work on a TV-adaptation of Alfred Döblin's *Berlin Alexanderplatz,* Fassbinder self-stylizes. We see him dictate a scene description into a machine: "Franz is seen in medium close-up through a door. He looks very lonely." Fassbinder (who often used the name Franz in various contexts—as actor and editor) later appears in exactly this set-up.

[24] See Miriam Hansen, "Cooperative *Auteur* Cinema and Oppositional Public Sphere," *New German Critique,* No. 24-25 (Fall/Winter 1981-2), pp. 36-56.

[25] In general liberal film critics like Hans C. Blumenberg *(Die Zeit)* and Wolfram Schütte *(Frankfurter Rundschau)* singled out the Fassbinder scene as the film's center piece. One finds an interesting comment in the notice written by the conservative Wilfried Wiegand, "Die sanften Filmfrauen im Vormarsch: Schlussbericht von der Berlinale," *Frankfurter Allgemeine Zeitung,* 8 March 1978: Fassbinder's scene, in the critic's estimation, "supplied the meat for the abstract montage of the [entire] film."

[26] Quoted in Zwerenz, p. 13.

[27] Benjamin, p. 257.

[28] *"Deutschland im Herbst:* Worin liegt die Parteilichkeit des Films?," p. 124.

PART FOUR
Appendices

"The strength of German film is its variety."
—"The Hamburg Declaration" of the Filmmakers (1979)

"And indeed, what else should one expect of foreign readings of a national cinema but that the experience of one culture be brought to bear, critically and with creative bias, upon the products of another?"
—David Bathrick

Appendix A

West German Film since Oberhausen: A Year-by-Year Checklist (1962-1981)

This checklist records the evolution of West German film since the 1962 Oberhausen Manifesto. It concentrates mainly on narrative feature films made by the *Jungfilmer*. In order, though, to provide a comprehensive overview of West German film culture, a survey that reflects the heterogeneity of FRG productions, the following sectors of the country's output have been included to some degree:

—films originally made for television which have not been shown in cinemas;

—short films;

—avant-garde, experimental, and independent films, particularly ones made by individuals whose work has gained attention outside of West Germany;

—documentary productions;

—films by foreigners based in the FRG or individuals who have received German backing while living abroad;

—children's films *(Kinderfilme)*.

The continued existence of *Papas Kino,* the older and conservative film branch, receives mention only when its products parallel or compete with the young filmmakers, e.g. during the literature adaptation crisis *(Literaturverfilmungskrise)* in the case of Manfred Purzer, Alfred Weidenmann, and others.

The inventory is not exhaustive or definitive. An attempt has been made to catalogue the growing riches of West German film culture over the past two decades with the hope of imparting a sense of the many different sorts of talent present in the FRG. Films have been listed according to their year of completion which quite often will vary from the date of their first public screenings. The titles have all been translated. In the case of films that do not enjoy distribution in the United States, unofficial renderings have been provided.

The main sources for this checklist include:

1. *Der junge deutsche Film: Dokumentation zu einer Ausstellung der Constantin-Film*. Ed. Leonhard H. Gmür. Munich: Constantin-Film, 1967.

2. *Neuer deutscher Film: Eine Dokumentation*. Mannheim: Verband der deutschen Filmklubs, 1967.

3. Handbuch VIII (1965-1970), IX (1971-1976), and X (1977-1980) der Katholischen Filmkritik. *Filme 1965-70, Filme 1971-76,* and *Filme 1977-80: Kritische Notizen aus Kino- und Fernsehjahren*. Ed. Elisabeth Uhländer. Cologne: J.P. Bachem, 1971, 1977, and 1981.

4. Bronnen, Barbara and Corinna Brocher. *Die Filmemacher: Der neue deutsche Film nach Oberhausen*. Munich/Gütersloh/Vienna: Bertelsmann, 1973.

5. *Die Information*. Ed. Ulrike Storch. Wiesbaden: Deutsches Institut für Filmkunde, 1973ff.

6. *Jahrbuch Film*. Ed. Hans Günther Pflaum. Munich: Hanser, 1977ff.

7. *Deutsche Filme 1977*. Ed. Rüdiger Koschnitzki. Wiesbaden: Deutsches Institut für Filmkunde, 1978.

8. *Kino 78: Bundesdeutsche Filme auf der Leinwand*. Ed. Doris Dörrie and Robert Fischer. Munich: Nüchtern, 1978. Subsequent yearbooks edited only by Fischer.

9. Pflaum, Hans Günther and Hans Helmut Prinzler. *Film in der Bundesrepublik Deutschland*. Munich: Hanser, 1979.

10. Jansen, Peter W. *The New German Film*. Munich: Goethe Institute, 1980.

11. Just, Lothar R. *Das Filmjahr*. Munich: Filmland Presse, 1980ff.

12. Möhrmann, Renate. *Die Frau mit der Kamera: Filmemacherinnen in der Bundesrepublik Deutschland*. Munich: Hanser, 1980.

13. Fischer, Robert and Joe Hembus. *Der neue deutsche Film 1960-1980*. Munich: Goldmann, 1981.

Pre-Oberhausen:

1955: Herbert Vesely—*nicht mehr fliehen/Stop Running*

1956: Georg Tressler—*Die Halbstarken/The Hooligans*

1957: Ottomar Domnick—*Jonas*
Georg Tressler—*Endstation Liebe/Last Stop Love*

1959: Wolfgang Staudte—*Rosen für den Staatsanwalt/Roses for the Prosecutor*
Bernhard Wicki—*Die Brücke/The Bridge*

1960: Ottomar Domnick—*Gino*
Alexander Kluge and Peter Schamoni—* *Brutalität in Stein (Die Ewigkeit von gestern)/Brutality in Stone (The Eternity of Yesterday)*
Wolfgang Staudte—*Kirmes/Fairground*

1961: Hans-Dieter Bove—*Immer, wenn es Nacht wird/Always at Nightfall*
Ferdinand Khittl—*Die Parallelstrasse/The Parallel Street*
Hansjürgen Pohland—*Tobby*
Will Tremper—*Flucht nach Berlin/Flight to Berlin*
Herbert Vesely—*Das Brot der frühen Jahre/The Bread of the Early Years*

1962-1980:

1962: Ottomar Domnick—*Ohne Datum/Undated*
Eberhard Hauff, Rob Houwer, Karl Schedereit, Walter Krüttner, Wolf Hart, Michael Blackwood, Franz Josef Spieker—*Hütet Eure Töchter/Guard Your Daughters*
Jean-Marie Straub and Danièle Huillet—* *Machorka-Muff*
Hans Rolf Strobel and Heinrich Tichawsky—* *Notabene Mezzogiorno*

1963: Vlado Kristl—* *Madeleine-Madeleine*
Will Tremper—*Die endlose Nacht/The Endless Night*
Herbert Vesely—*Sie fanden ihren Weg/They Found Their Way*
Bernhard Wicki—*Der Besuch/The Visit*

1964: Roland Klick—* *Ludwig*
Alexander Kluge—* *Porträt einer Bewährung/Portrait of a Man Who Proved Himself*

Vlado Kristl—*Der Damm/The Dam;* * *Autorennen/Car Race*
George Moorse—* *In side out*
Peter Nestler and Reinald Schnell—* *Mühlheim (Ruhr)*
Michael Pfleghar—*Die Tote von Beverly Hills/The Dead Woman from Beverly Hills*
Wolfgang Staudte—*Herrenpartie/Stag Outing*
Klaus Wildenhahn—* *Parteitag 64/Party Convention 64*

1965: George Moorse—*Zero in the Universe*
Peter Nestler and Reinald Schnell—* *Rheinstrom/The Rhein Flow*
Ulrich Schamoni—*Es/It*
Jean-Marie Straub and Danièle Huillet—* *Nicht versöhnt/Not Reconciled*
Hans-Jürgen Syberberg—*Fünfter Akt, Siebte Szene. Fritz Kortner probt Kabale und Liebe/Act Five, Scene Seven. Fritz Kortner Rehearses Love and Intrigue; Romy. Anatomie eines Gesichts/Romy. Anatomy of a Face.*

1966: Roger Fritz—*Mädchen, Mädchen*
Werner Herzog—* *Die beispiellose Verteidigung der Festung Deutschkreutz/The Unprecedented Defense of the Fortress Deutschkreutz*
Alexander Kluge—*Abschied von gestern/Yesterday Girl*
Vlado Kristl—*Der Brief/The Letter*
Peter Lilienthal—*Der Beginn/The Beginning*
Joachim Mock—*Rockys Messer/Rocky's Knife*
Rudolf Noelte—*Das Schloss/The Castle*
Michael Pfleghar—*Bel ami 2000*
Hansjürgen Pohland—*Katz und Maus/Cat and Mouse*
Edgar Reitz—*Mahlzeiten/Meal Times*
Christian Rischert—*Kopfstand, Madam!/Headstand, My Lady!*
Peter Schamoni—*Schonzeit für Füchse/Closed Season on Fox Hunting*
Volker Schlöndorff—*Der junge Törless/Young Törless*
Franz Josef Spieker—*Wilder Reiter GmbH./Wild Rider, Inc.*
Hans-Jürgen Syberberg—*Fritz Kortner spricht Monologe für eine Schallplatte/Fritz Kortner Recites Monologues for a Record*
Will Tremper—*Sperrbezirk/Blockade Area; Playgirl*
Wolfgang Urchs—*Die Begegnung/The Encounter*

1967: Horst Manfred Adloff—*Die goldene Pille/The Golden Pill*
Hellmuth Costard—* *Warum hast Du mich wachgeküsst?/Why Did You Wake Me with Kisses?*
Gustav Ehmck—*Spur eines Mädchens/Trace of a Girl*
Marran Gosov—*Engelchen oder Die Jungfrau von Bamberg/Engelchen or The Virgin from Bamberg*
Helmut Herbst and Marquard Bohm—* *Na und/So What*
Werner Herzog—*Lebenszeichen/Signs of Life*
Günther Hörmann—*Ruhestörung/Disturbance of the Peace*
Alexander Kluge—*Die Artisten in der Zirkuskuppel: ratlos/The Artists under the Big Top: Perplexed*
Klaus Lemke—*48 Stunden bis Acapulco/48 Hours to Acapulco; Negresco****-Eine tödliche Affäre/Negresco****-A Deadly Affair*
George Moorse—*Der Findling/The Foundling; Kuckucksjahre/Cuckoo Years*
Werner Nekes and Dore O.—* *jüm-jüm*
Peter Nestler and Reinald Schnell—* *Im Ruhrgebiet/In the Ruhr Valley*
Hansjürgen Pohland—*Tamara*
Johannes Schaaf—*Tätowierung/Tattooing*
Ulrich Schamoni—*Alle Jahre wieder/Once Every Year*
Volker Schlöndorff—*Mord und Totschlag/A Degree of Murder*
Eckhart Schmidt—*Jet Generation*
Haro Senft—*Der sanfte Lauf/The Gentle Course*
Franz Josef Spieker—*Mit Eichenlaub und Feigenblatt/With Oak and Fig Leaves*
May Spils—*Zur Sache, Schätzchen/Let's Get Down to Business, Darling*
Jean-Marie Straub and Danièle Huillet—*Chronik der Anna Magdalena Bach/Chronicle of Anna Magdalena Bach*
Michael Verhoeven—*Paarungen/Couplings*

1968: Robert Azderball—*Eine Frau sucht Liebe/A Woman Looks for Love*
Hellmuth Costard—* *Besonders wertvoll/Particularly Noteworthy*
Ottomar Domnick—*N.N.*
Gustav Ehmck—*Spielst du mit schrägen Vögeln/If You Keep Bad Company*

Rainer Erler—*Professor Columbus*
Peter Fleischmann—*Jagdszenen aus Niederbayern/Hunting Scenes from Lower Bavaria*
Helmut Förnbacher—*Sommersprossen/Freckles*
Roger Fritz, Eckhart Schmidt, and Hannes Dahlberg—*Erotik auf der Schulbank/Eroticism in the Classroom*
Roger Fritz—*Häschen in der Grube/Wake Up, Little Rabbit*
Hannes Fuchs—* *Film '68*
Hans W. Geissendörfer—*Der Fall Lena Christ/The Case of Lena Christ*
Marran Gosov—*Bengelchen liebt kreuz und quer/Bengelchen Gets Around*
Birgit and Wilhelm Hein—* *Rohfilm/Unexposed Film*
Werner Herzog—* *Letzte Worte/Last Words;* * *Massnahmen gegen Fanatiker/Preventive Measures against Fanatics*
Thomas Kiefer—* *Terror auch im Westen/Terror Also in the West*
Roland Klick—*Bübchen (Der kleine Vampir)/Bübchen (The Little Vampire)*
Alexander Kluge—* *Feuerlöscher E.A. Winterstein/Fireman E.A. Winterstein*
Theodor Kotulla—*Bis zum Happy End/To the Happy End*
Vlado Kristl—* *Sekundenfilme/Seconds-long Films*
George Moorse—*Der Griller/The Griller; Liebe und so weiter/Love, etc.*
Werner Nekes—*Kelek*
Edgar Reitz—*Uxmal*
Erika Runge—* *Warum ist Frau B. glücklich?/Why Is Mrs. B. Happy?*
Ulrich Schamoni—*Quartett im Bett/Quartet in Bed*
Peter Schneider—*Agilok und Blubo*
Werner Schroeter—* *Argila*
Ula Stöckl—*Neun Leben hat die Katze/The Cat Has Nine Lives*
Jean-Marie Straub and Danièle Huillet—* *Der Bräutigam, die Komödiantin und der Zuhälter/The Bridegroom, the Comedienne, and the Pimp*
Thomas Struck—* *Der warme Punkt/The Hot Dot*
Hans Rolf Strobel and Heinrich Tichawsky—*Eine Ehe/A Marriage*

Hans-Jürgen Syberberg—*Scarabea-Wieviel Erde braucht der Mensch?/Scarabea-How Much Earth Does a Person Need?*
Rudolf Thome—*Detektive/Detective*
Michael Verhoeven—*Engelchen macht weiter-hoppe, hoppe Reiter/The Further Adventures of Engelchen*
Peter Zadek—*Ich bin ein Elefant, Madame/I Am an Elephant, Madame*

1969: Hellmuth Costard—*Die Unterdrückung der Frau ist vor allem an dem Verhalten der Frauen selber zu erkennen/The Oppression of Woman Is Primarily Evident in the Behavior of Women Themselves*
Rainer Werner Fassbinder—*Liebe ist kälter als der Tod/Love Is Colder than Death; Katzelmacher; Götter der Pest/Gods of the Plague; Warum läuft Herr R. Amok?/Why Does Herr R. Run Amok?* (with Michael Fengler)
Roland Gall—*Wie ich ein Neger wurde/How I Became a Negro*
Hans W. Geissendörfer—*Jonathan*
Marran Gosov—*Der Kerl liebt mich-und das soll ich glauben?/The Guy Loves Me-And I'm Supposed to Believe That?*
Reinhard Hauff—*Die Revolte/The Revolt*
Werner Herzog—* *Die fliegenden Ärzte von Ostafrika/The Flying Doctors of East Africa*
Günther Hörmann—* *Aktiver Streik an der Frankfurter Universität/Active Strike at the Frankfurt University*
Alexander Kluge—*Die unbezähmbare Leni Peickert/The Indomitable Leni Peickert*
Vlado Kristl—* *Italienisches Capriccio/Italian Capriccio*
Peter Lilienthal—*Malatesta*
Edgar Reitz—*Cardillac*
Peter Schamoni—*Deine Zärtlichkeiten/Your Tender Embraces*
Ulrich Schamoni—*Wir-Zwei/We-Two*
Volker Schlöndorff—*Michael Kohlhaas-Der Rebell/Michael Kohlhaas; Baal*
Werner Schroeter—* *Neurasia; Eika Katappa; Nicaragua*
Haro Senft—*Fegefeuer/Purgatory*
Franz Josef Spieker—*Kuckucksei im Gangsternest/Cuckoo's Egg in the Gangster's Nest*
May Spils—*Nicht fummeln, Liebling/Don't Fondle Me, Love*

Jean-Marie Straub and Danièle Huillet—*Othon*
Hans-Jürgen Syberberg—*Sex-Business-made in Pasing*
Rudolf Thome—*Rote Sonne/Red Sun*
Michael Verhoeven—*Der Bettenstudent/The Bed-Hopping Student*
Wim Wenders—* *Alabama-2000 Light Years;* * *3 Amerikanische LPs/3 American LPs*
Klaus Wyborny—*Dämonische Leinwand/Haunted Screen*

1970: Robert Van Ackeren—*Blondie's Number One*
Horst Bienek—*Die Zelle/The Cell*
Hellmuth Costard—*Und niemand in Hollywood der versteht, dass schon viel zu viele Gehirne umgedreht wurden/And No One in Hollywood Understands That Far Too Many Brains Have Been Turned Already; Fussball wie noch nie/Football as Never Before*
Lutz Eisholz—*Bruno-der Schwarze/Bruno-The Black*
Ingemo Engström—*Dark Spring*
Rainer Werner Fassbinder—*Rio das mortes; Whity; Die Niklashauser Fahrt/The Niklashausen Journey; Der amerikanische Soldat/The American Soldier; Warnung vor einer heiligen Nutte/Beware of a Holy Whore*
Eberhard Fechner—*Klassenphoto/Class Photograph*
Peter Fleischmann—*Das Unheil/The Calamity*
Helmut Förnbacher—*Beiss mich, Liebling/Bite Me, Darling*
Roger Fritz—*Mädchen mit Gewalt/A Girl and Violence*
Hans W. Geissendörfer—*Eine Rose für Jane/A Rose for Jane*
Werner Herzog—*Fata Morgana; Auch Zwerge haben klein angefangen/Even Dwarfs Started Small*
Roland Klick—*Deadlock*
Alexander Kluge—*Der grosse Verhau/The Big Mess;* * *Ein Arzt aus Halberstadt/A Doctor from Halberstadt*
Vlado Kristl—*Film oder Macht/Film or Power*
George Moorse—*Lenz*
Rosa von Praunheim—*Macbeth Oper von Rosa von Praunheim/Macbeth, an Opera by Rosa von Praunheim; Die Bettwurst/The Bolster; Nicht der Homosexuelle ist pervers, sondern die Situation, in der er lebt/Not the Homosexual Is Perverse, but Rather the Situation in Which He Lives*
Edgar Reitz and Ula Stöckl—*Geschichten vom Kübelkind/Stories of the Dustbin Child*

Erika Runge—*Ich heisse Erwin und bin 17 Jahre/My Name Is Erwin and I'm 17*
Thomas Schamoni—*Ein grosser graublauer Vogel/A Large Gray-Blue Bird*
Volker Schlöndorff—*Der plötzliche Reichtum der armen Leute von Kombach/The Sudden Wealth of the Poor People of Kombach*
Eckhart Schmidt—*Männer sind zum Lieben da/Men Are There to Be Loved*
Werner Schroeter—*Der Bomberpilot*
Hans-Jürgen Syberberg—*San Domingo*
Rudolf Thome—*Supergirl*
Michael Verhoeven—*o.k.*
Volker Vogeler—*Jaider-der einsame Jäger/Jaider-The Lonely Hunter*
Matthias Weiss—*Blue Velvet*
Wim Wenders—* *Polizeifilm/Police Film; Summer in the City*

1971: Hark Bohm—* *Wie starb Roland S.?/How Did Roland S. Die?*
Uwe Brandner—*Ich liebe dich, ich töte dich/I Love You, I Kill You*
Gustav Ehmck—*Heiss and kalt/Hot and Cold*
Rainer Werner Fassbinder—*Pioniere in Ingolstadt/Pioneers in Ingolstadt; Der Händler der vier Jahreszeiten/The Merchant of Four Seasons*
Veith von Fürstenberg and Martin Müller—*Furchtlose Flieger/Fearless Fliers*
Theo Gallehr and Rolf Schübel—*Rote Fahnen sieht man besser/Red Flags Can Be Seen Better*
Hans W. Geissendörfer—*Carlos*
Reinhard Hauff—*Mathias Kneissl*
Werner Herzog—*Land des Schweigens und der Dunkelheit/Land of Silence and Darkness*
Alexander Kluge—*Willi Tobler und der Untergang der 6. Flotte/Willi Tobler and the Sinking of the Sixth Fleet*
Theodor Kotulla—*Ohne Nachsicht/Without Leniency*
Vlado Kristl—*Obrigkeitsfilm/Authority Film*
Peter Lilienthal—*Jakob von Gunten*
George Moorse—*Der Schattenreiter/The Shadow Rider*
Nicos Perakis, Ula Stöckl, Alf Brustellin, and Edgar Reitz—*Das goldene Ding/The Golden Thing*
Ottokar Runze—*Viola and Sebastian*

Helke Sander—* *Eine Prämie für Irene/A Prize for Irene*
Johannes Schaaf—*Trotta*
Ulrich Schamoni—*Eins/One*
Maximilian Schell—*Erste Liebe/First Love*
Niklaus Schilling—*Nachtschatten/Night Shadows*
Volker Schlöndorff—*Die Moral der Ruth Halbfass/The Morals of Ruth Halbfass*
Eberhard Schroeder and Rob Houwer— *§218—Wir haben abgetrieben, Herr Staatsanwalt/ §218—We Had an Abortion, Mr. Prosecutor*
Werner Schroeter—*Salome; Macbeth; Der Tod der Maria Malibran/The Death of Maria Malibran*
Wolfgang Urchs—*Das Fräulein von Stradonitz in memoriam/In Memory of the Lady of Stradonitz*
Wim Wenders—*Die Angst des Tormanns beim Elfmeter/The Goalie's Anxiety at the Penalty Kick*
Bernhard Wicki—*Das falsche Gewicht/The False Measure*

1972: Hark Bohm—*Tschetan, der Indianerjunge/Tschetan, the Indian Boy*
Uwe Brandner—*Kopf oder Zahl/Heads or Tails*
Klaus Emmerich—*Rosa und Lin*
Rainer Werner Fassbinder—*Die bitteren Tränen der Petra von Kant/The Bitter Tears of Petra von Kant; Wildwechsel/Jail Bait; Acht Stunden sind kein Tag/Eight Hours Don't Make a Day*
Theo Gallehr and Rolf Schübel—*Arbeitskampf/Labor Struggle*
Hans W. Geissendörfer—*Marie*
Werner Herzog—*Aguirre, der Zorn Gottes/Aguirre, the Wrath of God*
Ingo Kratisch and Marianne Lüdcke—*Die Wollands*
Norbert Kückelmann—*Die Sachverständigen/The Experts*
George Moorse—*Pan*
Werner Nekes—*T-WO-MEN I-IV*
Hans Noever—*Zahltag/Pay Day*
Nicos Perakis—*Die Wohngenossin/The Female Roommate*
Wolfgang Petersen—*Smog*
Peer Raben—*Adele Spitzeder*
Erika Runge—*Ich bin Bürger der DDR/I'm a Citizen of the GDR*
Helke Sander—* *Macht die Pille frei?/Does the Pill Liberate?*

Helma Sanders-Brahms—*Der Angestellte/The White-Collar Worker*
Volker Schlöndorff—*Strohfeuer/A Free Woman*
Daniel Schmid—*Heute nacht oder nie/Tonight or Never*
Jean-Marie Straub and Danièle Huillet— *Geschichtsunterricht/History Lessons;* * *Einleitung zu Arnold Schönbergs Begleitmusik zu einer Lichtspielscene/Introduction to Arnold Schönberg's Accompaniment to a Cinematographic Scene*
Hans-Jürgen Syberberg—*Ludwig-Requiem für einen jungfräulichen König/Ludwig; Theodor Hirneis oder: Wie man ehem. Hofkoch wird/Theodor Hirneis or: How to Become a Former Court Chef*
Rudolf Thome—*Fremde Stadt/Foreign City*
Wim Wenders—*Der scharlachrote Buchstabe/The Scarlet Letter*
Christian Ziewer—*Liebe Mutter, mir geht es gut/Dear Mother, I'm Doing Fine*

1973: Robert Van Ackeren—*Harlis*
Uwe Brandner—*Im Zeichen der Kälte/Under the Sign of Coldness*
Rainer Werner Fassbinder—*Welt am Draht/World on a Wire; Angst essen Seele auf/Ali: Fear Eats the Soul; Martha*
Peter Fleischmann—*Dorotheas Rache/Dorothy's Revenge*
Hans W. Geissendörfer—*Die Eltern/The Parents*
Wolf Gremm—*Ich dachte, ich wäre tot/I Thought I Was Dead*
Reinhard Hauff—*Die Verrohung des Franz Blum/The Brutalization of Franz Blum*
Roland Klick—*Supermarkt/Super Market*
Alexander Kluge—*Gelegenheitsarbeit einer Sklavin/Part-Time Work of a Domestic Slave*
Ingo Kratisch and Marianne Lüdcke—*Lohn und Liebe/Wages and Love*
Peter Lilienthal—*La Victoria*
Ulli Lommel—*Die Zärtlichkeit der Wölfe/The Tenderness of Wolves*
George Moorse—*Inki*
Werner Nekes—*Diwan*
Wolfgang Petersen—*Einer von uns beiden/One of the Two of Us*
Rosa von Praunheim—*Berliner Bettwurst/Berlin Bolster*
Edgar Reitz—*Die Reise nach Wien/The Trip to Vienna*

Ottokar Runze—*Der Lord von Barmbeck/The Lord of Barmbeck*
Helke Sander—* *Männerbünde/Male Bonding*
Helma Sanders-Brahms—*Die letzten Tage von Gomorrha/The Last Days of Gomorrha*
Johannes Schaaf—*Traumstadt/Dream City*
Ulrich Schamoni—*Chapeau Claque*
Maximilian Schell—*Der Fussgänger/The Pedestrian*
Volker Schlöndorff—*Übernachtung in Tirol/Overnight Stay in the Tyrol*
Werner Schroeter—*Willow Springs*
May Spils—*Hau drauf, Kleiner/Go to It, Shorty*
Ula Stöckl—*Ein ganz perfektes Ehepaar/A Completely Perfect Couple*
Michael Verhoeven—*Ein unheimlich starker Abgang/Apotheosis*
Volker Vogeler—*Verflucht, dies Amerika/Damn This America*
Wim Wenders—*Alice in den Städten/Alice in the Cities*
Max Willutzki—*Der lange Jammer/The Long Misery*
Klaus Wyborny—*Die Geburt der Nation/The Birth of a Nation*

1974: Herbert Achternbush—*Das Andechser Gefühl/The Andechs Feeling*
Rainer Werner Fassbinder—*Fontane Effi Briest/Effi Briest; Faustrecht der Freiheit/Fox and His Friends*
Eberhard Fechner—*Unter Denkmalschutz/Under Landmark Protection*
Michael Fengler—*Output*
Veith von Fürstenberg—*Ein bisschen Liebe/A Little Bit of Love*
Florian Furtwängler—*Zum Abschied Chrysanthemen/The Chrysanthemum Farewell*
Hans W. Geissendörfer—*Perahim-die zweite Chance/Perahim-The Second Chance*
Wolf Gremm—*Meine Sorgen möcht' ich haben/I'd Like to Have My Troubles*
Reinhard Hauff—*Zündschnüre/Fuses*
Helmut Herbst—*Die phantastische Welt des Matthew Madson/The Fantastic World of Matthew Madson*
Werner Herzog—* *Die grosse Ekstase des Bildschnitzers Steiner/The Great Ecstasy of the Sculptor Steiner; Jeder für sich und Gott gegen alle/The Mystery of Kaspar Hauser*

Alexander Kluge and Edgar Reitz—*In Gefahr und grösster Not bringt der Mittelweg den Tod/In Times of Danger and Greatest Peril, the Path of Compromise Leads to Death*
Norbert Kückelmann—*Die Schiessübung/Shooting Practice*
Lothar Lambert and Wolfram Zobus—*1 Berlin Harlem*
Peter Lilienthal—*Hauptlehrer Hofer/Schoolmaster Hofer*
Ulli Lommel—*Wachtmeister Rahn/Constable Rahn*
Ulf Miehe—*John Glückstadt*
Uschi Reich—*Anna*
Jochen Richter—*Die Ameisen kommen/The Ants Are Coming*
Ottokar Runze—*Im Namen des Volkes/In the Name of the People*
Helma Sander-Brahms—*Erdbeben in Chili/Earthquake in Chile; Unterm Pflaster ist der Strand/The Beach under the Sidewalk*
Volker Schlöndorff—*Georginas Gründe/Georgina's Reasons*
Daniel Schmid—*La Paloma*
Werner Schroeter—*Der schwarze Engel/The Black Angel*
Ula Stöckl—*Hase und Igel/Hare und Hedgehog*
Jean-Marie Straub and Danièle Huillet—*Moses und Aron/Moses and Aaron*
Hans-Jürgen Syberberg—*Karl May*
Karin Thome—*Amerika*
Rudolf Thome—*Made in Germany and USA*
Volker Vogeler—*Das Tal der tanzenden Witwen/The Valley of the Dancing Widows*
Wim Wenders—*Falsche Bewegung/Wrong Move*
Christian Ziewer—*Schneeglöckchen blühn im September/Snowdrops Bloom in September*

1975: Herbert Achternbusch—*Die Atlantikschwimmer/The Atlantic Swimmers*
Robert Van Ackeren—*Der letzte Schrei/The Latest Rage*
Hartmut Bitomsky—*Auf Biegen oder Brechen/By Hook or by Crook*
Walter Bockmayer and Rolf Bührmann—*Salzstangen-Geflüster/Pretzel Whispering*
Hark Bohm—*Nordsee ist Mordsee/North Sea Is Death Sea*
Jutta Brückner—*Tue recht und scheue niemand/Do Right and Fear No One*
Alf Brustellin and Bernhard Sinkel—*Berlinger*

Gustav Ehmck—*Mein Onkel Theodor/My Uncle Theodore*
Ingemo Engström—*Kampf um ein Kind/Battle over a Child*
Rainer Werner Fassbinder—*Mutter Küsters' Fahrt zum Himmel/ Mother Küsters Goes to Heaven; Angst vor der Angst/Fear of Fear*
Eberhard Fechner—*Tadellöser & Wolff/Right or Wrong: My Country*
Michael Fengler—*Eierdiebe/Egg Thieves*
Peter Fleischmann—*Der dritte Grad/The Third Degree*
Johannes Flütsch, Klaus Helle, and Marlis Kallweit—*Flöz Dickebank*
Reinhard Hauff—*Paule Pauländer*
Vojtech Jasny—*Ansichten eines Clowns/The Clown*
Klaus Kirschner—*Mozart-Aufzeichnungen einer Jugend/Mozart's Childhood*
Alexander Kluge—*Der starke Ferdinand/Strong Man Ferdinand*
Ingo Kratisch and Marianne Lüdcke—*Familienglück/Domestic Bliss*
Norbert Kückelmann—*Die Angst ist ein zweiter Schatten/Fear Is a Second Shadow*
Peter Lilienthal—*Es herrscht Ruhe im Lande/Calm Prevails over the Country*
Ulli Lommel—*Der zweite Frühling/The Second Spring*
Wolfgang Petersen—*Stellenweise Glatteis/Occasional Patches of Ice*
Manfred Purzer—*Das Netz/The Net*
Ottokar Runze—*Das Messer im Rücken/The Knife in the Back; Verlorenes Leben/A Life in Vain*
Sohrab Shahid Saless—*In der Fremde/Far from Home*
Helma Sanders-Brahms—*Shirins Hochzeit/Shirin's Wedding*
Peter Schamoni—*Potato Fritz (Zwei gegen Tod und Teufel)/Potato Fritz (Two against Death and the Devil)*
Volker Schlöndorff and Margarethe von Trotta—*Die verlorene Ehre der Katharina Blum/The Lost Honor of Katharina Blum*
Bernhard Sinkel—*Lina Braake*
Peter Stein—*Sommergäste/Summer Guests*
Hans-Jürgen Syberberg—*Winifried Wagner und die Geschichte des Hauses Wahnfried von 1914-1975/The Confessions of Winifried Wagner*
Rudolf Thome—*Tagebuch/Diary*

Michael Verhoeven —*MitGift/Deadly Dowry*
Herbert Vesely —*Depressionen/Depressions*
Klaus Wyborny —*Bilder vom verlorenen Wort/Pictures of the Lost Word*
Peter Zadek —*Eiszeit/Ice Age*

1976: Walter Bockmayer and Rolf Bührmann —*Salzstangen-Geschrei/Pretzel Screaming*
Rainer Boldt —*Menschenfresser/Man-Eater*
Peter F. Bringmann —*Aufforderung zum Tanz/Invitation to Dance*
Jutta Brückner —*Ein ganz und gar verwahrlostes Mädchen/A Fully Neglected Girl*
Rainer Werner Fassbinder —*Ich will doch nur, dass ihr mich liebt/I Only Want You to Love Me; Satansbraten/Satan's Brew; Chinesisches Roulette/Chinese Roulette*
Hans W. Geissendörfer —*Sternsteinhof/Sternstein Manor; Die Wildente/The Wild Duck*
Heidi Genée —*Grete Minde*
Wolf Gremm-*Die Brüder/The Brothers*
Werner Herzog —* *How Much Wood Would a Woodchuck Chuck; Herz aus Glas/Heart of Glass; * La Soufrière*
Vojtech Jasny —*Fluchtversuch/Attempted Escape*
Erwin Keusch —*Das Brot des Bäckers/The Baker's Bread*
Roland Klick —*Lieb Vaterland, magst ruhig sein/Rest Thou Tranquil, Beloved Country*
Thomas Körfer —*Der Gehülfe/The Assistant*
Theodor Kotulla —*Aus einem deutschen Leben/Death Is My Trade*
Ingo Kratisch and Marianne Lüdcke —*Die Tannerhütte/The Tanner Shack*
Ulli Lommel —*Adolf und Marlene*
Stefan Lukschy and Hartmann Schmige —*Krawatten für Olympia/Ties for Olympia*
Werner Nekes —*Amalgam I-IV*
Nicos Perakis —*Bomber und Paganini*
Rosa von Praunheim —*Underground and Emigrants; Ich bin ein Antistar/I Am an Anti-Star*
Manfred Purzer —*Die Elixiere des Teufels/The Devil's Elixirs*
Edgar Reitz —*Stunde Null/Zero Hour*
Christian Rischert —*Der Tod des Fischers Marc Leblanc/The Death of the Fisherman Marc Leblanc*

Sohrab Shahid Saless—*Reifezeit/Coming of Age*
Helma Sanders-Brahms—*Heinrich*
Niklaus Schilling—*Die Vertreibung aus dem Paradies/The Expulsion from Paradise*
Volker Schlöndorff—*Der Fangschuss/Coup de Grâce*
Daniel Schmid—*Schatten der Engel/Shadows of the Angels*
Werner Schroeter—*Goldflocken/Flocons d'Or/Goldflakes*
Franz Seitz—*Unordnung und frühes Leid/Disorder and Early Sorrow*
Ula Stöckl—*Erikas Leidenschaften/Erika's Passions*
Jean-Marie Straub and Danièle Huillet—*Fortini Cani*
Benno Trautmann and Brigitte Toni Lerch—*Der Umsetzer/The Displacer*
Michael Verhoeven—*Gefundenes Fressen/A Godsend*
Wim Wenders—*Im Lauf der Zeit/Kings of the Road*
Bernhard Wicki—*Die Eroberung der Zitadelle/The Conquest of the Citadel*
Klaus Wildenhahn—*Emden geht nach USA/Emden Goes to the USA* (with Gisela Tuchtenhagen)
Max Willutzki—*Vera Romeyke ist nicht tragbar/Vera Romeyke Is Not Acceptable*
Christian Ziewer—*Der aufrechte Gang/Walking Tall*

1977: Herbert Achternbusch—*Bierkampf/Beer Battle; Servus Bayern/Bye Bye, Bavaria*
Robert Van Ackeren—*Belcanto; Das andere Lächeln/The Other Smile*
Dagmar Beiersdorf—*Puppe kaputt/Dolly's Broken*
Wolfgang Berndt and Doris Dörrie—*Ob's stürmt oder schneit/Whether It Storms or Snows*
Susanne Beyeler, Rainer März, and Manfred Stelzer— * *Eintracht Borbeck*
Walter Bockmayer—*Jane bleibt Jane/Jane Is Jane Forever; Flammende Herzen/Flaming Hearts* (with Rolf Bührmann)
Hark Bohm—*Moritz, lieber Moritz/Moritz, Dear Moritz*
Rainer Boldt—*Fehlschuss/Bad Shot*
Uwe Brandner—*halbe-halbe/Fifty-Fifty*
Alf Brustellin and Bernhard Sinkel—*Der Mädchenkrieg/The Three Sisters*
Marian Czura and Tillmann Scholl—*Krautsand*
Gustav Ehmck—*Feuer um Mitternacht/Fire at Midnight*

Heinz Emigholz—* *Demon*
Klaus Emmerich—*Kreutzer; Heinrich Heine*
Ingemo Engström and Gerhard Theuring—*Fluchtweg nach Marseille/Escape Route to Marseilles*
Rainer Erler—*Operation Ganymed*
Rainer Werner Fassbinder—*Bolwieser/The Stationmaster's Wife; Frauen in New York/Women in New York; Eine Reise ins Licht/Despair*
Eberhard Fechner—*Winterspelt 1944*
Hans W. Geissendörfer—*Die gläserne Zelle/The Glass Cell*
Wolf Gremm—*Tod oder Freiheit/Liberty or Death*
Peter Handke—*Die linkshändige Frau/The Left-Handed Woman*
Thomas Hartwig—*Die Farbe des Himmels/The Color of the Sky*
Reinhard Hauff—*Der Hauptdarsteller/The Main Actor*
Helmut Herbst—*John Heartfield, Fotomonteur/John Heartfield, Photomontagist*
Christian Herrendoerfer and Joachim Fest—*Hitler-eine Karriere/Hitler-A Career*
Werner Herzog—*Stroszek*
Günther Hörmann—*Lernen ohne Zwang/Learning without Pressure*
Voytech Jasny—*Rückkehr/Return*
Alexander Kluge—*"Zu böser Schlacht schleich' ich heut nacht so bang"/"In Such Trepidation I Creep Off Tonight to the Evil Battle"*
Roald Koller—*Johny West*
Fritz Matthies—*Paulines Geburtstag oder Die Bestie von Notre Dame/Pauline's Birthday or The Beast of Notre Dame*
Werner Nekes—*Lagado*
Hans Noever—*Die Frau gegenüber/The Woman across the Way*
Rüdiger Nüchtern—*Anschi und Michael*
Wolfgang Petersen—*Die Konsequenz/The Consequence*
Alexander Petrović—*Gruppenbild mit Dame/Group Portrait with Lady*
Rosa von Praunheim—*Der 24. Stock/The 24th Floor*
Christian Rischert—*Venedig/Venice*
Ottokar Runze—*Die Standarte/The Standard*
Sohrab Shahid Saless—*Tagebuch eines Liebenden/Diary of a Man in Love*

Renate Sami and Matthias Weiss—*Jackpot*
Helke Sander—*Die allseitig reduzierte Persönlichkeit-REDUPERS/The All Round Reduced Personality-REDUPERS*
Niklaus Schilling—*Rheingold*
Volker Schlöndorff—* *Nur zum Spass-nur zum Spiel-Kaleidoskop Valeska Gert/Only for Fun and Games-Kaleidoscope Valeska Gert*
Daniel Schmid—*Violanta*
Bernhard Sinkel—*Taugenichts/Good-for-Nothing*
Hans-Christof Stenzel—*C'est la vie rrose-Ein Junggesellenspiel/ C'est la vie rrose-A Bachelor's Game*
Jean-Marie Straub and Danièle Huillet—* *Toute Révolution est un coup de dés/Every Revolution Is a Game of Dice*
Hans-Jürgen Syberberg—*Hitler, ein Film aus Deutschland/Our Hitler-A Film from Germany*
Karin Thome—*Also es war so/Well, It Was Like This*
Margarethe von Trotta—*Das zweite Erwachen der Christa Klages/The Second Awakening of Christa Klages*
Herbert Vesely—*Der kurze Brief zum langen Abschied/The Short Letter to the Long Goodbye*
Alfred Weidenmann—*Der Schimmelreiter/The Rider of the White Horse*
Wim Wenders—*Der amerikanische Freund/The American Friend*
Klaus Wyborny—*Der Ort der Handlung/The Scene of the Action;* * *Unerreichbar-Heimatlos/Unreachable-Homeless*

1978: Herbert Achternbusch—*Der junge Mönch/The Young Monk*
Karl Heinz Bieber—*Der Tiefstapler/The Two-bit Swindler*
Rainer Boldt—*Esch oder die Anarchie/Esch or Anarchy*
Peter F. Bringmann—*Der Tag, an dem Elvis nach Bremerhaven kam/The Day Elvis Came to Bremerhaven*
Alf Brustellin—*Der Sturz/The Fall*
Alf Brustellin, Rainer Werner Fassbinder, Alexander Kluge, Maximiliane Mainka, Edgar Reitz, Katja Rupé, Hans Peter Cloos, Volker Schlöndorff, and Bernhard Sinkel—*Deutschland im Herbst/Germany in Autumn*
Wolfgang Büld—*Brennende Langeweile/Bored Teenagers*
Bastian Clevé—*Der Deutschlandfahrer/The Traveler in Germany*

Hellmuth Costard—*Der kleine Godard an das Kuratorium junger deutscher Film/The Little Godard*
Helmut Dietl—*Der Durchdreher/The Man Who Flipped Out*
Doris Dörrie—* *Der erste Walzer/The First Waltz*
Gustav Ehmck—*Neues vom Räuber Hotzenplotz/The New Adventures of the Robber Hotzenplotz*
Klaus Emmerich—*Die erste Polka/The First Polka*
Harun Farocki—*Zwischen zwei Kriegen/Between Two Wars*
Rainer Werner Fassbinder—*Die Ehe der Maria Braun/The Marriage of Maria Braun; In einem Jahr mit 13 Monden/In a Year of 13 Moons*
Mischa Gallé—*Strauberg ist da/Strauberg Is There*
Wolf Gauer and Jorge Bodanzky—*Jakobine*
Günter Giesenfeld—*Die Katze und der Hahn/The Cat and the Cock*
Wolf Gremm—*Die Schattengrenze/Frontiers of Darkness*
Detlef Gumm and Hans-Georg Ullrich—*Deutschlandsgeschichten/Tales from Germany*
Michael Günther—*Der Pfingstausflug/The Pentecost Outing*
Walter Harrich, Claus Strigel, and Bertram Verhaag—*Was heisst 'n hier Liebe?/This Is Love, Isn't It?*
Reinhard Hauff—*Messer im Kopf/Knife in the Head*
Monika Held and Gisela Tuchtenhagen—*Sing, Iris-Sing*
Peter Heller—*Liebe zum Imperium/Love of the Empire*
Werner Herzog—*Nosferatu-Phantom der Nacht/Nosferatu-The Vampyre; Woyzeck*
Christian Hohoff—*Spiel der Verlierer/Losers' Game*
Erwin Keusch and Christian Weisenborn—*Was ich bin, sind meine Filme/I Am What My Films Are*
Klaus Kirschner—*h-moll-messe/Mass in B Minor*
Helmut Kopetzky—*Willi und die Kameraden/Willi and the Comrades*
Achim Kurz—*Grandison*
Klaus Lemke—*Ein komischer Heiliger/An Odd Kind of Saint*
Hans-Peter Maier—*Der ganz faire Prozess des Marcel G./The Completely Fair Trial of Marcel G.*
Elfi Mikesch—*Ich denke oft an Hawaii.../I Often Think of Hawaii...*

Hans-Rüdiger Minow—*Die Anstalt/The Asylum*
Werner Nekes—*Mirador*
Rüdiger Neumann—* *Zufalls-Stadt/Random City*
Hans Noever—*Die Nacht mit Chandler/The Night with Chandler*
Rüdiger Nüchtern—*Schluchtenflitzer/Whizzer*
Ulrike Ottinger—*Madame X-Eine absolute Herrscherin/Madame X-An Absolute Ruler*
Peter Patzak—*Das Einhorn/The Unicorn*
Cristina Perincioli—*Die Macht der Männer ist die Geduld der Frauen/The Power of Men Is the Patience of Women*
Wolfgang Petersen—*Schwarz und weiss wie Tage und Nächte/Black and White Like Day and Night*
Rosa von Praunheim—*Tally Braun, New York*
Uschi Reich—*Keiner kann was dafür/No One Can Help*
Edgar Reitz—*Der Schneider von Ulm/The Tailor of Ulm*
Josef Rödl—* *Am Wege stehen und nicht wissen wohin sich drehen/Standing on the Road Not Knowing Which Way to Turn; Albert-warum?/Albert-Why?*
W. Werner Schaefer—*Kalte Heimat/Cold Homeland*
Maximilian Schell—*Geschichten aus dem Wienerwald/Tales from the Vienna Forest*
Werner Schroeter—*Neapolitanische Geschwister/Regno di Napoli/Kingdom of Naples*
Eberhard Schubert—*Flamme empor/Flame on High*
Peter Schubert and Maximiliane Mainka—*Hafenarbeit im Roll-on, Roll-off Verkehr/Work on the Docks in Roll-on, Roll-off Traffic*
Haro Senft—*Ein Tag mit dem Wind/A Day with the Wind*
May Spils—*Wehe, wenn Schwarzenbeck kommt/Beware of Schwarzenbeck*
Wolfgang Staudte—*Zwischengleis/Yesterday's Tomorrow*
Peter Stein—*Trilogie des Wiedersehens/Trilogy of Farewell*
Gisela Stelly—*Liebe und Abenteuer/Love and Adventure*
Ula Stöckl—*Eine Frau mit Verantwortung/A Woman and Her Responsibilities*
Jean-Marie Straub and Danièle Huillet—*Dalla nube alle resistenza/From the Sky to the Resistance*
Hans Rolf Strobel—*Schritte ins Reich der Freiheit/Stepping into the Realm of Freedom*

Duccio Tessari—*Das 5. Gebot/The Fifth Commandment*
Volker Vogeler—*Die Strasse/The Street*
Gabriele Voss, Christoph Hübner, and Alfons Stiller—*Lebens-Geschichte des Bergarbeiters Alfons S./Life Story of the Coal Miner Alfons S.*
Max Willutzki—*Die Faust in der Tasche/Fist in the Pocket*
Adolf Winkelmann—*Die Abfahrer/On the Move*
Christian Ziewer—*Aus der Ferne sehe ich dieses Land/From the Distance I See This Country*

1979: Herbert Achternbusch—*Der Komantsche/The Comanche*
Susanne Beyeler and Andreas Soschynski—*Strahlende Zukunft/Glowing Future*
Hark Bohm—*Im Herzen des Hurrican/In the Heart of the Hurricane*
Luc Bondy—*Die Ortliebschen Frauen/The Women from Ortlieb*
Hans Borgelt—*Berlin-Dein Filmgesicht/Berlin-Your Film Face*
Job Crogier—*Capsule*
Rüdiger Daniel—*Narrenterror/Fools' Terror*
Wolfgang Dobrowolny and others—*Ashram in Poona-Bhagwans Experiment*
Thomas Draeger—*Metin*
Ingemo Engström—*Letzte Liebe/Last Love*
Rainer Erler—*Fleisch/Meat*
Rainer Werner Fassbinder—*Die dritte Generation/The Third Generation*
Eberhard Fechner—*Ein Kapitel für sich/A Story unto Itself*
Peter Fleischmann—*Die Hamburger Krankheit/The Hamburg Sickness*
Johannes Flütsch and Manfred Stelzer—*Monarch*
Bernd Friedmann, Wolfgang Krajewski, Rainer Lutter, Klaus Günther Otto, Hans Rombach, and Bernd Uhde—*Wer keinen Mut zum Träumen hat, hat keinen Mut zum Kämpfen/He Who Doesn't Have the Courage to Dream, Doesn't Have the Courage to Fight*
Uwe Friessner—*Das Ende des Regenbogens/The End of the Rainbow*
Hans W. Geissendörfer—*Theodor Chindler*
Heidi Genée—*1 + 1 = 3*

Wolf Gremm—*Fabian*
Klaus Michael Gruber—*Winterreise im Olympiastadion/Winter Trip in the Olympic Stadium*
Hans Andreas Guttner—** Alamanya Alamanya-Germania Germania*
Petra Haffter—*Wahnsinn, das ganze Leben ist Wahnsinn/Madness, This Whole Life Is Madness*
Frank Heinig—*Rache ist Blutwurst/Sweet Revenge*
Recha Jungmann—*Etwas tut weh/Something Hurts*
Thees Klahn—*Gitanes*
Alexander Kluge—*Die Patriotin/The Patriot*
Volker Koch—*Union Square*
Ingo Kratisch—*Henry Angst*
Werner Krüger—*Joseph Beuys-Jeder Mensch ist ein Künstler/Joseph Beuys-Everyone Is an Artist*
Norbert Kückelmann—*Die letzten Jahre der Kindheit/The Last Years of Childhood*
Reiner Kunze—*Die wunderbaren Jahre/The Wonderful Years*
Lothar Lambert—*Tiergarten/Zoo; Now or Never*
Klaus Lemke—*Arabische Nächte/Arabian Nights*
Peter Lilienthal—*David*
Marianne Lüdcke—*Die grosse Flatter/The Great Flutter*
Werner Masten and Michael Breining—*Baranski*
Klaus Müller-Laue and Herbert Rimbach—*Die Fluchtlinie/The Escape Route*
Werner Nekes—*Hurrycan*
Hans Noever—*Der Preis fürs Überleben/The Price of Survival*
Ulrike Ottinger—*Bildnis einer Trinkerin/Ticket of No Return*
Stefan Paul—*Reggae Sunsplash*
Werner Penzel—*Vagabundenkarawane/Vagabond Caravan*
Nicos Perakis—*Milo Milo*
Hansjürgen Pohland—*Warum die Ufos unseren Salat klauen/Why the Ufos Are Stealing Our Salad*
Rosa von Praunheim—*Armee der Liebenden oder Aufstand der Perversen/Army of the Lovers or The Revolt of the Perverse; Todesmagazin oder: Wie werde ich ein Blumentopf?/Death Magazine or: How to Become a Flower Pot?*
Peter Przygodda—*... als Diesel geboren/Born for Diesel*
Helga Reidemeister—*Von wegen "Schicksal"!/Who Says "Destiny"?*

Christian Rischert—*Lena Rais*
Ottokar Runze—*Der Mörder/The Murderer*
Sohrab Shahid Saless—*Die langen Ferien der Lotte H. Eisner/The Long Vacation of Lotte H. Eisner*
Helma Sanders-Brahms—*Deutschland, bleiche Mutter/Germany, Pale Mother*
Niklaus Schilling—*Der Willi-Busch-Report*
Volker Schlöndorff—*Die Blechtrommel/The Tin Drum*
Dietrich Schubert—*Das ist des Arbeitsmannes Los/Such Is the Fate of the Working Man*
Douglas Sirk—** Bourbon Street Blues*
Ulrich Stein—*Tag für Tag/Day for Day*
Hans-Christof Stenzel—*Sufferloh-Von heiliger Lieb und Trutz/Sufferloh*
George Tabori—*Frohes Fest/Merry Christmas*
Monica Teuber—*Primel macht ihr Haus verrückt/Primel Drives Everyone at Home Crazy*
Rudolf Thome and Cynthia Beatt—*Beschreibung einer Insel/Description of an Island*
Margarethe von Trotta—*Schwestern oder Die Balance des Glücks/Sisters or The Balance of Fortune*
Michael Verhoeven—*Sonntagskinder/Sunday Children*
Christian Virmond—*Der Unterhalter/The Entertainer*
Klaus G. Volkenborn, Johann Feindt, and Karl Siebig—*Unversöhnliche Erinnerungen/Irreconcilable Memories*
Christian Weisenborn and Michael Wulfes—*Profis/Pros*
Roswitha Ziegler, Niels-Christian Bolbrinker, and Bernd Westphal—*Die Herren machen das selber, dass ihnen der arme Mann Feyndt wird-Gorleben 1977-1979/It's the Gentlemen's Fault That the Poor Man Is Their Enemy-Gorleben 1977-1979*

1980: Herbert Achternbusch—*Der Neger Erwin/Black Erwin*
Robert Van Ackeren—*Die Reinheit des Herzens/Purity of Heart; Deutschland privat/Private Glimpses of Germany*
Claudia von Alemann—*Die Reise nach Lyon/The Trip to Lyon*
Stefan Aust, Alexander von Eschwege, Alexander Kluge, and Volker Schlöndorff—*Der Kandidat/The Candidate*
Ilona Baltrusch—*Flug durch die Nacht/Flight through the Night*
Uschi Barthelmess-Weller and Werner Meyer—*Die Kinder aus No. 67/The Children from No. 67*

Gloria Behrens—*Rosi und die grosse Stadt/Rosi and the Big City*
Friedemann Beyer—*Ein Haus steht im Wind-Leben meiner Grossmutter Marie Holder/A House Stands in the Wind-Life of My Grandmother Marie Holder*
Walter Bockmayer and Rolf Bührmann—*Looping*
Rainer Boldt—*Ich hatte einen Traum/I Had a Dream*
Wolfgang Brader—*Wie ein Fremder/Like a Stranger*
Thomas Brasch—*Engel aus Eisen/Iron Angels*
Heide Breitel and Eva Hammel—* *Die kleinen Kleberinnen/The Little Snippers*
Peter F. Bringmann—*Theo gegen den Rest der Welt/Theo against the Rest of the World*
Jutta Brückner—*Hungerjahre/Hunger Years; Laufen lernen/The First Steps*
Wolfgang Büld—*British Rock-Ready for the 80's*
Christel Buschmann—*Gibbi Westgermany*
Bastian Clevé—*Exit Sunset Boulevard*
Christoph Dreher and Heiner Mühlenbrock—*Okay Okay-Der moderne Tanz/Okay Okay-The Modern Dance*
Ulrich Edel—*Christiane F.-Wir Kinder vom Bahnhof Zoo/Christiane F.*
Klaus Emmerich—*Trokadero*
Rainer Werner Fassbinder—*Berlin Alexanderplatz; Lili Marleen*
Klaus-Peter Fischer—*Italienische Karriere/Italian Career*
Peter Fratzscher—*Asphaltnacht/Asphalt Night*
Peter Goedel—*Talentprobe/Talent Contest*
Vadim Glowna—*Desperado City*
Jörg Graser—*Der Mond ist nur a nackerte Kugel/The Moon Is Only a Naked Globe*
Rolf Gregan—*Didi Hallervorden-Alles im Eimer/Didi Hallervorden-Everything's Fouled Up*
Wolf Gremm—*Kein Reihenhaus für Robin Hood/No Tract Home for Robin Hood*
Martin Gressmann—*Heinrich auf der Erbse/Heinrich and the Pea*
Detlef Gumm and Hans-Georg Ullrich—*Von Überstehen der Sonne/The Survival of the Sun*
Matthias von Gunten—*Quelle Günther/Stoolie Günther*
Reinhard Hauff—*Endstation Freiheit/Slow Attack*
Peter Heller—*Usambara-Das Land, wo Glaube Bäume versetzen soll/Usambara-The Land Where Faith Is Supposed to Move*

Trees; *Der da ist tot und der beginnt zu sterben/This Man Is Dead and That One Is Dying* (with Wolf Reuter)

Oliver Herbrich—*Das stolze und traurige Leben des Mathias Kneissl/The Proud and Sad Life of Mathias Kneissl*

Dieter Hildebrandt—*Der gelbe Stern-Die Judenverfolgung von 1933 bis 1945/The Yellow Star-Persecution of the Jews from 1933 to 1945*

Claudia Holldack—*Don Quichottes Kinder/Don Quixote's Children*

Recha Jungmann—*Zwischen Mond und Sonne/Between the Sun and the Moon*

Alfred Jungraithmayr—**Bruno, wie geht's?/Bruno, How Are You?*

Hartmut Kaminski and Dieter Vervuurt—*Alles andere kann ich sehen, doch solche Menschen nicht/I Can Look at Anything except Those People*

Erwin Keusch—*Soweit das Auge reicht/As Far as the Eye Can See*

Rainer Klaholz—*Herbstkatzen/Autumn Cats*

Peter Krieg—*Septemberweizen/September Wheat*

Christoph Kühn—*Falsche Bilder/False Images*

Micky Kwella—*Die von der Strasse/The Street People*

Lothar Lambert—*Die Alptraumfrau/The Nightmare Woman*

Klaus Lemke—*Flitterwochen/Honeymoon*

Peter Lilienthal—*Der Aufstand/La Insurreccion/The Insurrection*

Udo Lindenberg—*Panische Zeiten/Panic-ridden Times*

Gerhard Mandler—*Day-Die Zeiten haben sich geändert/Day-Times Have Changed*

Jeanine Meerapfel—*Malou*

Dieter Meier—*Jetzt und alles/Now and Everything*

Elfi Mikesch—*Was soll'n wir denn machen ohne den Tod?/What Are We Supposed to Do without Death?*

Lutz Mommartz—*Tango durch Deutschland/Tango through Germany*

Hans Noever—*Total vereist/The Wake*

Gertrud Pinkus—*Das höchste Gut einer Frau ist ihr Schweigen/Il valore della donna e il suo silenzio/The Most Important Thing a Woman Owns Is Her Silence*

Werner Possardt and Frank Döhmann—*Fünf Flaschen für Angelika/Five Noodles for Angelika*

Udo Radek and Lothar Woite—*"... und wenn wir nicht wollen?"*

oder: Wer saniert hier wen?/"... And If We Don't Want to?" or: Who Is Cleaning Out Whom?
Edgar Reitz—*Geschichten aus den Hunsrückdörfern/Stories from the Hunsrück Villages*
Jochen Richter—*Nullpunkt/Point Zero*
Frank Ripploh—*Taxi zum Klo/Taxi to the Loo*
Josef Rödl—*Franz-der leise Weg/Franz-The Gentle Path*
Ottokar Runze—*Stern ohne Himmel/A Skyless Star*
Sohrab Shahid Saless—*Ordnung/Order*
Helke Sander—*Der subjektive Faktor/The Subjective Factor*
Ulrich Schamoni—*Das Traumhaus/The House of My Dreams*
Roland Schraut—*Stückgut/Piece Goods*
Werner Schroeter—*Palermo oder Wolfsburg/Palermo or Wolfsburg; Die Generalprobe/La Répétition générale/The Dress Rehearsal; * Weisse Reise/White Trip*
Dietrich Schubert—* *365 Tage im Jahr/365 Days a Year*
Katrin Seybold—* *Schimpft uns nicht Zigeneuner/Gypsy's No Term of Abuse*
Christian Sievers and Steven Adamczewski—*Kreuzberg "Ahoi"*
Bernhard Sinkel—*Kaltgestellt/Put on Ice*
Phillip Sonntag—*Die Momskys oder Nie wieder Sauerkraut/The Momskys or Never Again Sauerkraut*
Peter Stein—*Gross und klein/Large and Small*
Ulrich Stein—* *Postcards from America*
Thomas Tanner—*Am Piano Jack Trommer/At the Piano Jack Trommer*
Rudolf Thome—* *Hast du Lust, mit mir einen Kaffee zu trinken?/Would You Like to Have Coffee with Me?; Berlin Chamissoplatz*
Muscha and Trini Trimpop—*Humanes Töten/Humane Killing*
Wolfgang Tumler—*Der rote Strumpf/The Red Stocking*
Klaus Tuschen—*Catch Up Paradise*
Herbert Vesely—*Egon Schiele-Exzesse/Egon Schiele-Excesses*
Christian Weisenborn and Michael Wulfe—*Der Rasen ihrer Träume/The Pitch of Their Dreams*
Franz Weisz—*Charlotte*
Wim Wenders and Nicholas Ray—*Nick's Film-Lightning over Water*
Wigbert Wicker—*Car-Napping*

Klaus Wildenhahn—*Der Nachwelt eine Botschaft-Ein Arbeiterdichter/A Message for Posterity-A Working-Class Poet*
Klaus Wyborny—* *Potpourri aus östlich von keinem Westen/Potpourri from East of No West;* * *Das szenische Opfer/The Scenic Sacrifice*

1981: Herbert Achternbusch—*Das letzte Loch/The Last Hole*
Percy Adlon—*Céleste*
Marie Bardischewski and Ursula Jeshel—*Tino Modotti-Fotografin und Revolutionärin 1896-1942/Tino Modotti-Photographer and Revolutionary 1896-1942*
Gabriele Bartels, Barbara Etz, Niels Christian Bolbrinker, Barbara Hennings, Christoph Marzian, Helmut Nierychlo, Barbare Rhode, Klaus Salge, Wolfgang Schikrafft—*Schade, dass Beton nicht brennt/Too Bad Concrete Doesn't Burn*
Alfred Behrens—*Berliner Stadtbahnbilder/Berlin S-Bahn Pictures*
Dagmar Beiersdorf—*Dirty Daughters-Die Hure und der Hurensohn/Dirty Daughters-The Whore and Her Son*
Werner Biedermann—*Des Lebens ganze Fülle oder Das goldene Zeitalter/The Richness of Life or The Golden Age*
Hartmut Bitomsky—*Highway 40/West-Reise in Amerika/Highway 40/West-A Trip through America*
Christian Boekel and Beate Rose—*Der lange Atem/The Deep Breath*
Christel Buschmann—*Comeback*
Richard Claus—*Bananen Paul/Banana Paul*
Hellmuth Costard and Jürgen Ebert—*Witzleben*
Elbe-Film Gruppe—*Beispiel Elbe-Zerstörung eines Lebensraums/The Elbe for Instance-Destruction of a Landscape*
Heinz Emigholz—*Normalsatz/The Basis of Makeup I*
Torsten Emrich—*Die Boonekamp-Affäre/The Boonekamp Affair*
Axel Engstfeld—*Von Richtern und anderen Sympathisanten/About Judges and Other Sympathizers*
Harun Farocki—*Etwas wird sichtbar/Something Becomes Visible*
Rainer Werner Fassbinder—*Lola; Theater in Trance*
Pia Frankenberg, Horst Edler, Robert Berghoff, Stefan Limmroth, Klaus Bueb, Ingo Helm, Tillmann Scholl—*Nachtbilder/Images of Night*
Roger Fritz—*Frankfurt, Kaiserstrasse*

Veith von Fürstenberg—*Feuer und Schwert-Die Legende von Tristan und Isolde/Tristan and Isolde*
Radu Gabrea—*Fürchte dich nicht, Jakob!/Don't Be Afraid, Jakob!*
Hans W. Geissendörfer—*Der Zauberberg/The Magic Mountain*
Heidi Genée—*Stachel im Fleisch/Thorn in the Flesh*
Thomas Giefer and Ulrich Tilgner—*Schah matt/Shahmate*
Helmut Christian Görlitz—*Das Ende vom Anfang/The End of the Beginning*
Wolf Gremm—*Nach Mitternacht/After Midnight*
Michael de Groot—*Amphitryon*
Alexandra von Grote—*Weggehen um anzukommen/Depart to Arrive*
Hans Andreas Guttner—*Familie Villano kehrt nicht zurück/The Villanos Aren't Coming Back*
Peter Hajek—*Sei zärtlich, Pinguin/Be Gentle, Penguin*
"Arnold Hau"—*Das Casanova-Projekt*
Helmut Herbst—*Eine deutsche Revolution/A German Revolution*
Werner Herzog—*Fitzcarraldo*
Michael Hoffmann and Harry Raymon—*Regentropfen/Raindrops*
Monika Hoffmann—*Die alten Leute vom Kreuzberger Kiez/The Old People of Kreuzberg*
Claudia Holldack—*Vor den Vätern sterben die Söhne/The Sons Die before Their Fathers*
Bert Holterdorf, Andreas Oswald, and Ralph Sotscheck—*Belfast*
Rebecca Horn—*La Ferdinanda*
Christoph Hübner and Gabriele Voss—*Die Einwanderer/The Immigrants*
Stephan Kayser—*Magma-Reise von hier nach dort/Magma-Journey from Here to There*
Angelika Kettelhack—*Jonas und der aufrechte Gang/Jonas: To Walk Upright*
Erwin Keusch and Norbert Wiedmer—*Wunden und Narben/Wounds and Scars*
Beate Klöckner—*Kopfschuss/Nightfall*
Erwin Kneihsl—*Gemischter Salat-French Dressing/Mixed Salad-French Dressing*

Horst Königstein and Heinrich Breloer—*Das Beil von Wandsbek/The Axe of Wandsbek*
Lothar Lambert—*Fucking City*
Klaus Lemke—*Wie die Weltmeister/Like World Champions*
Helmer von Lützelburg—*Die Nacht des Schicksals/The Fateful Night*
Stefan Lukschy and Christian Rateuke—*Wer spinnt da, Herr Doktor?/Who's Crazy, Dear Doctor?*
Jeanine Meerapfel—*Im Land meiner Eltern/In the Country of My Parents*
Dorothea Neukirchen—*Dabbel Trabbel/Double Trouble*
Rüdiger Nüchtern—*Nacht der Wölfe/Night of the Wolves*
Ulrike Ottinger—*Freak Orlando*
Wolfram Paulus Jr.—*Wochenend/Weekend*
Wolfgang Petersen—*Das Boot*
Berengar Pfahl—*Komm doch mit nach Monte Carlo/Come On Along to Monte Carlo*
Werner Possardt—*Strommberg-Die letzte Nacht/Strommberg-The Last Night*
Rosa von Praunheim—*Rote Liebe/Red Love; Unsere Leichen leben noch/Our Bodies Are Still Alive*
Peer Raben—*Heute spielen wir den Boss/Today We'll Be the Boss*
Christian Rateuke and Hartmann Schmige—*Der Mann im Pyjama/The Man in Pyjamas*
Helma Sanders-Brahms—*Die Berührte/No Mercy No Future*
Carl Schenkel—*Kalt wie Eis/Cold as Ice*
Niklaus Schilling—*Zeichen und Wunder/Signs and Miracles*
Volker Schlöndorff—*Die Fälschung/Circle of Deceit*
Eckhart Schmidt—*Der Fan/The Fan*
Edith Schmidt and David H. Wittenberg—*Das Land, das wir uns nehmen/The Land We Take for Ourselves*
Werner Schroeter—*Tag der Idioten/Day of the Idiots; Liebeskonzil/Lovers' Council*
Friedemann Schulz—*Der Tod in der Waschstrasse/Death in the Carwash*
Manfred Stelzer—*Perle der Karibik/Pearl of the Caribbean*
Hans Stempel and Martin Ripkens—*Wie geht ein Mann?/To Go as a Man*

Hans-Christof Stenzel—*Marmor, Stein und Eisen bricht/Iron Bends and Marble Breaks; Obszön/Obscene*
Jean-Marie Straub and Danièle Huillet—*Zu früh, zu spät/Trop tôt, trop tard/ Too Early, Too Late*
Antje Strost and Hans-Helmut Grotjahn—*Marika und Caterina*
Monica Teuber—*Kenn ich...Weiss ich...War ich schon/I Know...I See...I Already Was*
Margarethe von Trotta—*Die bleierne Zeit/Marianne und Juliane*
Tuwat-Wochenschau Filmkollektiv—* *Tuwat*
Verband Deutscher Nachwuchsfilm—*Heimatkunde/Social Studies*
Gisela Weilemann, Helmer von Lützelburg, Dominik Graf, Johann Schmid, Wolfgang Büld—*Neonstadt/Neon City*
Aribert Weis—*Das Haus im Park/The House in the Park*
Klaus Werner and Uschi Madeisky—*Kleiner Mann-was tun?/What To Do, Little Man?*
Karsten Wichniarz—*Kein Land/No Country*
Klaus Wildenhahn—* *Bandonion (1)-Deutsche Tangos/Bandonion (1)-German Tangos;* * *Bandonion (2)-Tango im Exil/Bandonion (2)-Tango in Exile*
Adolf Winkelmann—*Jede Menge Kohle/A Lot of Bills to Pay*
Klaus Wyborny—*Am Arsch der Welt/To Have and To Be*
Roswitha Ziegler, Bernd Westphal, and Niels-Christian Bolbrinker—*Gorleben-der Traum von einer Sache/Gorleben-The Dream of a Cause*

* short- and medium-length films

Appendix B

Readings in English on West German Film: A Selected Bibliography

The following entries serve as a basic guide through the large amount of critical and scholarly writing on West German Film produced in the English language between 1962 and early 1982. No attempt has been made to be complete. At best the catalogue can list *only the more representative literature* on the subject. Certain criteria guided the selection process:

—scholarly and critical commentaries were preferred to more ephemeral coverage (short reviews and interviews);

—certain reviews and occasion-bound articles were included due to their importance for the reception of New German Cinema as a whole or of individual directors;

—an effort was made to list articles written on directors less well-known in the United States as well as ones devoted to the more heralded filmmakers;

—in the case of Fassbinder/Herzog/Syberberg/Wenders, I have tried to single out only the most significant work devoted to these figures. Especially in these instances, the word "selected" truly does apply for this bibliography.

For lengthy bibliographies of recent German (and other foreign) literature on West German film, these works have proven to be helpful:

Fisher, Robert and Joe Hembus. *Der neue deutsche Film 1960-1980*. Munich: Goldmann, 1981.

Jansen, Peter W. and Wolfram Schütte, ed. *Herzog/Kluge/Straub*. Munich: Hanser, 1976.

―――. *Rainer Werner Fassbinder*. 3rd rev. ed. Munich: Hanser, 1979.
―――. *Werner Herzog*. Munich: Hanser, 1979.
―――. *Werner Schroeter*. Munich: Hanser, 1980.
Künzel, Uwe. *Wim Wenders: Ein Filmbuch*. Freiburg: Dreisam, 1981.
Lewandowski, Rainer. *Die Filme von Alexander Kluge*. Hildesheim/New York: Olms, 1980.

―――. *Die Filme von Volker Schlöndorff*. Hildesheim/New York: Olms, 1981.

Möhrmann, Renate. *Die Frau mit der Kamera: Filmemacherinnen in der Bundesrepublik Deutschland*. Munich: Hanser, 1980.

Pflaum, Hans Günther and Hans Helmut Prinzler. *Film in der Bundesrepublik Deutschland*. Munich: Hanser, 1979.

Abbreviations:

AF	*American Film*
BFI	British Film Institute
FC	*Film Comment*
FQ	*Film Quarterly*
IFG	*International Film Guide*
Kino	*Kino: German Film* (West Berlin)
LFQ	*Literature/Film Quarterly*
NGC	*New German Critique*
NYT	*New York Times*
QRFS	*Quarterly Review of Film Studies*
S & S	*Sight & Sound*
VV	*Village Voice*

General Introductions, Surveys, and Updates

Adorno, Theodor W. "Transparencies on Film." Trans. Thomas Y. Levin. *NGC*, No. 24-25 (Fall/Winter 1981-2), pp. 199-205.

Baker, Rob. " 'New German Cinema': A Fistful of Myths." *Soho Weekly News*, 23 March 1978, pp. 21-23.

Bean, Robin. "Bubis Kino." *Films and Filming*, February 1967, pp. 49-56.

―――. "Nein Neue Welle." *Films and Filming*, April 1962, pp. 12, 44.

Bucher, Felix. *Germany: An Illustrated Guide*. London: Zwemmer (Screen Series), 1970.

Canby, Vincent. "The German Renaissance—No Room for Laughter or Love." *NYT*, 11 Dec. 1977.

Clarke, Gerald. "Seeking Planets That Do Not Exist: The new German cinema is the liveliest in Europe." *Time*, 20 March 1978, pp. 51-53.

Cockrell, Edward D. "A Festival of New German Cinema." *Preview*, Nov.-Dec. 1980, pp. 15-29.

Cohen, Jules. "The Chronic Crisis in West German Film." *FC*, Winter 1965, pp. 32-35.

Collins, Richard and Vincent Porter. *WDR and the Arbeiterfilm: Fassbinder, Ziewer and others*. London: BFI, 1981.

_____. "West German Television: the crisis of public service broadcasting." *S & S*, Summer 1980, pp. 172-77.

_____. "*Westdeutscher Rundfunk* and the *Arbeiterfilm* (1967-1977)." *QRFS*, Spring 1980, pp. 233-51.

Cook, David A. "Germany: Das Neue Kino." In *A History of Narrative Film*. New York/London: Norton, 1981, pp. 604-23.

Dawson, Jan. "The Industry: German Weasels (*Filmverlag* Follies)." *FC*, May-June 1977, pp. 33-34.

_____. "A Labyrinth of Subsidies: The Origins of the New German Cinema." *S & S*, Winter 1980/81, pp. 14-20.

Donner, Wolf. "Films Around the World: The Germans Are Coming." *Atlas*, March 1976, pp. 29-30.

Durgnat, Raymond. "From Caligari to *Hitler*." *FC*, July-August 1980, pp. 59-70.

Eidsvik, Charles. "Behind the Crest of the Wave: An Overview of the New German Cinema." *LFQ*, Vol. 7, No. 3 (1979), pp. 167-81.

_____. "The State as Movie Mogul." *FC*, March-April 1979, pp. 60-66.

Elsaesser, Thomas. "The Postwar German Cinema." In *Fassbinder*. Ed. Tony Rayns. 2nd rev. ed. London: BFI, 1979, pp. 1-16.

Fehervary, Helen, Claudia Lenssen, and Judith Mayne. "From Hitler to Hepburn: A Discussion of Women's Film. Production and Reception." *NGC*, No. 24-25 (Fall/Winter 1981-2), pp. 172-85.

Gambaccini, Peter. "The New German Film Makers." *Horizon*, June 1980, pp. 22-33.

Greenspun, Roger. "Germans Turn History Into Cinema." *NYT*, 12 May 1972.

Gregor Ulrich. *The German Experimental Film of the Seventies*. Munich: Goethe Institute, 1980.

_____. "The German Film in 1964: Stuck at Zero." *FQ*, Winter 1964, pp. 7-21. See also rebuttal and reply in Fall 1965, pp. 63-64.

Himes, Geoffrey. "Breaking Through: New German Images on Film." *Unicorn Times*, February 1980, pp. 19-21.

Holloway, Ronald. "A German Breakthrough?" *Kino*, No. 1 (October 1979), pp. 4-17.

_____. "The German Cameraman." *Kino*, No. 6 (Spring 1982), pp. 41-45.

_____. "German Film Tour 1980." *Kino*, No. 2 (Spring 1980), pp. 41-61.

_____. "New German Cinema Seeks Way Out of 20-Yr. Deadend." *Variety*, 28 Feb. 1979, pp. 32ff.

_____. "Oskar in Amerika." *Kino*, No. 3 (Summer 1980), pp. 3-10.

_____. "Who's Who in West German Film Industry: A Directory of Directors and Filmmakers Over the Period 1957-1977." *Variety*, 2 June 1977, pp. 51ff.

Jacobs, Diane. "Hitler's Ungrateful Grandchildren: Today's German Filmmakers." *AF,* May 1980, pp. 34-40.

Jansen, Peter W. *The New German Film.* Munich: Goethe Institute, 1980.

Johnston, Sheila. "The Author as Public Institution: The 'New' Cinema in the Federal Republic of Germany." *Screen Education,* Nos. 32/33 (Autumn-Winter 1979/80), pp. 67-78.

Lenssen, Claudia. *Woman's Cinema in Germany.* Munich: Goethe Institute, 1980.

Lubow, Arthur. "Cinema's New Wunderkinder." *New Times,* 14 Nov. 1975, pp. 50ff.

Manvell, Roger and Heinrich Fraenkel. "The Nineteen-sixties and the New German Cinema." In *The German Cinema.* New York/Washington: Praeger, 1971, pp. 124-33.

McCormick, Ruth. "Metropolis Now: The New German Cinema." *In These Times,* 30 July 1979, pp. 20-21.

Mekas, Jonas. "Movie Journal." *VV,* 13 April 1972, p. 77.

Moeller, Hans-Bernhard. "Brecht and 'Epic' Film Medium: The Cineaste, Playwright, Film Theoretician and His Influence." *Wide Angle,* Vol. 3, No. 4 (1980), pp. 4-11. (Brecht's influence on Young German Film)

———. "New German Cinema and Its Precarious Subsidy and Finance System." *QRFS,* Spring 1980, pp. 157-68.

Overbey, David L. "From Murnau to Munich. New German Cinema." *S & S,* Spring 1974, pp. 101-03, 115.

Patalas, Enno. "German Cinema since 1945." In *Cinema: A Critical Dictionary.* Ed. Richard Roud. 2 vols. New York: Viking, 1980, pp. 423-36.

Petzke, Ingo. *German Experimental Films: From the Beginnings to 1970.* Munich: Goethe Institute, 1981.

Prinzler, Hans Helmut. *Satire, Irony, Humour in Federal German Film.* Munich: Goethe Institute, 1980.

Rentschler, Rick. *Misère-en-scène:* Young German Filmmakers on Dangerous Ground." *Movietone News,* No. 49 (April 1976), pp. 18-24.

Rickey, Carrie. "Beyond Sorrow and Pity." *VV,* 14 Jan. 1981, p. 46.

Roth, Wilhelm. *The Federal Republic of Germany as Reflected in its Documentary Films.* Munich: Goethe Institute, 1980.

Rumler, Fritz. "Hurrahs for the Wunderkinder." Trans. J. Turnbull. *Thousand Eyes,* April 1976, pp. 4-5.

Sandford, John. *The New German Cinema.* Totowa, NJ: Barnes & Noble, 1980.

———. "The New German Cinema." *German Life and Letters,* April 1979, pp. 206-28.

Sarris, Andrew. "The Germans Are Coming! The Germans Are Coming!" *VV,* 27 Oct. 1975, pp. 137-38.

Scheib-Rothbart, Ingrid, ed. *New German Cinema in the American Press 1979: A Selection.* New York: Goethe House, 1980.

Silberman, Marc. "Cine-Feminists in West Berlin." *QRFS,* Spring 1980, pp. 217-32.

_____. "Women Filmmakers in West Germany: A Catalog." *camera obscura*, No. 6 (1980), pp. 122-52.
Stein, Elliott. "Germany in Winter." *FC,* May-June 1981, pp. 20-23.
Strout, Andrea. "West Germany's Film Miracle." *AF,* May 1980, pp. 37-39.
A Tribute to Das Kleine Fernsehspiel/ZDF. Alternative Filmmaking in Television. Berkeley/San Francisco: University Art Museum, Pacific Film Archive, and Goethe Institute San Francisco, 1979.
Vogel, Amos. "A Nation Comes out of Shell-Shock." *VV,* 4 May 1972, pp. 87-88.
Whitney, Craig R. "New German Movie Directors Are Winning Acclaim." *NYT,* 26 Jan. 1979.
Wiseman, Carter and others. "The German Film Renaissance." *Newsweek* (International Edition), 2 Feb. 1976, pp. 42-46.
Women's Cinema in Germany. Munich: Goethe Institute, 1979.
"Young German Film" (reprinted from *Der Spiegel*). *FC,* Spring 1970, pp. 32-44.
Zurbach, Werner. "Young German Directors." *FQ,* Spring 1961, p. 65.

Individual Directors

Herbert Achternbusch:
Achternbusch, Herbert. "Achternbusch on Chaplin: The Throne is Vacant." Trans. Ronald Holloway. *Kino,* No. 1 (October 1979), pp. 21-23.
Kael, Pauline. "Enfant Terrible." *New Yorker,* 13 Nov. 1978, pp. 223-28. *(Bye Bye, Bavaria)*

Percy Adlon:
Milne, Tom. "A mystery passage: *Céleste.*" *S & S,* Spring 1982, pp. 132-33.

Horst Bienek:
White, J.J. "Horst Bienek's *Die Zelle*—Novel and Film." *German Life and Letters,* April 1979, pp. 229-47. *(The Cell)*

Walter Bockmayer and Rolf Bührmann:
Canby, Vincent. "Screen: Jane since Tarzan." *NYT,* 7 April 1978. *(Jane Is Jane Forever)*

Hark Bohm:
Holloway, Ronald. *"Moritz, lieber Moritz."* *Variety,* 29 March 1978, p. 22. *(Moritz, Dear Moritz)*

Uwe Brandner:
Vierling, David L. "A Conversation with Uwe Brandner." *Kino,* No. 1 (October 1979), pp. 24-26. *(Fifty-Fifty)*

Hellmuth Costard:
  Dawson, Jan, ed. *The Films of Hellmuth Costard.* London: Riverside Studios, 1979.
  Dawson, Jan. "Germany in Autumn & Eine Kleine Godard [sic]." *Take One,* November 1978, pp. 14–15, 44–45. *(The Little Godard)*

Ulich Edel:
  Maslin, Janet. "Film: A Child Awry in *Christiane F.*" *NYT,* 19 March 1982.

Ingemo Engström and Gerhard Theuring:
  Engström, Ingemo and Gerhard Theuring. "Dossier: *Escape Route to Marseilles.*" Trans. Barry Ellis-Jones with intro. by Steve Neale and Paul Willemen. *Framework,* No. 18(1982), pp. 22-29.

Rainer Werner Fassbinder:
  Aitken, Will. "*Despair.*" *Take One,* January 1979, pp. 6–8.
  Alvarado, Manuel. "*Eight Hours are not a Day* (and Afterword)." In *Fassbinder.* Ed. Tony Rayns. 2nd rev. ed. London: BFI, 1979, pp. 70-78.
  Badder, D.J. "Rainer Werner Fassbinder." *Film Dope,* September 1978, pp. 16-18.
  Berman, Bruce. "*Merchant of the Four Seasons.*" *Take One,* Nov.-Dec. 1972, pp. 39-40.
  Borchardt, Edith. "Leitmotif and Structure in Fassbinder's *Effie* [sic] *Briest.*" *LFQ,* Vol. 7, No. 3 (1979), pp. 201-07.
  Borden, Diane M. "German Chamber Film: Fassbinder vs. Syberberg." *Proceedings of the Purdue University Fifth Annual Conference on Film.* West Lafayette: Purdue Univ., 1980, pp. 244-49. *(The Bitter Tears of Petra von Kant)*
  Britton, Andrew. "*Fox and his Friends:* Foxed." *Jump Cut,* No. 16 (November 1977), pp. 22-23.
  Canby, Vincent. "Rainer Fassbinder—The Most Original Talent Since Godard." *NYT,* 6 March 1977.
  Cant, Bob. "Fox and his Friends: Fassbinder's *Fox.*" *Jump Cut,* No. 16 (November 1977), p. 22.
  Combs, Richard. "*Chinese Roulette* and *Despair.*" *S & S,* Autumn 1978, pp. 258-60.
  Dawson, Jan. "The Sacred Terror: shadows of terrorism in the new German cinema." *S & S,* Autumn 1979, pp. 242-45. *(The Third Generation* and other films)
  ———. "Women—present tense." *Take One,* July 1979, pp. 10-12. *(The Marriage of Maria Braun)*
  ——— and Joe Medjuck. "Misc: Fassbinder: A Year (or so) in the Life." *Take One,* vol. 4, No. 12 (1975), p. 26.
  Denby, David. "The Brilliant, Brooding Films of Rainer Fassbinder." *NYT,* 1 Feb. 1976.
  Dyer, Richard. "Reading Fassbinder's Sexual Politics." In *Fassbinder.* Ed. Tony Rayns. 2nd rev. ed. London: BFI, 1979, pp. 54-64.

Elsaesser, Thomas. "A Cinema of Vicious Circles (and Afterword)." In *Fassbinder.* Ed. Tony Rayns. 2nd rev. ed. London: BFI, 1979, pp. 24-53.

_____. "Primary Identification and the Historical Subject: Fassbinder and Germany." *Ciné-Tracts,* No. 11 (Fall 1980), pp. 43-52.

Farber, Manny and Patricia Patterson. "R.W. Fassbinder." *FC,* Nov.-Dec. 1975, pp. 5-7.

Fassbinder. Trans. Ruth McCormick. New York: Tanam, 1981.

Fassbinder, R.W. "Fassbinder on Sirk." Trans. Thomas Elsaesser. *FC,* Nov.-Dec. 1975, pp. 22-24.

_____. "Insects in a Glass Cage: random thoughts on the films of Claude Chabrol." Trans. Derek Prouse. *S & S,* Autumn 1976, pp. 205-06, 252.

Fell, John L. *"Despair." FQ,* Fall 1979, pp. 59-61.

Figge, Richard C. "The Modus Operandi of Rainer Werner Fassbinder." *Die Unterrichtspraxis,* Fall 1979, pp. 19-26.

Franklin, James C. "The Films of Fassbinder: Form and Formula." *QRFS,* Spring 1980, pp. 169-81.

_____. "Method and Message: Forms of Communication in Fassbinder's *Angst Essen Seele Auf." LFQ,* Vol. 7, No. 3 (1979), pp. 182-200. *(Ali: Fear Eats the Soul)*

Gilliatt, Penelope. "Fassbinder." *New Yorker,* 14 June 1976, pp. 93-96. *(The Bitter Tears of Petra von Kant)*

_____. "No Sadness That Art Cannot Quell." *New Yorker,* 28 March 1977, pp. 118-22. *(Mother Küsters Goes to Heaven)*

Gow, Gordon. "Obsession." *Films and Filming,* March 1976, pp. 12-17.

Greenspun, Roger. "Phantom of Liberty. Thoughts on Fassbinder's *Fist-Right of of Freedom." FC,* Nov.-Dec. 1975, pp. 8-10. *(Fox and His Friends)*

Harrigan, Renny. *"Effi Briest. The Marquise of O . . . :* Women Oppressed!" *Jump Cut,* No. 15 (July 1977), pp. 3-5.

Hughes, John, "Why Herr R. Ran Amok. Fassbinder and Modernism." *FC,* Nov.-Dec. 1975, pp. 11-13.

_____ and Ruth McCormick. "Rainer Werner Fassbinder and the Death of Family Life." *Thousand Eyes,* April 1977, pp. 4-5ff.

_____ and Brooks Riley. "A New Realism: Fassbinder Interviewed." *FC,* Nov.-Dec. 1975, pp. 14-17.

Iden, Peter. "Making an Impact—Rainer Werner Fassbinder and the Theatre." In *Fassbinder.* Ed. and trans. Tony Rayns. 2nd rev. ed. London: BFI, 1979, pp. 17-23.

Jaehne, Karen. *"Lili Marleen." FQ,* Winter 1981-1982, pp. 42-46.

Johnson, Catherine. "The Imaginary & *The Bitter Tears of Petra von Kant." Wide Angle,* Vol. 3, No. 4 (1980), pp. 20-25.

Johnston, Sheila. "A Star is Born: Fassbinder and the New German Cinema." *NGC,* No. 24-25 (Fall/Winter 1981-2), pp. 57-72.

Karsunke, Yaak. "History of Anti-Teater: The Beginnings." In *Fassbinder.* Trans. Ruth McCormick. New York: Tanam, 1981, pp. 1-10.

Kling, Vincent. "The Dynamics of Defeat: Aspects of Rainer Werner Fassbinder's Art." *1976 Film Studies Annual.* West Lafayette: Purdue Research Foundation, 1976, pp. 157-66.

Leaming, Barbara. "Rainer Werner Fassbinder's *Fear of Fear.*" *Take One,* July-August 1977, pp. 14-15.

———. "Structures of Alienation: *The Merchant of Four Seasons.*" *Jump Cut,* No. 10/11 (June 1976), pp. 39-40.

Lellis, George, "Retreat from Romanticism: Two Films from the Seventies." *FQ,* Summer 1975, pp. 16-20. *(The Merchant of Four Seasons)*

Limmer, Wolfgang. *Fassbinder.* Munich: Goethe Institute/Filmverlag der Autoren, 1973.

Linnett, Richard. *"The Third Generation."* *Cineaste,* Winter 1980-81, pp. 39-42.

Margretta, William R. "Reading the Writerly Film: Fassbinder's *Effi Briest* (1974)." In *Modern European Filmmakers and the Art of Adaptation.* Ed. Andrew S. Horton and Joan Magretta. New York: Ungar, 1981, pp. 248-62.

Mayne, Judith. "Fassbinder and Spectatorship." *NGC,* No. 12 (Fall 1977), pp. 61-74. *(Ali: Fear Eats the Soul)*

McCormick, Ruth. "Fassbinder and the Politics of Everyday Life." *Cineaste,* Vol. 8, No. 2 (1977), pp. 22-30.

———. "Fassbinder's Reality: An Imitation of Life." In *Fassbinder.* New York: Tanam, 1981, pp. 84-97.

———. *"The Marriage of Maria Braun."* *Cineaste,* Spring 1980, pp. 34-36.

Morris, George. "Fassbinder X 5." *FC,* Sept.-Oct. 1981, pp. 59-65. *(Jail Bait, Martha, I Only Want You to Love Me, Satan's Brew, Women in New York)*

Noonan, Tom. *"The Marriage of Maria Braun."* *FQ,* Spring 1980, pp. 40-45.

Rayns, Tony, ed. *Fassbinder.* 2nd rev. ed. London: BFI, 1979.

———. "Fassbinder, Form and Syntax." In *Fassbinder.* 2nd rev. ed. London: BFI, 1979, pp. 79-81.

———. "Forms of Address: Tony Rayns Interviews Three German Film Makers." *S & S,* Winter 1974/75, pp. 2-7. (Fassbinder, Syberberg, Wenders)

Rignall, John. "Rainer Werner Fassbinder's *An American Soldier* [sic]." *Monogram,* No. 2 (Summer 1971), pp. 20-21.

Sarris, Andrew. "Can Fassbinder Break the Box-Office Barrier?" *VV,* 22 Nov. 1976, p. 57.

———. "Fassbinder and Sirk: The Ties That Unbind." *VV,* 3 Sept. 1980, pp. 37-38. *(The Third Generation)*

———. "Further Thoughts on Fassbinder." *VV,* 11 July 1977, p. 39.

———. "Is History Merely an Old Movie?" *VV,* 8 July 1981, p. 33. *(Lili Marleen)*

———. "Lost Love, Found Despair." *VV,* 22 Nov. 1973, pp. 77-78. *(The Merchant of Four Seasons)*

Schütte, Wolfram. "Franz, Mieze, Reinhold, Death and the Devil: Rainer Werner Fassbinder's *Berlin Alexanderplatz.*" In *Fassbinder.* Trans. Ruth McCormick. New York: Tanam, 1981, pp. 98-109.

Sparrow, Norbert. " 'I Let the Audience Feel *and* Think' — An Interview with Rainer Werner Fassbinder." *Cineaste,* Vol. 8, No. 2 (1977), pp. 20-21.

Thieringer, Thomas. "Memories of Fassbinder's TV Work." In *Fassbinder.* Trans. Barrie Ellis-Jones. Ed. Tony Rayns. 2nd rev. ed. London: BFI, 1979, pp. 65-69.

Thomas, Paul. "Fassbinder: The Poetry of the Inarticulate." *FQ*, Winter 1976-77, pp. 2-17.

Thompson, Bill. "Germany, Fassbinder and Those Waves." *Cinegram*, No. 3 (1976/77), pp. 38-42.

Thomsen, Christian Braad. "Fassbinder's Holy Whores." *Take One*, Vol. 4, No. 6 (1974), pp. 12-16.

———. "Five Interviews with Fassbinder." In *Fassbinder*. Ed. Tony Rayns. 2nd rev. ed. London: BFI, 1979, pp. 82-101.

Thomson, David. "Rainer Werner Fassbinder." In *A Biographical Dictionary of Film*. 2nd rev. ed. NY: Morrow, 1981, pp. 182-83.

Whitney, Craig R. "Fassbinder: A New Director Movie Buffs Dote On." *NYT*, 16 Feb. 1977.

Wiegand, Wilfried. "The Doll in the Doll: Observations on Fassbinder's Films." In *Fassbinder*. Trans. Ruth McCormick. New York: Tanam, 1981, pp. 24-55.

———. "Interview with Rainer Werner Fassbinder." In *Fassbinder*. Trans. Ruth McCormick. New York: Tanam, 1981, pp. 56-82.

Wilson, David. "Anti-Cinema: Rainer Werner Fassbinder." *S & S*, Spring 1972, pp. 99-100, 113.

———. "Rainer Werner Fassbinder." *IFG 1976*. Ed. Peter Cowie. London: Tantivy, 1975, pp. 61-67.

———. "Rainer Werner Fassbinder." In *Cinema: A Critical Dictionary*. Ed. Richard Roud. 2 vols. New York: Viking, 1980, pp. 335-39.

Peter Fleischmann:
Fabrikant, Geraldine. "The Hunters and the Hunted." *VV*, 14 June 1973, p. 81. *(Hunting Scenes from Lower Bavaria)*

Fleischmann, Peter. "Not a Film." Trans. Charlotte Vokes-Dudgeon. *Framework*, No. 12 (1980), p. 15. *(Holocaust)*

Hans W. Geissendörfer:
Hoberman, J. "Excuse the Expressionism." *VV*, 5 Feb. 1979, p. 42. *(The Glass Cell)*

Steene, Birgitta. "Film as Theater: Geissendörfer's *The Wild Duck* (1976)." In *Modern European Filmmakers and the Art of Adaptation*. Ed. Andrew S. Horton and Joan Magretta. New York: Ungar, 1981, pp. 295-312.

Germany in Autumn:
Canby, Vincent. "Film: 13 Directors Make *Germany in Autumn*." *NYT*, 5 April 1979.

Coleman, J. "Films: Angst and After." *New Statesman*, 1 Dec. 1978, p. 762.

McCormick, Ruth. *"Germany in Autumn." Cineaste*, Spring 1979, pp. 53-54.

Peter Handke:
Hoberman, J. "She Vants To Be Alone." *VV*, 7 April 1980, p. 40. *(The Left-Handed Woman)*

Perlmutter, Ruth. "Visible Narrative, Visible Woman." *Millennium Film*

Journal, No. 6 (Spring 1980), pp. 18-30. *(The Left-Handed Woman* and other films)
  Strick, Philip, *"The Left-Handed Woman." S & S,* Summer 1979, p. 195.

Reinhard Hauff:
  Canby, Vincent. "German *Knife in the Head." NYT,* 23 April 1980.
  Fox, Terry Curtis. "MOMA's Boys." *VV,* 10 April 1978, pp. 48-49. *(The Main Actor* and *Paule Pauländer)*
  Kauffmann, Stanley. "Changing the World." *New Republic,* 26 April 1980, pp. 24-25. *(Knife in the Head)*
  Reinhard Hauff and his Films. Munich: Goethe Institute, n.d.
  Sarris, Andrew. "Starting from Ground Zero." *VV,* 28 April 1980, p. 45. *(Knife in the Head)*

Birgit and Wilhelm Hein:
  Hein, Birgit. "The Avantgarde and Politics." *Millennium Film Journal,* No. 2 (Spring-Summer 1978), pp. 23-28.
  Kiernan, Joanna. "Birgit & Wilhelm Hein: From Structural Studies to Now." *Millennium Film Journal,* No. 6 (Spring 1980), pp. 95-97.

Helmut Herbst:
  Hoberman, J. "Modernist Reds." *VV,* 3 Feb. 1982, p. 48. *(John Heartfield, Photomontagist)*

Werner Herzog:
  Andrews, Nigel. "Dracula in Delft." *AF,* October 1978, pp. 32-38. *(Nosferatu)*
  Bachmann, Gideon. "The Man on the Volcano: Werner Herzog." *FQ,* Fall 1977, pp. 2-10.
  Barthelme, Donald. "The Earth As An Overturned Bowl." *New Yorker,* 10 Sept. 1979, pp. 120-22. *(Woyzeck)*
  Benelli, Dana. "The Cosmos and Its Discontents." *Movietone News,* No. 56 (Nov. 1977), pp. 8-16. *(Aguirre, the Wrath of God* and *Signs of Life)*
  ———. "Mysteries of the Organism." *Movietone News,* No. 54 (June 1977), pp. 28-33. *(The Mystery of Kaspar Hauser)*
  Cairns, Francis. *"Fitzcarraldo." S & S,* Summer 1981, pp. 180-81.
  Cleere, Elizabeth. "Three Films by Werner Herzog: Seen in the Light of the Grotesque." *Wide Angle,* Vol. 3, No. 4 (1980), pp. 12-19. *(Even Dwarfs Started Small, Aguirre, the Wrath of God,* and *Fata Morgana)*
  Cocks, Jay. "Down and Out; Pleading Insanity; Grave New World." *Time,* 3 Nov. 1975, pp. 70ff. *(The Mystery of Kaspar Hauser)*
  Combs, Richard. "Werner Herzog." In *Cinema: A Critical Dictionary.* Ed. Richard Roud. 2 vols. New York: Viking, 1980, pp. 486-87.
  ———. *"Woyzeck." S & S,* Autumn 1979, pp. 259-60.
  Cott, Jonathan. "Signs of Life." *Rolling Stone,* 18 Nov. 1976, pp. 48-56. (Interview with Herzog)

Coursen, David. "Two Films by Werner Herzog." *Cinemonkey*, No. 16 (Winter 1979), pp. 22-24. *(Aguirre, the Wrath of God* and *Even Dwarfs Started Small)*

Davidson, David. "Borne Out of Darkness: The Documentaries of Werner Herzog." *Film Criticism*, Fall 1980, pp. 10-25.

Dawson, Jan. "Herzog's Magic Mountain." *S & S*, Winter 1977/78), pp. 57-58. *(Stroszek)*

Dorr, John H. *"Even Dwarfs Started Small." Take One*, Vol. 3, No. 6 (1972), pp. 35-36.

Eder, Richard. "A New Visionary in German Films." *NYT*, 10 July 1977.

Eisler, Ken. *"Aguirre, the Wrath of God." Movietone News*, No. 29 (Jan.-Feb. 1974), pp. 43-44.

———. "Offing the Pig: *Even Dwarfs Started Small." Movietone News*, No. 36 (October 1974), pp. 8-11.

Eisner, Lotte H. "Herzog in Dinkelsbuehl." *S & S*, Fall 1974, pp. 212-13. *(The Mystery of Kaspar Hauser)*

Elsaesser, Thomas. "The Cinema of Irony." *Monogram*, No. 5 (1974), pp. 1-2. (On Herzog and others)

Fell, John L. *"Heart of Glass." FQ*, Spring 1979, pp. 54-55.

Finger, Ellis. "Kaspar Hauser Doubly Portrayed: Peter Handke's *Kaspar* and Werner Herzog's *Every Man for Himself and God Against All." LFQ*, Vol. 7, No. 3 (1979), pp. 235-43.

Forbes, Jill. *"Heart of Glass." S & S*, Autumn 1977, pp. 255-56.

Gilliatt, Penelope. "Gold." *New Yorker*, 11 April 1977, pp. 127-28. *(Aguirre, the Wrath of God)*

Greenberg, Alan, Herbert Achternbusch, and Werner Herzog. *Heart of Glass*. Munich: Skellig, 1976.

Herzog, Werner. *Of Walking in Ice*. New York: Tanam, 1980.

———. *Screenplays*. New York: Tanam, 1980.

———. "Why Is There 'Being' at All, Rather than Nothing?" Trans. Stephen Lamb. *Framework*, No. 3 (Spring 1976), pp. 24-27.

Hoberman, J. "Over the Volcano." *VV*, 22 May 1978, p. 48. *(How Much Wood Would a Woodchuck Chuck* and *La Soufrière)*

Horak, Jan-Christopher. "Werner Herzog's *Écran Absurde." LFQ*, Vol. 7, No. 3 (1979), pp. 223-34. *(The Mystery of Kaspar Hauser)*

Kael, Pauline. "Metaphysical Tarzan." *New Yorker*, 20 Oct. 1975, pp. 142-49. *(The Mystery of Kaspar Hauser)*

Kauffmann, Stanley. "Secret Places, Secret Parts." *New Republic*, 1 Nov. 1975, pp. 22-23. *(The Mystery of Kaspar Hauser)*

Kawin, Bruce. *"Nosferatu." FQ*, Spring 1980, pp. 45-47.

Kent, Liticia. "Werner Herzog: 'Film Is Not the Art of Scholars, But of Illiterates.' " *NYT*, 11 Sept. 1977.

Lloyd, Peter. " 'Objectivity' as irony: Werner Herzog's *Fata Morgana." Monogram*, No. 5 (1974), pp. 8-9.

McCormick, Ruth and Pat Aufderheide. "Werner Herzog's *Heart of Glass*—Pro and Contra." *Cineaste*, Vol. 8, No. 4 (1978), pp. 32-34.

Mitgutsch, Waltraud. "Faces of Dehumanization: Werner Herzog's Reading of Büchner's *Woyzeck.*" *LFQ,* Vol. 11, No. 3 (1981), pp. 152-60.
Morris, George. *"Stroszek."* Take One, November 1977, pp. 8-9.
―――. "Werner Herzog." *IFG 1979.* Ed. Peter Cowie. London: Tantivy, 1978, pp. 28-33.
O'Toole, Lawrence. "The Great Ecstasy of the Filmmaker Herzog." *FC,* Nov.-Dec. 1979, pp. 34-39.
―――. " 'I Feel That I'm Close to the Center of Things.' " *FC,* Nov.-Dec. 1979, pp. 40-50. (Interview with Herzog)
Overbey, David L. *"Every Man for Himself."* S & S, Spring 1975, pp. 73-75.
Perlmutter, Ruth. "The Cinema of the Grotesque." *Georgia Review,* Vol. 33, No. 1 (1979), pp. 169-93.
Rayns, Tony. *"Aguirre, Wrath of God."* S & S, Winter 1974/75, pp. 56-57.
―――. "Even Dwarfs Started Small." S & S, Winter 1972/73, pp. 49-50.
Sarris, Andrew. "Werner Herzog Makes a Real Movie." *VV,* 1 Aug. 1977, pp. 88 and 37. *(Stroszek)*
Silverman, Kaja. "Kaspar Hauser's 'Terrible Fall' into Narrative." *NGC,* No. 24-25 (Fall/Winter 1981-2), pp. 73-93.
Simon, Andrea. "Werner Herzog's *Aguirre, Wrath of God."* Monogram, No. 6 (1975), pp. 26-27.
Simon, John. "Cinematic Illiterates." *New York,* 20 Oct. 1975, pp. 86-87. *(The Mystery of Kaspar Hauser)*
Strick, Philip. *"Nosferatu—The Vampyre."* S & S, Spring 1979, pp. 127-28.
Thomson, David. "Werner Herzog." In *A Biographical Dictionary of Film.* 2nd rev. ed. New York: Morrow, 1981, pp. 265-66.
Todd, Janet M. "The Class-ic Vampire." In *The English Novel and the Movies.* Ed. Michael Klein and Gillian Parker. New York: Ungar, 1981, pp. 197-210. *(Nosferatu* and Bram Stoker's *Dracula)*
Trojan, Judith. *"How Much Wood Would a Woodchuck Chuck. La Soufriere." Take One,* January 1979, pp. 11-13.
Van Wert, William F. "Hallowing the Ordinary, Embezzling the Everyday: Werner Herzog's Documentary Practice." *QRFS,* Spring 1980, pp. 183-90. *(Land of Silence and Darkness)*
Vogel, Amos. "In Paradise Man Is Born Dead." *VV,* 25 Nov. 1971, p. 88. *(Fata Morgana)*
―――. "On Seeing a Mirage." *FC,* Jan.-Feb. 1981, pp. 76-78. *(Fata Morgana)*
Walker, Beverly. "Werner Herzog's *Nosferatu."* S & S, Autumn 1978, pp. 202-05.
Waller, Gregory A. "Satire and the Grotesque in Herzog's *Even Dwarfs Started Small."* Proceedings of the Purdue University Fifth Annual Conference on Film. West Lafayette: Purdue Univ., 1980, pp. 3-10.
―――. *"The Great Ecstasy of the Woodsculptor Steiner:* Herzog and the 'Stylized' Documentary." *Film Criticism,* Fall 1980, pp. 26-35.
Walsh, Gene, ed. *"Images at the Horizon": A Workshop with Werner Herzog Conducted by Roger Ebert.* Chicago: Facets Multimedia, 1979.

Young, Vernon. "Werner Herzog and Contemporary German Cinema." *Hudson Review.* Vol. 30, No. 3 (1977), pp. 409-14.

Alexander Kluge:
Acuff, Skip [James Terry]. "Excerpts from *Big Business Bolshevik:* The Genesis of Alexander Kluge's *Strong Man Ferdinand.*" *QRFS,* Spring 1980, pp. 193-204.

_____. "Toward a Realistic Method: Commentaries on the Notion of Antagonistic Realism. A Translation of Alexander Kluge's *Zur realistischen Methode."* M.A. Thesis Univ. Texas 1980.

_____ and Hans-Bernhard Moeller. "Selected Writings by Alexander Kluge: Theory and Literary-Cinematic Practice of the *Auteur* Film." *Wide Angle,* Vol. 3, No. 4 (1980), pp. 26-33.

Dawson, Jan, ed. *Alexander Kluge & The Occasional Work of a Female Slave.* Perth: Perth Film Festival, 1975.

_____. "Alexander Kluge Interview." *FC,* Nov.-Dec. 1974, pp. 51-57.

_____. "*Strong-Man Ferdinand.*" *Take One,* January 1978, p. 12.

Franklin, J.C. "Alienation and the Retention of the Self: The Heroines in *Der gute Mensch von Sezuan, Abschied von gestern,* and *Die verlorene Ehre der Katharina Blum.*" *Mosaic,* Summer 1979, pp. 87-98. *(Yesterday Girl)*

Hansen, Miriam. "Cooperative Auteur Cinema and Oppositional Public Sphere: Alexander Kluge's Contribution to *Germany in Autumn.*" *NGC,* No. 24-25 (Fall/Winter 1981-2), pp. 36-56.

_____. "Introduction to Adorno, 'Transparencies on Film' (1966)." *NGC,* No. 24-25 (Fall/Winter 1981-2), pp. 186-98. (On Kluge's film theory)

Kay, Karyn. *"Part-Time Work of a Domestic Slave."* *FQ,* Fall 1975, pp. 52-57.

Kluge, Alexander. "On Film and the Public Sphere." Trans. Thomas Y. Levin and Miriam B. Hansen. *NGC,* No. 24-25 (Fall/Winter 1981-2), pp. 206-20.

Moeller, Hans-Bernhard and Carl Springer. "Directed Change in the Young German Film: Alexander Kluge and *Artists Under the Big Top: Perplexed.*" *Wide Angle,* Vol. 2, No. 1 (1977), pp. 14-21.

Rosenbaum, Jonathan and Yehuda Safran. *"Occasional Work of a Female Slave."* *S & S,* Winter 1974/75, pp. 19-20.

Thomson, David. "Alexander Kluge." In *A Biographical Dictionary of Film.* 2nd rev. ed. New York: Morrow, 1981, p. 311.

Vierling, David. "Quinzaine: *Die Patriotin.* Alexander Kluge: 'A Question of *Zusammenhang.*' " *Kino,* No. 2 (Spring 1980), pp. 22-28.

Peter Lilienthal:
Canby, Victor. "Film: *Calm Prevails.*" *NYT,* 6 April 1978.

Hoberman, J. "Bring Me the Head of Anastasio Somoza." *VV,* 12 Aug. 1981, p. 48. *(The Insurrection)*

_____. "Hard To Be a Jew." *VV,* 20 Jan. 1982, p. 48. *(David)*

Holloway, Ronald. "A Peter Lilienthal Retro." *Variety,* 1 March 1978, p. 38.

Insdorf, Annette. "A Passion for Social Justice: An Interview with Peter Lilienthal." *Cineaste,* Vol. 11, No. 4 (1982), pp. 36-38.

Ziemann, Ulla. "Interview Peter Lilienthal." *Kino,* No. 1 (October 1979), pp. 27-31. *(David)*

Elfi Mikesch:
Hoberman, J. "Das Blaue Hawaii." *VV,* 3 Dec. 1980, p. 74. *(I Often Think of Hawaii...)*

George Moorse:
Holloway, Ronald. "Interview George Moorse: The American in Munich." *Kino,* No. 2 (Spring 1980), pp. 33-37.

Ulrike Ottinger:
Carter, Erika. "Interview with Ulrike Ottinger." *Screen Education,* No. 41 (Winter/Spring 1982), pp. 34-42.
Mueller, Roswitha. "Interview with Ulrike Ottinger." *Discourse,* No. 4 (Winter 1981-82), pp. 108-26.
Rickey, Carrie. "Beyond Sorrow and Pity." *VV,* 14 Jan. 1981, p. 46. *(Ticket of No Return)*

Wolfgang Petersen:
Clarens, Carlos. "Horst maneuver." *Soho Weekly News,* 23 Feb. 1982, pp. 45-46. *(Das Boot)*
Hoberman, J. "This is America." *VV,* 6 May 1981, p. 58. *(Black and White Like Day and Night)*
Jameson, Richard T. "The financial extravagance of *Das Boot* pays off." *The Weekly* (Seattle), 21 April 1982.
Rickey, Carrie. "In Which We Sink." *VV,* 10 Feb. 1982, p. 60. *(Das Boot)*

Rosa von Praunheim:
Kelley, Keith. "The Sexual Politics of Rosa von Praunheim." *Millennium Film Journal,* No. 3 (Winter/Spring 1979), pp. 115-18.

Edgar Reitz:
Reitz, Edgar. "Inquiry on *Holocaust:* A generation to which we belong." Trans. Charlotte Vokes-Dudgeon. *Framework,* No. 12 (1980), pp. 10-11.

Helke Sander:
Canby, Vincent. "Movie: Feminist Film from Germany." *NYT,* 24 April 1979. *(REDUPERS)*
Hoberman, J. "MOMA's Got a Brand New Bag." *VV,* 30 April 1979, p. 54. *(REDUPERS)*
Mayne, Judith. "Female Narration, Women's Cinema: Helke Sander's *The All-Round Reduced Personality/Redupers.*" *NGC,* No. 24-25 (Fall/Winter 1981-2), pp. 155-71.
"Women Working: *All Around Reduced Personality.*" Trans. Elisabeth Lyon from Basis-Film publicity dossier. *camera obscura,* No. 3/4 (1979), pp. 224-27.

Niklaus Schilling:
  Sprengel, Mareike. "Border Fantasy in Friedheim." *Kino,* No. 2 (Spring 1980), pp. 16-18. *(The Willi-Busch-Report)*
  Youngblood, Gene. "Flamingo Hours." *Take One,* September 1978, pp. 42-43. *(Rheingold)*

Volker Schlöndorff:
  Allen, Tom. "Losers." *VV,* 6 Feb. 1978, p. 40. *(Coup de Grâce)*
  Callenbach, Ernest. *"Young Törless." FQ,* Winter 1966-67, pp. 42-44.
  Canby, Vincent. "Coup de Grace, a Film Parable." *NYT,* 6 Feb. 1978.
  Cetinich, Daniel. *"The Lost Honor of Katharina Blum:* Who's The Terrorist in West Germany?" *Jump Cut,* No. 19 (December 1978), pp. 4-5.
  Cocks, Jay. *"Free Woman." Time,* 8 July 1974, p. 60.
  Friedman, Lester D. "Cinematic Techniques in *The Lost Honor of Katharina Blum." LFQ,* Vol. 7, No. 3 (1979), pp. 244-52.
  Gilliatt, Penelope. "Private Nose." *New Yorker,* 1 July 1974, pp. 70-72. *(A Free Woman)*
  Harcourt, Peter. *"The Sudden Wealth of the Poor People of Kombach." FQ,* Fall 1980, pp. 60-63.
  Haskell, Molly "Katharina Blum Loses Honor and Finds Sainthood." *VV,* 5 Jan. 1976, p. 80.
  _____. "White Russians and Mad Doctors." *New York,* 13 Feb. 1978, pp. 71-73. *(Coup de Grâce)*
  Head, David. " 'Der Autor muss respektiert werden'—Schlöndorff/Trotta's *Die verlorene Ehre der Katharina Blum." German Life and Letters,* April 1979, pp. 248-64.
  Holloway, Ronald. "Volker Schlöndorff." *IFG 1982.* Ed. Peter Cowie. London: Tantivy, 1981, pp. 30-35.
  Hughes, John. *"The Tin Drum:* Volker Schlöndorff's 'Dream of Childhood.' " *FQ,* Spring 1981, pp. 2-10.
  Kauffmann, Stanley. "Living Through Wars." *New Republic,* 5 April 1980, pp. 26-27. *(The Tin Drum)*
  Margretta, William R. and Joan. "Story and Discourse: Schlöndorff & von Trotta's *The Lost Honor of Katharina Blum* (1975)." In *Modern European Filmmakers and the Art of Adaptation.* Ed. Andrew S. Horton and Joan Magretta. New York: Ungar, 1981, pp. 278-94.
  Maslin, Janet. "Film: *Circle of Deceit,* War Reporter in Beirut." *NYT,* 11 Feb. 1982.
  Morris, George. "Neo-Brechtian Numbness." *VV,* 14 Nov. 1974, p. 100. *(The Sudden Wealth of the Poor People of Kombach)*
  Pachter, Henry. *"The Tin Drum." Cineaste,* Fall 1980, pp. 31-32.
  Phillips, Klaus. "History Reevaluated: Volker Schlöndorff's *The Sudden Wealth of the Poor People of Kombach." 1978 Film Studies Annual.* West Lafayette: Purdue Research Foundation, 1979, pp. 33-39.
  Sarris, Andrew. "Banging the Tin Drum Slowly." *VV,* 21 April 1980, p. 47.
  _____. "The Father, the Son, and the Holy Revolution(II)." *VV,* 2 March 1982, p. 45. *(Circle of Deceit)*

Thomson, Barry and Greg. "Volker Schlondorff [sic]: An Interview." *Film Criticism*, Winter 1976-77, pp. 26-37.
Thomson, David. "Volker Schlöndorff." In *A Biographical Dictionary of Film*. 2nd rev. ed. New York: Morrow, 1981, p. 547.
Vincour, John. "After 20 Years, *The Tin Drum* Marches to the Screen." *NYT*, 6 April 1980.
Zipes, Jack. "The Political Dimensions of *The Lost Honor of Katharina Blum*." *NGC*, No. 12 (Fall 1977), pp. 75-84.

Werner Schroeter:
Canby, Vincent. "Film: *Kingdom of Naples*, 32 Years in the Life of an Italian Family." *NYT*, 28 April 1979.
Corrigan, Timothy. "Werner Schoreter's Operatic Cinema." *Discourse*, No. 3 (Spring 1981), pp. 46-59. *(Willow Springs)*
Hoberman, J. "MOMA's Got a Brand New Bag." *VV*, 30 April 1979, p. 54. *(Kingdom of Naples)*
Indiana, Gary. "Scattered Pictures: The Movies of Werner Schroeter." *Art Forum*, March 1982, pp. 46-51.

Jean-Marie Straub and Danièle Huillet:
Bachmann, Gideon. "*Nicht Versöhnt.*" *FQ*, Summer 1966, pp. 51-55. *(Not Reconciled)*
Bennett, E. "The Films of Straub Are Not 'Theoretical.' " *Afterimage*, No. 7 (Summer 1978), pp. 4-11.
Dermody, Susan. "Jean-Marie Straub and Danièle Huillet: The Politics of Film Practice." *Cinema Papers*, Sept.-Oct. 1976, pp. 126-30.
Engel, Andi. "Andi Engel Talks to Jean-Marie Straub, and Danièle Huillet Is There Too." *Enthusiasm*, December 1975, pp. 1-25.
Fieschi, Jean-André. "Jean-Marie Straub." In *Cinema: A Critical Dictionary*. Ed. Richard Roud. 2 vols. New York: Viking, 1980, pp. 969-73.
Greene, Naomi. "Report from Venice: Cinema and Ideology." *Praxis*, No. 2 (1976), pp. 249-65.
Heath, Stephen. "From Brecht to Film: Theses, Problems (on *History Lessons* and *Dear Summer Sister*)." *Screen*, Winter 1975/6, pp. 34-45.
Huillet, Danièle. "Notes on Gregory's Work Journal." *Enthusiasm*, December 1975, pp. 32-55.
Jenkins, Bruce L. "The Counter Cinemas of Straub/Huillet and Robbe-Grillet." *1976 Film Studies Annual*. West Lafayette: Purdue Research Foundation, 1976, pp. 144-56.
Lellis, George. "Jean-Marie Straub's *Moses and Aaron*." *Take One*, Vol. 4, No. 12 (December 1975), pp. 37-39.
Magisos, Melanie. "*Not Reconciled:* The Destruction of Visual Pleasure." *Wide Angle*, Vol. 3, No. 4 (1980), pp. 35-41.
Nash, Mark and Steve Neale. "Reports from the Edinburgh Festival: Film: 'History/Production/Memory.' " *Screen*, Winter 1977/78, pp. 77-91. *(Fortini/Cani)*

Nowell-Smith, Geoffrey. "After *Othon*, Before *History Lessons*: Geoffrey Nowell-Smith Talks to Jean-Marie Straub and Danièle Huillet." *Enthusiasm*, December 1975, pp. 26-31.

⸺. "Introduction" [to *Fortini/Cani*]. *Screen*, Summer 1978, pp. 9-10.

Orr, Christopher. "The Adventures of the Signifier: The Driving Sequences in *History Lessons*." *Proceedings of the Purdue University Fifth Annual Conference on Film*. West Lafayette: Purdue Univ., 1980, pp. 250-55.

Perez, Gilberto. "Modernist Cinema: The History Lessons of Straub and Huillet." *Artforum*, October 1978, pp. 46-55.

Rogers, Joel. "Jean-Marie Straub and Danièle Huillet Interviewed: *Moses and Aaron* as an Object of Marxist Reflection." *Jump Cut*, No. 12/13 (December 1976), pp. 61-64.

Roud, Richard. "Jean-Marie Straub." In *Cinema: A Critical Dictionary*. Ed. Richard Roud. 2 vols. New York: Viking, 1980, pp. 967-69.

⸺. *Straub*. New York: Viking, 1972.

Straub, Jean-Marie and Danièle Huillet. *"Fortini-Cani-*Script." *Screen*, Summer 1978, pp. 11-40.

⸺. "Scenarios of *History Lessons* and Introduction to Arnold Schoenberg's *Accompaniment to a Cinematograph Scene*." *Screen*, Spring 1976, pp. 54-83.

Thomson, David. "Jean-Marie Straub." In *A Biographical Dictionary of Film*. 2nd rev. ed. New York: Morrow, 1981, pp. 585-86.

Turim, Maureen. *"Écriture Blanche:* The Ordering of the Filmic Text in *The Chronicle of Anna Magdalena Bach*." *1976 Film Studies Annual*. West Lafayette: Purdue Research Foundation, 1976, pp. 177-92.

Walsh, Martin. *The Brechtian Aspect of Radical Cinema*. London: BFI, 1981.

⸺. "The Frontiers of Language: Brecht and Straub/Huillet: *History Lessons*" *Afterimage*, No. 7 (Summer 1978), pp. 12-31.

⸺. "Introduction to Arnold Schoenberg's 'Accompaniment for a Cinematographic Scene': Straub/Huillet: Brecht: Schoenberg." *camera obscura*, No. 2 (Fall 1977), pp. 34-39.

⸺. *"Moses and Aaron:* Straub and Huillet's Schoenberg." *Jump Cut*, No. 12/13 (December 1976), pp. 57-61.

⸺. "Political Formations in the Cinema of Jean-Marie Straub." *Jump Cut*, No. 4 (Nov.-Dec. 1974), pp. 12-18.

Woods, Gregory. "A Work Journal of the Straub/Huillet Film *Moses and Aaron*." *Enthusiasm*, December 1975, pp. 32-55.

Hans-Jürgen Syberberg:

Andrews, Nigel. "Hitler as Entertainment." *AF,* April 1978, pp. 50-53.

Brunette, Peter. *"Ludwig: Requiem for a Virgin King."* *FQ,* Spring 1981, pp. 59-61.

Christie, I., ed. "The Syberberg Statement." *Framework,* No. 6 (Autumn 1977), pp. 12-18.

Elsaesser, Thomas. "Myth as the Phantasmagoria of History: H.J. Syberberg, Cinema and Representation." *NGC,* No. 24-25 (Fall/Winter 1981-2), pp. 108-54.

Hoberman, J. "The Führer Furor: Film As Fever Dream." *VV,* 14 Jan. 1980, pp. 28, 30. *(Our Hitler)*
———. "Life with Führer." *VV,* 27 March 1978, p. 39. *(The Confessions of Winifried Wagner)*
Jaehne, Karen. "Old Nazis in New Films." *Cineaste,* Vol. 9, No. 1 (1978), pp. 32-35. *(Our Hitler and other films)*
Jameson, Frederic. " 'In the Destructive Element Immerse': Hans-Jürgen Syberberg and Cultural Revolution." *October,* No. 17 (Summer 1981), pp. 99-118.
Landy, Marcia. "Politics, Aesthetics, and Patriarchy in *The Confessions of Winifried Wagner.*" *NGC,* No. 18 (Fall 1979), pp. 151-66.
Layton, Lynne. "The Case of Syberberg: *Hitler, Ein Film aus Deutschland.*" *Proceedings of the Purdue University Fifth Annual Conference on Film.* West Lafayette: Purdue Univ., 1980, pp. 238-43.
Mueller, Roswitha. "Hans-Jürgen Syberberg's *Hitler*—an Interview-Montage." *Discourse,* No. 2 (Summer 1980), pp. 60-82.
Pachter, Henry. "Our Hitler, or His?" *Cineaste,* Spring 1980, pp. 25-27.
Pym, John. "Syberberg and the Tempter of Democracy." *S & S,* Autumn 1977, pp. 227-30 *(Our Hitler)*
Scheib-Rothbart, Ingrid, ed. *Hans-Jürgen Syberberg's Our Hitler: A Film from Germany. A Documentation.* New York: Goethe House, 1980.
Sharrett, Christopher. "Epiphany for Modernism: Anti-Illusionism and Theatrical Tradition in Syberberg's *Our Hitler.*" *Millennium Film Journal,* Nos. 10/11 (Fall/Winter 1981-82), pp. 141-57.
Sontag, Susan. "Eye of the Storm." *New York Review of Books,* 21 Feb. 1980, pp. 36-43. Reprinted in *Under the Sign of Saturn.* New York: Vintage, 1980, pp. 135-65 as "Syberberg's Hitler."
Syberberg, Hans-Jürgen. "Form Is Morality: *Holocaust,* a symptom of the biggest crisis in our intellectual life." Trans. Barrie Ellis-Jones. *Framework,* No. 12 (1980), pp. 11-15.
Thomson, David. "Hans-Jürgen Syberberg." In *A Biographical Dictionary of Film.* 2nd rev. ed. New York: Morrow, 1981, pp. 592-94.
Wasserman, Steven. "The Führer Furor: Filmmaker as Pariah." *VV,* 14 Jan. 1980, pp. 29-31. *(Our Hitler)*

Margarethe von Trotta:
Canby, Vincent. "Screen: *Christa Klages.*" *NYT,* 17 May 1979.
Garafola, Lynn. "*The Second Awakening of Christa Klages.*" *Cineaste,* Fall 1979, pp. 48-49.
Hoberman, J. "Brecht-Fest Epiphanies." *VV,* 28 May 1979, p. 51. *(The Second Awakening of Christa Klages)*
Insdorf, Annette. "Von Trotta: By Sisters Obsessed." *NYT,* 31 Jan. 1982.
Rickey, Carrie. "The Sisters Grimm." *VV,* 3 Feb. 1982, p. 44. *(Sisters)*
———. "Some Moving Pictures (and Some That Aren't)." *VV,* 27 April 1982, pp. 52-54. *(Marianne and Juliane)*

Wim Wenders:

Andrews Nigel. "The Goalie's Fear of the Penalty Kick." *S & S,* Winter 1972/73, pp. 6-7.

Brunette, Peter. "Filming Words: Wenders's *The Goalie's Anxiety at the Penalty Kick* (1971)." In *Modern European Filmmakers and the Art of Adaptation.* Ed. Andrew S. Horton and Joan Magretta. New York: Ungar, 1981, pp. 188-202.

Burnett, Ron. "Wim Wenders, Nicholas Ray, and *Lightning Over Water.*" *Ciné-Tracts,* Nos. 14/15 (Summer/Fall 1981), pp. 11-14.

Clarens, Carlos. "King of the Road. Wim Wenders Interviewed." *FC,* Sept.-Oct. 1977, pp. 42-46.

Combs, Richard. *"Lightning Over Water." S & S,* Spring 1981, pp. 96-97.

―――――. "Wim Wenders." *IFG 1980.* Ed. Peter Cowie. London: Tantivy, 1979, pp. 43-46.

Corrigan, Timothy J. "The Realist Gesture in the Films of Wim Wenders: Hollywood and the New German Cinema." *QRFS,* Spring 1980, pp. 205-16.

―――――. "Wender's [sic] *Kings of the Road:* The Voyage from Desire to Language." *NGC,* No. 24-25 (Fall/Winter 1981-2), pp. 94-107.

Covino, Michael. "Wim Wenders: A Worldwide Homesickness." *FQ,* Winter 1977-78, pp. 9-19.

Dawson, Jan. "Filming Highsmith." *S & S,* Winter 1977/78, pp. 30-36. *(The American Friend)*

―――――. *Wim Wenders.* Toronto: Festival of Festivals, 1976.

―――――. "Wim Wenders." In *Cinema: A Critical Dictionary.* Ed. Richard Roud. 2 vols. New York: Viking, 1980, pp. 1070-72.

Elley, Derek. *"Alice in the Cities." Films and Filming,* December 1975, pp. 35-36.

―――――. *"The Goalkeeper's Fear of the Penalty Kick." Films and Filming,* February 1976, pp. 36-37.

Fell, John L. *"Wrong Movement." FQ,* Winter 1978-79, pp. 49-50.

Fox, Terry Curtis. "Wim Wenders Crosses the Border." *VV,* 3 Oct. 1977, pp. 42-43, 46. *(The American Friend)*

Frisch, Shelley. "The Disenchanted Image: From Goethe's *Wilhelm Meister* to Wenders' *Wrong Movement.*" *LFQ,* Vol. 7, No. 3 (1979), pp. 208-14.

Geist, Kathe. "The Cinema of Wim Wenders 1967-1977." Diss. Univ. Michigan 1981.

―――――. *"Lightning Over Water." FQ,* Winter 1981-82, pp. 46-51.

Harcourt, Peter. "Adaptation through Inversion: Wenders's *Wrong Movement* (1974)." In *Modern European Filmmakers and the Art of Adaptation.* Ed. Andrew S. Horton and Joan Magretta. New York: Ungar, 1981, pp. 263-77.

Hoberman, J. "Wenders in Wanderland." *VV,* 13 Nov. 1978, p. 78. *(Wrong Move)*

Jaehne, Karen. "The American Fiend." *S & S,* Spring 1978, pp. 101-03. *(The American Friend* and *Stroszek)*

Johnston, Sheila, ed. *Wenders.* London: BFI, 1981.

Jost, Jon. "Wrong Move." *S & S,* Spring 1981, pp. 94-96. *(Lightning over Water)*

Kael, Pauline. "Heart/Soul." *New Yorker,* 17 Oct. 1977, pp. 173-79. *(The American Friend)*

Kass, Judith M. "At Home on the Road." *Movietone News,* No. 57 (February 1978), pp. 2-11. (Interviews with Wenders)

Kauffmann, Stanley. "Wenders." *New Republic,* 29 Jan. 1977, pp. 26-27.

Kinder, Marsha. *"The American Friend."* FQ, Winter 1978-79, pp. 45-49.

Lehman, Peter, Robin Wood, and Edward Lachmann. "Wim Wenders: An Interview." *Wide Angle,* Vol. 2, No. 4 (1978), pp. 72-79.

Monaco, James. *"Alice in the Cities:* Alice is alive and well." *Take One,* Vol. 4, No. 11 (1975), pp. 30-31.

Morris, George. *"The American Friend."* *Take One,* January 1978, p. 11.

Ruppert, Peter. "Audience Engagement in Wenders's *The American Friend* and Fassbinder's *Ali: Fear Eats the Soul."* In *Narrative Strategies: Original Essays in Film and Prose Fiction.* Ed. Syndy M. Conger and Janice R. Welsch. Western Illinois Univ., 1980, pp. 61-77.

Schlunk, Jürgen E. "The Image of America in German Literature and in the New German Cinema: Wim Wenders' *The American Friend." LFQ,* Vol. 7, No. 3 (1979), pp. 215-22.

Simon, John. "Of Men and Justice: A Platonic Relationship." *New York,* 25 Oct. 1976, pp. 90-92. *(Kings of the Road)*

Stamelman, Peter. "Wenders at Warners." *S & S,* Autumn 1978, p. 225.

Thomson, David. "Wim Wenders." In *A Biographical Dictionary of Film.* 2nd rev. ed. New York: Morrow, 1981, pp. 656-57.

Welsh, James. M. "Wim Wenders Bibliography." *Wide Angle,* Vol. 2, No. 4 (1978), pp. 80-81.

_____ and Richard C. Keenan. "Wim Wenders and Nathanial Hawthorne: From *The Scarlet Letter* to *Der scharlachrote Buchstabe." LFQ,* Vol. 6, No. 2 (Spring 1978), pp. 175-179.

Wenders, Wim and Fritz Müller-Scherz. *The Film by Wim Wenders: Kings of the Road (In the Course of Time).* Trans. Christopher Doherty. Munich: Filmverlag der Autoren, 1976.

Wenders, Wim and Chris Sievernich. *Nick's Film: Lightning Over Water.* Frankfurt: Zweitausendeins, 1981.

Youngblood, Gene. "A New Nostalgia." *Take One,* October 1976, pp. 33-34. *(Alice in the Cities)*

Klaus Wyborny:

Christie, Ian. "Before and After Narrative: Klaus Wyborny." *Afterimage,* No. 8/9 (Spring 1981), pp. 110-11.

_____ and Tony Rayns. "An Interview." *Afterimage,* No. 8/9 (Spring 1981), pp. 133-55.

Hoberman, J. "The Best of the Apples and Pears." *VV,* 1 Jan. 1979, p. 41. *(Unreachable Homeless)*

_____. "Eine Kleine Eye Musik." *VV,* 1 May 1978. p. 40.

Wyborny, Klaus. "Random Notes on the Conventional Narrative Film." Trans. Philip Drummond. *Afterimage,* No. 8/9 (Spring 1981), pp. 112-32.

INDEX OF FILMS

The following list catalogues all the film titles mentioned in the text and footnotes. To avoid confusions in the case of remakes and different films with the same titles, the date of production is listed in some cases.

ACTIVE STRIKE AT THE FRANKFURT UNIVERSITY, 18
AGUIRRE, THE WRATH OF GOD, 47, 51
ALBERT — WHY?, 110, 124
ALI: FEAR EATS THE SOUL, 51, 75, 78
ALICE IN THE CITIES, 75, 186, 188
ALL ROUND REDUCED PERSONALITY — REDUPERS, THE, 152
ALL THAT HEAVEN ALLOWS, 85
ALL THE PRESIDENT'S MEN, 55
AMERICAN FRIEND, THE, 67, 76, 87-88, 89, 133, 134
AREN'T WE WONDERFUL?, 36
ARTISTS UNDER THE BIG TOP: PERPLEXED, THE, 33, 45-46, 57, 75
ASSISTANT, THE, 132
ATLANTIC SWIMMERS, THE, 52

BAAL, 111
BEACH UNDER THE SIDEWALK, THE, 18
BEER BATTLE, 142, 166, 182-84
BELCANTO, 132
BERLIN ALEXANDERPLATZ (1980), 72, 90, 140, 196, 199, 202
BERLIN S-BAHN PICTURES, 26
BERLIN, SYMPHONY OF A BIG CITY, 26
BERLINGER, 51
BEWARE OF A HOLY WHORE, 46, 57
BITTER TEARS OF PETRA VON KANT, THE, 75, 98
BLACK ERWIN, 27, 124
BLACK FOREST GIRL (1950), 108
BLOOD OF THE WALSUNGS, 40
BLUE ANGEL, THE (1930), 137
BLUE LIGHT, THE, 107
BOOT, DAS, 59, 74
BREAD OF THE EARLY YEARS, THE, 37
BROTHERS, THE (1976), 131
BRUTAL BARTER, THE, 123
BRUTALITY IN STONE (THE ETERNITY OF YESTERDAY), 12
BUDDENBROOKS (1959), 138, 144
BYE BYE, BAVARIA, 55, 124, 190

CALM PREVAILS OVER THE COUNTRY, 52

CANDIDATE, THE (1980), 196, 202
CHINESE ROULETTE, 98
CHRISTIANE F., 74
CHRONICLE OF ANNA MAGDALENA BACH, 75, 156, 177
CLOSED SEASON ON FOX HUNTING, 41, 43, 61, 138
CONFESSIONS OF THE CONFIDENCE MAN FELIX KRULL (1957), 138
CONQUEST OF THE CITADEL, THE, 132, 155
CONSEQUENCE, THE, 133
CONVERSATION, THE, 177
COUP DE GRÂCE, 27, 132, 135

DAMM THIS AMERICA, 111-12, 123, 127
DAMNED, THE, 99
DEADLOCK, 19
DEATH IS MY TRADE, 132
DEATH OF MARIA MALIBRAN, THE, 46
DEGREE OF MURDER, A, 45
DESPAIR, 55, 73, 76, 130, 132, 134
DESTINY, 26
DEVIL PROBABLY, THE, 99
DEVIL'S ELIXIRS, THE, 132, 134, 145
DEVIL'S GENERAL, THE, 36
DIARY, 141
DISORDER AND EARLY SORROW, 132, 144-45
DOCTEUR POPAUL, 98
DRESS REHEARSAL, THE, 128, 200

EDELWEISS KING, THE (1957), 112-13
EFFI BRIEST (1974), 140
EIGHT HOURS DON'T MAKE A DAY, 72
END OF THE RAINBOW, THE, 156
ESCAPE ROUTE TO MARSEILLES, 55, 132, 143, 155-56
EVEN DWARFS STARTED SMALL, 75, 78
EXPULSION FROM PARADISE, THE, 20, 142

FAIRGROUND, 36
FALL, THE, 133
FAN, THE (1981), 74
FATA MORGANA, 47, 75, 76, 86
FAUST (1926), 137
FEAR OF FEAR, 52, 75
FIFTY-FIFTY, 19, 55, 142
FILM OR POWER, 157, 185
FILM '68, 18
FIRST POLKA, THE, 133
FISHERWOMAN FROM LAKE CONSTANCE, THE (1956), 108
FISTFUL OF DOLLARS, A, 111
FITZCARRALDO, 62, 73, 76

INDEX OF FILMS

The following list catalogues all the film titles mentioned in the text and footnotes. To avoid confusions in the case of remakes and different films with the same titles, the date of production is listed in some cases.

ACTIVE STRIKE AT THE FRANKFURT UNIVERSITY, 18
AGUIRRE, THE WRATH OF GOD, 47, 51
ALBERT — WHY?, 110, 124
ALI: FEAR EATS THE SOUL, 51, 75, 78
ALICE IN THE CITIES, 75, 186, 188
ALL ROUND REDUCED PERSONALITY — REDUPERS, THE, 152
ALL THAT HEAVEN ALLOWS, 85
ALL THE PRESIDENT'S MEN, 55
AMERICAN FRIEND, THE, 67, 76, 87-88, 89, 133, 134
AREN'T WE WONDERFUL?, 36
ARTISTS UNDER THE BIG TOP: PERPLEXED, THE, 33, 45-46, 57, 75
ASSISTANT, THE, 132
ATLANTIC SWIMMERS, THE, 52

BAAL, 111
BEACH UNDER THE SIDEWALK, THE, 18
BEER BATTLE, 142, 166, 182-84
BELCANTO, 132
BERLIN ALEXANDERPLATZ (1980), 72, 90, 140, 196, 199, 202
BERLIN S-BAHN PICTURES, 26
BERLIN, SYMPHONY OF A BIG CITY, 26
BERLINGER, 51
BEWARE OF A HOLY WHORE, 46, 57
BITTER TEARS OF PETRA VON KANT, THE, 75, 98
BLACK ERWIN, 27, 124
BLACK FOREST GIRL (1950), 108
BLOOD OF THE WALSUNGS, 40
BLUE ANGEL, THE (1930), 137
BLUE LIGHT, THE, 107
BOOT, DAS, 59, 74
BREAD OF THE EARLY YEARS, THE, 37
BROTHERS, THE (1976), 131
BRUTAL BARTER, THE, 123
BRUTALITY IN STONE (THE ETERNITY OF YESTERDAY), 12
BUDDENBROOKS (1959), 138, 144
BYE BYE, BAVARIA, 55, 124, 190

CALM PREVAILS OVER THE COUNTRY, 52

CANDIDATE, THE (1980), 196, 202
CHINESE ROULETTE, 98
CHRISTIANE F., 74
CHRONICLE OF ANNA MAGDALENA BACH, 75, 156, 177
CLOSED SEASON ON FOX HUNTING, 41, 43, 61, 138
CONFESSIONS OF THE CONFIDENCE MAN FELIX KRULL (1957), 138
CONQUEST OF THE CITADEL, THE, 132, 155
CONSEQUENCE, THE, 133
CONVERSATION, THE, 177
COUP DE GRÂCE, 27, 132, 135

DAMM THIS AMERICA, 111-12, 123, 127
DAMNED, THE, 99
DEADLOCK, 19
DEATH IS MY TRADE, 132
DEATH OF MARIA MALIBRAN, THE, 46
DEGREE OF MURDER, A, 45
DESPAIR, 55, 73, 76, 130, 132, 134
DESTINY, 26
DEVIL PROBABLY, THE, 99
DEVIL'S ELIXIRS, THE, 132, 134, 145
DEVIL'S GENERAL, THE, 36
DIARY, 141
DISORDER AND EARLY SORROW, 132, 144-45
DOCTEUR POPAUL, 98
DRESS REHEARSAL, THE, 128, 200

EDELWEISS KING, THE (1957), 112-13
EFFI BRIEST (1974), 140
EIGHT HOURS DON'T MAKE A DAY, 72
END OF THE RAINBOW, THE, 156
ESCAPE ROUTE TO MARSEILLES, 55, 132, 143, 155-56
EVEN DWARFS STARTED SMALL, 75, 78
EXPULSION FROM PARADISE, THE, 20, 142

FAIRGROUND, 36
FALL, THE, 133
FAN, THE (1981), 74
FATA MORGANA, 47, 75, 76, 86
FAUST (1926), 137
FEAR OF FEAR, 52, 75
FIFTY-FIFTY, 19, 55, 142
FILM OR POWER, 157, 185
FILM '68, 18
FIRST POLKA, THE, 133
FISHERWOMAN FROM LAKE CONSTANCE, THE (1956), 108
FISTFUL OF DOLLARS, A, 111
FITZCARRALDO, 62, 73, 76

Index of Films

FLAMING HEARTS, 55
FOR A FEW DOLLARS MORE, 111
FOREST FEVER (1977), 133, 145
400 BLOWS, THE, 42
FOX AND HIS FRIENDS, 75
FRANZ — THE GENTLE PATH, 124
FREAK ORLANDO, 20
FRIEDRICH SCHILLER, 137
FROM THE DISTANCE I SEE THIS COUNTRY, 72, 134
FRONTIERS OF DARKNESS, 134

GERMANY IN AUTUMN, 24, 55-56, 82, 94, 125, 128, 151-52, 159, 191-200, 201, 202
GLASS CELL, THE, 132, 134
GOALIE'S ANXIETY AT THE PENALTY KICK, THE, 47, 188
GOOD-FOR-NOTHING, 133, 146-47, 156
GOOD, THE BAD, AND THE UGLY, THE, 111
GREAT TEMPTATION, THE, 36
GREEN IS THE HEATHER (1951), 108
GRETE MINDE, 54, 131, 143, 144, 146, 155
GROUP PORTRAIT WITH LADY, 54, 133, 134, 135, 143, 155

HAMMETT, 73, 87
HANDS UP, 144
HEART OF GLASS, 76, 99, 123
HEINRICH, 54, 132, 135, 143, 145-46, 155
HEINRICH HEINE, 132
HISTORY LESSONS, 75
HITLER — A CAREER, 25, 154
HOLOCAUST, 148
HUBERTUS PALACE (1954), 108
HUNGER YEARS, 159
HUNTING SCENES FROM LOWER BAVARIA, 109, 110, 127

I LOVE YOU, I KILL YOU, 103-04, 109, 114-23, 124
IN A YEAR OF 13 MOONS, 76, 201
IN TIMES OF DANGER AND GREATEST PERIL,
   THE PATH OF COMPROMISE LEADS TO DEATH, 19, 26
IT, 41, 43, 59, 61, 145

JAIDER — THE LONELY HUNTER, 109, 118
JAIL BAIT, 111, 123, 127
JANE IS JANE FOREVER, 142
JOHN GLÜCKSTADT, 52, 128, 140
JONAS, 12, 37
JOYLESS STREET, THE, 27

KATZELMACHER, 29, 111, 161
KINGS OF THE ROAD, 20, 57, 75, 87, 177

LAGADO, 25, 142
LAND OF SILENCE AND DARKNESS, 75
LAST HOLE, THE, 200
LAST YEARS OF CHILDHOOD, THE, 156
LEFT-HANDED WOMAN, THE, 55, 76, 133, 134, 166-73, 181, 187
LETTER, THE, 42, 185
LIBERTY OR DEATH, 132, 143, 144, 156
LIFE IN VAIN, A, 52
LIGHTNING OVER WATER, 76, 87
LILI MARLEEN, 74, 82, 97, 98, 161
LINA BRAAKE, 51
LITTLE GODARD, THE, 14, 80-81, 94, 150-51, 157, 201
LODGER, THE, 26
LOLA, 98
LONG VACATION OF LOTTE H. EISNER, THE, 20, 27
LOOPING, 74
LOST HONOR OF KATHARINA BLUM, THE, 51, 53, 75, 78, 96, 128

MACHORKA-MUFF, 36, 141
MAN IN PYJAMAS, THE, 74
MARQUISE OF O***, THE, 75
MARRIAGE OF MARIA BRAUN, THE, 66, 76, 84, 98
MARTHA, 72, 140
MATHIAS KNEISSL, 103-04, 109, 110, 111, 114-23, 124, 127
MERCHANT OF FOUR SEASONS, THE, 46, 75, 76, 77, 82-83, 96
MICHAEL KOHLHAAS, 45, 140
MIGRATING BIRDS, 108
MOON IS ONLY A NAKED GLOBE, THE, 123
MOSES AND AARON, 75, 78
MYSTERY OF KASPAR HAUSER, THE, 26, 27, 51, 75, 78, 90, 96, 100, 160

NETWORK, 55
NEW ADVENTURES OF THE ROBBER HOTZENPLOTZ, THE, 133
NIBELUNGEN, DIE (1966), 40
NIGHT SHADOWS, 48, 123
NOSFERATU (1921), 26, 47, 62
NOSFERATU (1978), 20, 62, 73, 76, 86-87, 99, 134
NOT RECONCILED, 36, 42, 141, 186

ON THE MOVE, 156
ONCE UPON A TIME IN THE WEST, 111, 176
ONLY FOR FUN AND GAMES — KALEIDOSCOPE VALESKA GERT, 27
OTHON, 75, 186
OUR HITLER — A FILM FROM GERMANY, 20, 55, 99, 160, 161, 186
OUT OF THE BLUE, 196, 202

PANDORA'S BOX (1928), 137
PARALLEL STREET, THE, 37

Index of Films

PARSIFAL, 76
PART-TIME WORK OF A DOMESTIC SLAVE, 75, 80, 155
PARTICULARLY NOTEWORTHY, 151
PASSION DE JEANNE D'ARC, LA, 189
PATRIOT, THE, 58-59, 101, 104, 125, 185, 186, 200, 202
PAULINE'S BIRTHDAY OR THE BEAST OF NOTRE DAME, 133
PIONEERS IN INGOLSTADT, 75, 76, 111
POLICE FILM, 18

RED FLAGS CAN BE SEEN BETTER, 48
REST THOU TRANQUIL, BELOVED COUNTRY, 131
RETURN OF THE MOUNTED CORPSES, THE, 177, 189
RHEINGOLD, 123
RIDER OF THE WHITE HORSE, THE (1977), 133, 134, 144-45
ROSE FOR JANE, A, 19
ROSES FOR THE PROSECUTOR, 36
RULES OF THE GAME, THE, 150

SAN DOMINGO, 141
SATAN'S BREW, 98
SCHOOLMASTER HOFER, 52
SECOND AWAKENING OF CHRISTA KLAGES, THE, 152
SHADOWS OF THE ANGELS, 132, 156-57
SHE WORE A YELLOW RIBBON, 167
SHORT LETTER TO THE LONG GOODBYE, THE, 133, 188
SIGNS OF LIFE, 75, 140
SOMEONE'S YODELING UNDER MY DIRNDL, 109
SOMETHING HURTS, 13
SOUFRIÈRE, LA, 76, 184
STANDARD, THE, 133
STARK NAKED IN UPPER BAVARIA, 109
STATE OF THINGS, THE, 74
STATIONMASTER'S WIFE, THE, 76, 132
STERNSTEIN MANOR, 123, 131
STOP RUNNING, 37 126
STRONG MAN FERDINAND, 52, 55, 75, 136
STROSZEK, 55, 136
SUBJECTIVE FACTOR, THE, 18, 25, 200
SUDDEN WEALTH OF THE POOR PEOPLE OF KOMBACH, THE,
    103-04, 106, 109, 111, 114-23, 124, 127, 128
SUFFERLOH, 123
SUMMER IN THE CITY, 47, 186

TAILOR OF ULM, THE, 57
TALES FROM THE VIENNA FOREST, 134
TATTOOING, 145

TAXI TO THE LOO, 76
THEODOR CHINDLER, 90
THIRD GENERATION, THE, 57, 85, 99
THREE AMERICAN LPS, 174
THREE SISTERS, THE, 132, 143, 146, 155
THREEPENNY OPERA, THE (1931), 27, 137
TIEFLAND, 107
TIGER OF ESCHNAPUR, THE, 20
TIN DRUM, THE, 31, 58-59, 66, 73, 155, 156, 161
TOKYO CHORUS, 169
TONIO KRÖGER, 40, 144
TRACE OF A GIRL, 145
TRILOGY OF FAREWELL, 134
TRIP, THE, 50
TROKADERO, 123
TSCHETAN, THE INDIAN BOY, 127

UNICORN, THE, 134
UNTIL WE MEET AGAIN, 36

VACATION FROM MYSELF, 126
VACATION GREETINGS FROM THE LOWER REACHES, 109
VAMPYR, 48
VERONIKA VOSS, 76, 98
VICTORIA, LA, 177
VIOLANTA, 133

WAR AND PEACE (1983), 196, 202
WEDDING IN BLOOD, 98
WHEN THEY PLAY MUSIC IN THE VILLAGE ON SUNDAY EVENING, 115
WHO CARES, 20
WILD DUCK, THE, 131, 147
WILD RIDER, INC., 57, 185
WINNETOU I, 40
WINTERSPELT, 132, 150, 157
WOMEN IN NEW YORK, 72, 132
WORLD ON A WIRE, 72
WOYZECK (1978), 134
WRITTEN ON THE WIND, 85
WRONG MOVE, 20, 27, 52, 87, 88, 99, 142, 174-78, 188, 189

YESTERDAY GIRL, 41-42, 58, 75, 76, 138-39, 145
YOUNG EAGLE, 144
YOUNG MONK, THE, 179
YOUNG MR. LINCOLN, 167
YOUNG TÖRLESS, 31, 38, 40, 42, 43, 58, 75, 138, 156, 161